John Babington Macaulay Baxter

Historical Records of the New Brunswick Regiment, Canadian Artillery

John Babington Macaulay Baxter

Historical Records of the New Brunswick Regiment, Canadian Artillery

ISBN/EAN: 9783744743372

Printed in Europe, USA, Canada, Australia, Japan

Cover: Foto ©Thomas Meinert / pixelio.de

More available books at **www.hansebooks.com**

Presented to

The University of Toronto

by the New Brunswick Regiment, Canadian Artillery,
with the compliments of

Historical Records

OF THE

New Brunswick Regiment Canadian Artillery.

COMPILED BY

Captain JOHN B. M. BAXTER,

(A member of the N. B. Historical Society)

AND

PUBLISHED BY THE OFFICERS OF THE CORPS

FOR PRIVATE DISTRIBUTION.

ST. JOHN, N. B.
THE SUN PRINTING COMPANY, LIMITED.
1896.

TO
LIEUTENANT-COLONEL DE LA CHEROIS T. IRWIN,
(*late R. A.*)
Assistant Adjutant-General for Artillery,
THIS VOLUME
IS RESPECTFULLY INSCRIBED
BY THE AUTHOR
AS A RECOGNITION OF HIS EFFORTS IN PLACING
BEFORE THE ARTILLERY OF CANADA
THE HIGHEST STANDARD OF EXCELLENCE
FOR THEIR IMITATION.

PREFACE.

In presenting his work for the consideration of the reader the author trusts that it will be considered rather as a compilation than as a history and judged accordingly with greater leniency. From imperfect records, during brief intervals of leisure, the material has been gathered, and so far as possible its accuracy has been ensured. There must, however, be many things in 'the life which all men live yet few men notice' that have escaped both recollection and chronicle, and it is in the hope that the artilleryman of the next century who takes up the thread of the story may find it less difficult to trace, that the writer lays down his pen warmly thanking the many friends who have assisted him in the task which he accepted with all its difficulties underestimated.

JOHN B. M. BAXTER.

St. John, N. B.,
February, 1896.

INDEX TO CONTENTS.

Chapter	Period	Page
Chapter I	1793	1
Chapter II	1794-1811	16
Chapter III	1812-1815	24
Chapter IV	1816-1837	32
Chapter V	1838	45
Chapter VI	1839	54
Chapter VII	1840-1843	63
Chapter VIII	1844-1859	72
Chapter IX	1859	82
Chapter X	1860	91
Chapter XI	1861	100
Chapter XII	1862-1864	117
Chapter XIII	1865-1868	129
Chapter XIV	1869-1876	141
Chapter XV	1877-1884	154
Chapter XVI	1885-1893	169
Chapter XVII	THE SERGEANT-MAJOR AND NON-COMMISSIONED OFFICERS.	186
Chapter XVIII	THE BAND.	191
Chapter XIX	THE FORTIFICATIONS.	197
Chapter XX	1893-1896—Conclusion.	207

CONTENTS.

APPENDICES.

Centennial Battery Rolls—1893	225
Regimental Field and Staff Officers—1838-1896	228
Officers' Service Lists	234
The Colville company	234
Captain Nicholson's battery	236
" B. L. Peters' "	236
" Ranney's "	237
" McLauchlan's "	237
" Pick's, No. 1, "	238
" Adams', No. 2, "	240
" Hurd Peters', No. 3 "	242
" Kerr's, No. 4, "	243
" Lander's, No. 5, "	245
Charlotte County Artillery	246
Westmoreland County Artillery	247
Fredericton, York County Artillery	248
Captain Travis' battery	249
" Osburn's "	249
Woodstock (No. 5) "	250
St. George (No. 6) "	251
Chatham (No. 7) "	251
St. Stephen (No. 8) "	252
St. George (No. 9) "	252
Index	253

HISTORICAL RECORDS

OF THE

New Brunswick Regiment

CANADIAN ARTILLERY.

1793-1896.

CHAPTER I.

1793.

The Loyalists—War with France—Formation of the First Company—The Muster Roll—Preparations for Defence—Notes on the First Members.

THE history of the New Brunswick Regiment of Artillery, if it were written after years of research, would be almost a history of the province whose name it bears. A single company formed a hundred years ago, in a city that was then but a village, has become the regiment of today, and the city is now the commercial metropolis of New Brunswick. That company was founded at a time when the province had just been brought into existence by the efforts of a few men whose example of loyalty and devotion has been a watchword and rallying cry throughout the succeeding years.

On the eighteenth day of May, 1783, there had landed on the inhospitable shore at the mouth of the river Saint John about three thousand men, women and children, who had left the scenes of their childhood and the homes of their age rather than submit to a form of government in the principles of which they could not concur. A few months later, in September of that year another band arrived numbering nearly two thousand souls, and thus passed into history a name that shall live through the ages—the Loyalists of 1783. So was founded the city of St. John, as the district of Parrtown was afterwards known, when it received a royal charter on the eighteenth day of May, 1785. In such a community the ranks of the pioneer artillery company were ten years later filled by men who had been in close touch with those mighty events which caused the political division of this continent, and by others, who, coming from the mother country had cast in their lot with those who upheld in the new province the principles and institutions to which they were devotedly attached. The muster rolls of our artillery for the past century contain the names of men whose patriotism, ability and influence have been at the service of their country in whatever capacity she has required them. It is, therefore, of great moment to the present members of the corps that its record should be perpetuated during the coming years, in the hope that the illustrious example of the past may be followed in the present and the future.

A history, like all things finite, must have a beginning, but in a work like this, it is somewhat difficult to fix the proper period for commencement. That the origin of the regiment can be traced to the Reign of Terror is a statement which seems at first sight to be more fanciful than exact, yet that series of events which shed such a lurid light upon the last decade of the eighteenth century, is really the cause of which our organization today is the indirect result. While on the 21st January, 1793, the infuriated populace of Paris was exulting over the death of Louis XVI, Colonel BONAPARTE, the young Corsican officer, commanded the artillery of the republic at Toulon. Years afterwards a future commander of our regiment of artillery was an officer on the island station where the great emperor was imprisoned. The crash of the guillotine and the thunder of the guns at Toulon, roused the nations of Europe. War was declared by France against Great Britain, Holland, Spain, Austria and Prussia, and counter declarations were made. In consequence of this the then Colonial Secretary, Mr. HENRY DUNDAS, sent a letter dated at Whitehall, 9th February, 1793, to the lieutenant-governor of Nova Scotia informing him that the persons exercising the supreme authority in France had declared war against the king of England on the first of that month— that letters of marque or commissions of privateer would be granted in the usual manner and giving assurance to all owners of armed ships and vessels that his majesty would consider them as having a just claim to the king's share of all French ships and property of which they might make prize. A similar despatch was probably sent to the lieutenant-governor of New Brunswick. At the same time a circular letter was sent to the lieutenant-governors of both provinces requiring them to raise provincial corps of six hundred men each, the subsistence and equipment of which was to be a charge upon the royal exchequer. On the 4th May, 1793, Governor (Brigadier-General) THOMAS CARLETON wrote to Major-General CLARKE, then in command, stating that he had appointed EDWARD WINSLOW, Esq., Muster-master General of the late provincial forces, to muster and inspect the recruits for one of these corps, the King's N. B. Regiment. This regiment was entirely distinct from the militia which at the same time was being organized as rapidly as possible.

The peace which followed the American rebellion, had left the provinces in a supine state with respect to military organization and defences. An act providing for the enrolment of the militia had been passed in 1787 but does not appear to have been acted upon. Another law, repealing the former, was enacted in 1792, and under this the enrolment of the militia began, while the regiment for service with troops of the line was also being mustered. In those times the militia represented not alone the lads and young men of the community but in reality every able bodied man from sixteen to sixty years of age with the exception of a very few exempts. The feeling of danger was immediate and personal and there was a commensurate sense of responsibility. Many of the citizens were men who had fought for their homes and lost everything in their struggle for king and conscience. Such men were the leaders of public opinion in our province, and under the stimulus of their example it is quite probable that the ranks were quickly and willingly filled. Under such circumstances and from such splendid material, on the fourth day of May, 1793, there was enrolled in the Loyal Company of Artillery of the city of Saint John the following patriotic men:—

>John Colville, captain.
>Thomas Gilbert, 1st lieutenant.
>John Ward, 2nd lieutenant.
>Oliver Bourdette, John Chubb, sergeants.

Privates:—

Alex. McPherson,	Samuel Smiler,	Stephen Potter,
Timothy Perry,	Arthur Dingwall,	Beach Sealy,
Lewis DeBlois,	John Mills,	Daniel Belding,
Timothy Thomson,	William Thompson,	Thomas Robson,
Lawrence Robinson,	William Olive,	Daniel Leavitt,
John McLeod,	Robert Andrews,	William Chappell,
Josiah Butler,	Nathaniel Worrell,	Geo. Symers (Stymest?)
James Hoyt,	Anthony Reece,	Samuel Whitney,
James Gaynor,	Samuel Stephen,	Stephen Bourdette,
William Barlow,	Archibald McNeill,	Asa Cutler,

Wm. Margeston,
Samuel Miley,
Humphrey Peel,
Lawrence Hartwick,
James Gregor,
Robert Alden,
John Morrill,
Geo. Younghusband,
Joseph Canby,
Thos. Smith,
Ezekiel Barlow,
John Waterbury,
Henry Anthony,
Thomas Clapp,
Aaron Moses Beek,
Thos. Lawton,
Wm. Roden,
Andrew Crookshank,
Thomas Hanford,
George Smith,

James Kavanaugh,
Robert Reid,
Charles Thomas, jr.,
William Pagan,
Bradford Gilbert,
Robert Laidley,
Daniel DeVoe,
Joseph Forrester,
Jacob Pearson,
Jonathan Leavitt,
William Young,
Samuel Mason,
Thomas Jennings,
Captain Watt,
John Garrison,
Benjamin Burgess,
Simeon Parker,
Nicholas Lake,
John Shaw,
Barth'w Coxetter,

William Donald,
John Belyea,
Thomas Green,
Robert E. Boyd,
John Darragh,
Henry Finch,
Aquilla Rich,
Richard Longmuir,
Robert Patullo,
Thomas Reed,
Benjamin Stanton,
Samuel Boyer,
Charles Thomas, sr.,
Joseph Gorham,
Thomas Thomas,
William Harper,
James Hume,
Peter Boura,
Robert Green.

The muster roll was completed not a day too soon. On the 6th May news was received at Saint John that a French privateer of ten guns and forty-five men was cruising in the Bay of Fundy. A night patrol was immediately established and Capt. ROBERT REED of the 'Independent Volunteers' took the first tour of duty. Some proposed to fit out an armed vessel to go after the belligerent stranger. Another guard-house was provided for the watch, and a double guard was placed at the Lower Cove battery—probably Dorchester battery. This fort was then armed with 18-pr. guns which it is gravely stated, were 'so excellently situated as to prevent the possibility of an 'enemy's ship coming into the harbor.' The expected vessel never came and the night patrol exerted its vigilance for nothing. Later on, in August, there was another scare caused by the report that a large naval force of the enemy had arrived on this continent. Governor CARLETON hastened to St. John, which was in a state of alarm, and directed the erection of some fortifications which were thought to render the city perfectly safe against attack by sea. Again, in October, a report was spread that two thousand four hundred French troops among which were 'a banditti of miscreants' and some deserters from Galbaud's corps, were ready to embark at New York. They were said to have forty horses and sixteen pieces of field artillery but were badly clothed. Governor CARLETON did not suppose that New Brunswick would be the objective point of this expedition but as a matter of precaution he ordered forty artillerymen (Royal) and a detachment of about eighty men of the King's New Brunswick Regiment, commanded by Major MURRAY, to St. John. Capt. CLINCH's company of that regiment was stationed at Passamaquoddy and the remaining companies at Fredericton and the upper posts. The governor reviewed the militia of the city of St. John and five hundred and eleven non-commissioned officers and men responded. He set them to work preparing fascines and throwing up temporary works for the protection of the harbor. This was the first military employment of the militia artillery. At this time the common council of the city had under consideration the obtaining of some lots in St. James street for the purposes of fortification but the project appears to have been abandoned. Despite the danger, either malice or mischief was not suppressed as the following extract from the minutes of common council of 8th November, 1793, will shew:—

"Information having been given to this board that the Centi-
"nals posted at the batteries have in several instances been as-
"saulted by some evil disposed persons who have thrown stones
"at them in the dark

"Ordered, that the Clark do prepare an advertisement to "send to the publick papers offering in the name of the cor- "poration 20 dollars reward to any person who shall discover "the offender or offenders to be paid on conviction."

No further reports appear to have been received during the winter and there was no further reference to the unfortunate sentinels. The alarm of the French revolution, however, had, among other things, caused the formation of a company of artillery which has unbroken historical continuity with the or- ganization of today. It will be noticed that the term 'company' is used in referring to the artillery of that time. It was then and until about 1862 continued to be the correct designation of artillery. It is a fact, worthy of note, that Captain COL-VILLE's company was organized only seventy-seven years later than the formation of that splendid regiment which shares in every victory of British arms and proudly writes *'Ubique'* on its shield. The Royal artillery having been organized with two companies claim regimental history from 1716, while their New Brunswick kinsman must be content with the record of a single company until 1833. At first our company formed a part of the Saint John County militia and was accorded the honor due to artillery of occupying the right flank at inspections and reviews. When the annual parade states were made up the staff officers and non-commissioned officers were always included in the state of the artillery. Another and a very special distinction was accorded to this company—that of wearing gold facings instead of those at that time usually worn by colonial corps.

The personnel of the first muster-roll is an interesting study to a resident of St. John. Many of the names are still borne by the descendants of the old artillerymen while others have completely died out. JOHN COLVILLE, the first captain, was a man of wealth and position in the little community. By the city charter he had been appointed assistant to the alderman for Kings ward, a position which gave him a seat at the common council, in the minutes of which he is frequently referred to by his military title. In 1794, after several years of absence from the board, he was elected alderman for the same ward, and in 1795 having been again chosen to that position he appeared at the council and declined re-election. He had also held several minor offices under the city. Captain COLVILLE was the founder of the commercial firm of CROOKSHANK & JOHNSTON, which flourished for many years. The senior member of that firm was ANDREW CROOKSHANK, whose mother had married Captain COLVILLE. ANDREW CROOKSHANK afterwards succeeded to the command of the artillery company.

Captain COLVILLE is buried in the Church of England burying ground at St. John. The following is the inscription on his tombstone:—

JOHN COLVILLE.
Died Nov. 7, 1808,
In the 71st year of his age.

Mr. COLVILLE came to this province with the Loyalists in 1783, and was for many years a merchant in this city, during which time his unflinching integrity won for him the sincere esteem of every honest man, to whom he was known.

RACHEL NORRIS,
widow of
JOHN COLVILLE,
Died June 6, 1823.

THE CROOKSHANK HOUSE.
(Residence of Captain John Colville.)

The 'Crookshank house' as it is now known was the residence of JOHN COLVILLE. It was situated on Prince William street opposite the Bank of British North America, and at its destruction in 1895 was the oldest house in St. John. The material for its construction was brought to the city by packet. Its owner drew Nos. 50 and 159 in the original distribution of lots on the eastern side of the harbor among the loyalist settlers of the city.

THOMAS GILBERT, the first lieutenant, was one of the Gilbert family of which there are a number of descendants in the province today.

JOHN WARD, second lieutenant, was one of the very few of the original members of the company who was destined to witness the celebration of its fiftieth anniversary. His name is still fresh and his record bright while nearly all of his companions have faded out of recollection. A later chapter will deal with the history of this excellent officer in some detail.

OLIVER BOURDETTE, sergeant, was, like his brother Stephen, who was a private in the company, 'a respectable citizen of St. John.'

JOHN CHUBB, sergeant, was a loyalist who came to this province in 1783. He carried on the business of a shoemaker and tanner in company with Jehiel Partelow. His son was HENRY CHUBB, the editor and proprietor of the 'Courier,' one of the early newspapers of the city, from the files of which much interesting material has been gathered for this work. JOHN CHUBB died October 15th, 1822, aged 69 years.

ALEXANDER McPHERSON, one of the privates, died on the 5th January, 1819, at the age of 64 years. He was then an old and respected inhabitant of the city. There was a lieutenant in the New Jersey volunteers of the same name.

TIMOTHY PERRY is one of the many whose record seems to have been lost. He may have been a relation of JOHN PERRY, a Massachusetts loyalist, who died at St. John in 1803.

LEWIS DEBLOIS was a Massachusetts loyalist and a prominent merchant in St. John. His daughter married JAMES WHITE who was sheriff of St. John city and county from 1816 to 1847. DEBLOIS died in 1802.

TIMOTHY THOMSON. No record.

LAWRENCE ROBINSON. No record.

JOHN MCLEOD. A loyalist. Was a merchant of St. John, and died there in 1805, aged 45 years.

JOSIAH BUTLER. A loyalist. Died at St. John in 1812, aged 50 years.

JAMES HOYT, came from Connecticut. Was a loyalist and a merchant of St. John. Died in Kings county in 1803.

JAMES GAYNOR. A loyalist. Died at St. John in 1803, aged 72.

WILLIAM BARLOW was one of a family of shipwrights and merchants. The others were Thomas, Joseph and Ezekiel.

WILLIAM MARGESTON. A loyalist. No further record.

SAMUEL MILEY. No record.

HUMPHREY PEEL. A block and pump maker in St. John. He was a loyalist and 'a very respectable man.'

LAWRENCE HARTWICK. No record.

JAMES GREGOR. A merchant. He died at Hampton, Kings county, July 21st, 1823, aged 71.

ROBERT ALDEN. No record.

JOHN MORRILL. A loyalist from Long Island, N. Y. He died at St. John in 1817, aged 69.

GEORGE YOUNGHUSBAND was a loyalist, and in 1803 was an alderman of St. John.

JOSEPH CANBY was a Pennsylvania loyalist. He fell from a

wharf and died at St John on October 8th, 1814, aged 56 years. He was a merchant.

THOMAS SMITH. Of him there is no record unless he was the Thos. Smith, of Ridgefield, Conn., who was captain of a privateer during the Revolutionary war. If so, he was a friend and fellow prisoner of EBENEZER HATHEWAY. This Smith died at St. John.

EZEKIEL BARLOW. See WILLIAM BARLOW.

JOHN WATERBURY. A Connecticut loyalist. Was a merchant in St. John where he died in 1817, at the age of 68 years.

HENRY ANTHONY was a loyalist. Anthony's cove near Courtenay bay was named after him. ROBERT CHESTNUT of Fredericton married a daughter of ANTHONY. He was one of the three survivors who was present at the celebration of the fiftieth anniversary of the formation of the company.

THOMAS CLAPP. No record.

AARON MOSES BEEK may have been related to JOSEPH BEEK, a loyalist who came to St. John, otherwise no record.

THOMAS LAWTON. A loyalist from Rhode Island, who died in 1803.

WILLIAM RODEN. No record.

ANDREW CROOKSHANK. A son of Capt. GEO. CROOKSHANK, a loyalist. He was afterwards captain of the company.

THOMAS HANFORD was a Connecticut loyalist and a prominent citizen and merchant of St. John. He died in 1826, at the age of 78 years.

GEORGE SMITH was a builder. He was the first W. M. of St. John's Lodge, F. & A. M.

SAMUEL SMILER was a loyalist. He died November 9th, 1820, at the age of 56 years, and 'filled many public offices with the greatest integrity.'

ARTHUR DINGWALL was a loyalist and a merchant of St. John. He was drowned on a passage to England.

JOHN MILLS. A loyalist. No further record.

WILLIAM THOMPSON. A loyalist No further record.

WILLIAM OLIVE. A loyalist. He died at Carleton in 1822, and was 'an upright and most respectable citizen.'

ROBERT ANDREWS. No record.

NATHANIEL WORRELL. A loyalist. Thought to have gone to Halifax, N. S.

ANTHONY REECE. No record.

SAMUEL STEPHEN. No record. He may have been a brother of SOLOMON STEPHEN, a New Hampshire loyalist who died at Musquash, St. John county, in 1819.

ARCHIBALD MCNEILL was a loyalist. He died on the St. John River in 1808.

JAMES KAVANAUGH. No record.

ROBERT REID. A loyalist. No further record.

CHARLES THOMAS, jr. He was probably a son of CHARLES THOMAS, a Connecticut loyalist, who died in 1818, aged 75.

WILLIAM PAGAN was a native of Glasgow, Scotland. He was a merchant in New York at the time of the Revolution and came with the loyalists to this province in 1783. He was a representative of the county of Saint John in the first general assembly of the Province of New Brunswick, and was one of the aldermen of the city of Saint John appointed by the charter.

BRADFORD GILBERT. A loyalist. Was a merchant of St. John, and in 1803 was an alderman of the city. He died in 1814, aged 68 years.

ROBERT LAIDLEY. He died October 16th, 1817, and was one of the early settlers, 'an honest and industrious man.' He was a dealer in tinware, and resided on King street, St. John.

DANIEL DEVOE. Was a soldier in the Revolutionary war in a company in which JOHN WARD was an officer. He probably followed his old commander into the Artillery company. On 13th June, 1818, DEVOE while walking down King street, was accidentally shot by BARTON WALLOP who, with his brother NEWTON, was playing with an old horse pistol, not knowing it to be loaded. These boys were grandsons of JOHN WARD.

JOSEPH FORRESTER. A loyalist. Died in Boston in 1804, aged 46 years.

JACOB PEARSON. A loyalist. Was a pilot of the port of St. John.

JONATHAN LEAVITT. Came from New Hampshire in 1763 in the company of colonists brought by FRANCIS PEABODY from New England. He was a shipmaster, shipowner and trader, doing a considerable business. He had six sons and several daughters. All of Jonathan's descendants in the province spell their name 'Leavitt,' while those of DANIEL, his brother, spell it 'Lovett.' Both brothers were grantees of lots in Carleton, Jonathan having seventeen lots and Daniel three.

WILLIAM YOUNG. A Pennsylvania loyalist. Died at Carleton, St. John, in 1804, aged 49 years.

SAMUEL MASON. A loyalist. Died in 1827, at the age of 66 years, 'a respectable inhabitant and a good mechanic.'

THOMAS JENNINGS. A loyalist. Died 1805.

CAPTAIN WATT was a shipmaster, captain of the *Dardalus*. He died at Quebec, October 28th, 1817.

JOHN GARRISON. A loyalist and member of the House of Assembly. He died on the St. John River, in 1810.

BENJAMIN BURGESS, SIMEON PARKER, NICHOLAS LAKE. No record.

John Shaw. A loyalist. At the time of the peace he was in the lumber trade. He went to Shelburne, N. S.

Bartholomew Coxetter was a loyalist and a very respectable inhabitant of St John. He died in 1836.

Stephen Potter. No record. He was probably related to James Potter mentioned as a captain of artillery.

Beach Sealy. No record.

Daniel Belding. Was one of the three survivors who participated in the jubilee of the company in 1843.

Thomas Robson, who died October 16th, 1841, aged 74 years, was the oldest shipmaster of the port of St. John, and for many years had been harbor master.

Daniel Leavitt was also a shipmaster. He died October 16th, 1833, aged 88 years.

William Chappell. A loyalist, is thought to have removed to P. E. Island.

George Symers, (probably Stymest) is not mentioned, but Jasper Stymest was a Long Island loyalist who died in 1826, aged 75 years. They were probably related.

Samuel Whitney. A loyalist. Died in 1815, aged 61 years, having been for many years a merchant of St. John. He was the father of James Whitney, a steamboat proprietor.

Stephen Bourdette, a brother of Oliver Bourdette. Both well known as 'respectable citizens of St. John.'

Asa Cutler. No record.

William Donald was a Scotchman and a prominent merchant of the city. He afterwards was a lieutenant in the company. He died June 22nd, 1828, aged 74.

John Belyea. This name is spelled indifferently, Bulyea, Beryea or Belyea. He was a loyalist who settled in Kings county.

THOMAS GREEN. A Pennsylvania loyalist who died about 1815.

ROBERT E. BOYD, JOHN DARRAGH. No record.

HENRY FINCH. A Georgia loyalist who died at St. John in 1814.

AQUILLA RICH. No record.

RICHARD LONGMUIR was a shipmaster. His daughter was the first wife of Hon. CHARLES SIMONDS.

ROBERT PATULLO. A respectable citizen who lived on King street, next to THATCHER SEARS' house.

THOMAS REED. He married the daughter of one JOHN CLARK in 1819.

BENJAMIN STANTON. A Rhode Island loyalist and a very respectable citizen. He died in 1823, aged 68.

SAMUEL BOYER. No record. There were two of this name, both loyalists. The name is still extant both in St. John and Carleton counties.

CHARLES THOMAS, sr., was a Connecticut loyalist who died in St. John in 1818, at the age of 75 years.

JOSEPH GORAM, (now spelled Gorham), a loyalist. There was also a JOSEPH A. GORHAM, also a loyalist.

THOMAS THOMAS. A loyalist. There were several of this name who settled in St. John at the end of the war.

WILLIAM HARPER. No record.

JAMES HUME. A Georgia loyalist. No further record.

PETER BOURA. A loyalist. Was a shipmaster, and died in 1804, aged 49 years, while on a passage from Jamaica.

ROBERT GREEN. No record. Several of this name were loyalists.

CHAPTER II.

1794-1811.

Visit of the Duke of Kent—Address—Perilous Times—The Artillery Company Contribute to the National Defence Fund—Nelson and the Navy—Muster Rolls—New Officers—Arms and Accoutrements.

THE events in Europe ceased to affect the colonies in America, so far as the danger of invasion was concerned after the year 1793, though commerce was considerably interfered with. An era of comparative quiet began which was not materially disturbed for many years. The next event of importance to the young artillery company, and indeed to the city of Saint John, was the visit of a royal prince, the first of many occasions on which members of the royal family have been received in this province. PRINCE EDWARD, Duke of Kent, a son of GEORGE III, and the father of our present Most Gracious Sovereign was, at this time, in military command at Quebec. In 1794 he visited Halifax, and after staying there for a time, proceeded to Annapolis on June 14th, where he embarked in the *Zebra* sloop of war, for Saint John. Here he arrived on the 19th June. The Royal Gazette of 24th June of that year in a letter thus describes his visit :—

On Wednesday last (18th June) arrived in this city from Fredericton, His Excellency Major-General CARLETON, Governor of this province, to meet His Royal Highness PRINCE EDWARD, who was hourly expected from Digby, to which place he had passed through the country from Halifax on a visit to this province. His Excellency was received by a salute from the Royal Artillery here upon his landing, and yesterday, (19th June) at 4 o'clock p. m., arrived His Majesty's ship of war *Zebra*, commanded by Capt. VAUGHAN, having on board His Royal Highness attended by Capt. VEZEY, one of his aides-de-camp. A royal salute was fired from Dorchester battery as the ship passed. At 6 o'clock His Royal Highness left the ship, which immediately fired a royal salute, and in a few minutes he came ashore at the public landing which was crowded and surrounded by a great concourse of loyal subjects, who had collected, eager to testify their joy upon this very pleasing and flattering occasion. * * * * * * * * *

Prince William street was lined on both sides from the landing to Mr. CHIPMAN'S house (where rooms were prepared for the reception of His Royal Highness) by the Cadet company in their uniform, the Artillery company of the city and several of the companies of the militia under arms, who made a very good appearance and with which His Royal Highness appeared to be much pleased.

Immediately upon his landing royal salutes were fired by the Artillery Company of the City and from the armed brig *Union* and His Royal Highness with that complacency and dignity which so strongly mark his character passed between the lines, and attended as he was, received at the landing to Mr. CHIPMAN'S house.

At seven o'clock in the evening His Royal Highness received an address from the Mayor, Aldermen and Commonalty of the City. He left St. John the following day for Fredericton and returned on the succeeding Monday. On Tuesday, after holding a levee and inspecting the fortifications, he re-embarked for Digby *en route* to Halifax.

The Chipman house is still standing in a state of good preservation. More than half a century later it was destined to receive H. R. H. the PRINCE OF WALES on his visit to the provinces. From the height on which it is situated may be seen the site of old Fort La Tour, memorable for its gallant defence by the heroic French lady of that name ; Fort Howe, in the garrison of which COBBETT was a private soldier ; and the gray old Martello Tower on Carleton Heights which stands a lonely sentinel of the historic past.

Another incident connecting PRINCE EDWARD with Saint John may be noticed here. In 1799 he became Commander-in-Chief of H. M. forces in British North America, and on this occasion the common council of Saint John, at a meeting held 27th November of that year voted the following address to His Royal Highness :—

To His Royal Highness Prince Edward, Duke of Kent and Strathern, Knight of the most Noble Order of the Garter and of the most Illustrious Order of Saint Patrick, General and Commander-in-Chief of all His Majesty's forces in British North America, etc.

May it please Your Excellency :—

The Mayor, Aldermen and Commonalty of the City of Saint John beg leave in an humble address to approach your Royal Highness with sentiments of loyalty, gratitude and respect in the expression of which language fails to give utterance to the fulness of their hearts.

When we reflect that the city and the province of which it is a part, both yet in their infancy, are the offspring of loyalty to the best of sovereigns and of attachment to a constitution the birth right of British subjects and the envy and admiration of surrounding nations, we feel those principles of our origin indissolubly strengthened and confirmed by His Majesty's most gracious favor in appointing to the chief military command of his dominion in this part of the world so illustrious a branch of his august family and one in so eminent a degree inheriting his father's virtues.

The pleasure with which our bosoms beat high when your Royal Highness heretofore condescended to visit this province still vibrates in our breasts ; we then experienced a high and proud satisfaction from your residence in a part of the country so near to us. But when we find the safety, interest, and welfare of this part of the empire the distinguished and favored object of your voluntary patronage and care—sensations of unbounded gratitude arise in quick succession to our most gracious sovereign for conferring, and to your Royal Highness for accepting, the high and important trust committed to your hands. From these signal instances of royal benevolence and attention the most public benefits are naturally anticipated, and the knowledge we have of the character drawn from the conduct of your Royal Highness on past occasions encourages our indulgence of the most sanguine hopes.

While virtue, talents and exalted rank happily united shall be respected among mankind—while high command in all its just arrangements and minute operations directed solely to the public safety and the public welfare—shall claim the esteem and applause of the virtuous and the good—the name of your Royal Highness will stand eminently conspicuous on the rolls of fame.

That your Royal Highness thro' a long life yet to come may enjoy the satisfaction and happiness and your country the benefits resulting from the exercise of qualities so enviable and so great will be our ardent and unceasing prayer.

(Signed) WM. CAMPBELL, Mayor.
(Signed) CHARLES J. PETERS,
Common Clerk.

Scarcely anything could be imagined more adulatory than this address, but the people of the time must be credited with deep feeling of the sentiments which they rather effusively expressed. At the time of passing the address JOHN WARD, the lieutenant, and OLIVER BOURDETTE, one of the sergeants, named in the first muster roll, occupied seats at the council, the former as alderman for Kings and the latter as assistant for Queens ward.

In the year 1798 Britain was engaged in a life and death struggle with the combined powers of France and Spain. BONAPARTE contemplated and made preparation for the invasion of England. The resources of parliament were at a low ebb and the national existence was at stake. An appeal was made to the nation at large, and the response was hearty and immediate.

Books for voluntary subscriptions were opened at the Bank of England—all subscriptions to be annual during the war, or so long as required. The king headed the list with £200,000 sterling, and contributions flowed in from all quarters from thousands of pounds down to sixpences, even the mite of the widow and the infant helping to swell the general fund. In a short time £5,000,000 sterling was raised in Great Britain. The colonies loyally united with the mother country, the infant province of New Brunswick, with a population of perhaps fifteen thousand, contributing £3,000 towards the national defence. Lieutenant-Governor CARLETON headed the list with £500. Chief Justice LUDLOW contributed £100 and others in proportion. On June 15th, 1798, the Adjutant-General of New Brunswick by command of His Excellency the Lieutenant-Governor addressed a circular to the colonels of the militia regiments requesting them to bring the matter of contributing to the fund for national defence before their captains in order that the men of their companies might have the opportunity of subscribing such sums as they could afford, the same to be transmitted to the Duke of Portland, one of His Majesty's Principal Secretaries of State. The following sums were contributed by Captain COLVILLE's company of Militia Artillery:

John Colville,	£10 0 0	James Lawton,	£2 10 0
John Ward,	10 0 0	John Dillon,	2 6
Thomas Jennings,	20 0 0	Lewis DeBlois,	2 10 0
Arthur Dingwall,	10 0 0	Daniel Lovett,	5 0 0
John Bentley,	10 0 0	Thomas Lawton, .	5 0 0
James Gregor,	7 10 0	Timothy Thomson,	1 3 4
George Younghusband,	10 0 0	James Reid,	2 0 0
William Roden,	2 10 0		

£98 5 10

Exclusive of the above sum £110 was paid by different members of the company, under the head of "City and County of Saint John" which makes the total amount that the company subscribed £208 5 10.

The news of NELSON's victory at the battle of the Nile, fought August 1st, 1798, reached Saint John by the ship *William*, Capt. HUNTER, about the 23d November following. It was received with universal exultation. The Saint John Gazette records :—'as soon as the agreeable intelligence reached this 'loyal city the forts and shipping in the harbour were decorated 'with their flags flying, and universal joy diffused itself through 'every order of the people. At 12 o'clock a salute of 21 guns 'was fired by the Royal Artillery, followed by a discharge of 'three volleys from the troops in garrison, which was returned 'by the same number of guns from the City Artillery and 'ship *William*, Capt. HUNTER.'

There was a spontaneous desire for illumination which was duly carried into effect, and that night Saint John held high carnival. The houses of Hon. GEO. LEONARD, JOHN BLACK, Esq., and many others "flamed away from top to bottom." The shipping in the harbour was brilliantly illuminated, cannon were discharged from the Artillery park and the battery by the garrison and City Artillery, the streets resounded with cheers for NELSON and the Navy, and altogether the night was one of the most memorable in the early days of Saint John.

The next muster roll of the corps which is extant is that of 1809. That many changes had taken place in the sixteen years since formation will readily be seen by a glance at the names which appear as follows :—

Andrew Crookshank, captain.
William Donald, 1st lieutenant.
David Waterbury, 2nd lieutenant.
John Chubb, John Freeman, Thos. Hunter, sergeants.
John Gamble, Humphrey Peele, Sam'l Nichols, corp'ls.
Privates :—

Henry Anthony,
Ezekiel Barlow,
Thomas Barlow,
John Booth,
George Bonsall,
Thomas Bean,
William Burtis,
John Bentley,
John W. Bliss,
Lawton Bedell,
John Bernie,
Daniel Cables,
Joseph Canby,
Barthol'w Coxetter,
Peter Cables,
James Cables,
George Clark,
Isaac Clark,
Noah Disbrow,

George Donald,
John Faught,
James Gregor,
Henry Gardner, jr.
Harry Gilbert,
Thomas Gilbert
Robert Green,
Arcb'd Henderson,
Alex. Hethburn,
William Hedden,
William Harper,
Hugh Johnston,
James Johnston,
Ralph Jarvis,
Daniel Lovett, sr.,
James Lawton,
Samuel Miles, jr.
Alex. McKenzie,
Richard Mott,

Solomon Nichols,
Daniel Pettingal,
George Pagan,
Thomas Pettingal,
James Pettingal,
William Robinson,
Philip Schurman,
George Swiney,
Tartelus Theall,
Whitney Traverse,
William Tell,
John Waterbury, jr.
John Ward, jr.
Robert Wood,
Stephen Wiggins,
Charles Ward.
Josiah Butler,
Thomas Handford,
James Henderson.

October 25th, 1810, was the fiftieth anniversary of the accession of GEORGE III. The rolls of 1810 shew the following changes since the previous year :—

DISCHARGED.

John H. Bliss,
Wm. Harper,
James Johnston,
James Lawton,
John Ward, jr., promoted.
Josiah Butler,
Thomas Handford,

JOINED.

Lewis Bliss,
John Downie,
William Gaynor,
Alex. Johnston,
Thos. Merritt,
Robt. Robertson,
Jas. Waterberry.

The roll was made up on 2nd August, 1810, and if there was any military observance of the old King's jubilee at Saint John, the Artillery company was sure to have taken part in it.

On August 12th, 1811, the Artillery was mustered again. A few more changes had taken place in the ranks as the following will shew:—

DISCHARGED.	JOINED.
Henry Gilbert,	Amos Addams,
Robert Green,	Ezekiel Barlow, jr.,
Richard Mott,	Samuel Ferris,
Thomas Pettingal,	Thomas Fowler,
James Pettingal,	W. Tyng Peters,
Whitney Traverse,	John Wood.

Upon the death of Capt. COLVILLE, in 1808, ANDREW CROOKSHANK had become captain of the company, and at some time previous to 1812, WILLLIAM DONALD had succeeded to the first lieutenancy and DAVID WATERBURY had been appointed second lieutenant. ANDREW CROOKSHANK as before stated, was the stepson of JOHN COLVILLE, and was a merchant of the city. He represented King's ward in 1813 and 1814 as alderman. In the latter year DAVID WATERBURY was assistant for the same ward.

A return of arms and accoutrements in 1808, shows that the Artillery company then had two 6-pr. guns, complete, but they were without muskets or side arms. The belts were only round belts or a strap and frog which 'had to answer all purposes.'

CHAPTER III.

1812 1815.

The Right of Search—Drifting towards War—Military Governors Appointed—War Declared—Letter from the People of Eastport—March of the 104th—Loss of Materiel—A Prize in the Port of St. John—Recollections—End of the War.

THE bitter feelings engendered by the revolution of the American colonies were not destined to quickly die out. Though nominally at peace with England, yet many of the states saw in the great struggle between that nation and France, an opportunity for striking another blow at the mother land. This feeling was confined to the Southern and Western states, while those in the North-eastern portion of the Union sympathized with the British colonies across the line. The great naval contest in which Britain was then engaged made the obtaining of seamen a matter of vital importance. Desertions were frequent under the rough discipline of those days and, alluring as their tales of glory now may be, it was necessary to resort to impressment and other severe measures to keep up the supply and prevent unauthorized abandonment of the service. The American merchant service was growing and that nation being at peace with all the world employment in her marine was eagerly sought. Men who had served in the British Navy were of course most desirable seamen and by that class the American vessels were principally manned. Great Britain resolved to put an end to desertions and claimed a "right of search" of all vessels on the high seas for that purpose. So early as 1807, a collision occurred on this subject which angered the Americans. H. M. S. *Leopard* stopped the U. S. ship *Chesapeake*, when sailing out of Hampton Roads. There was some resistance and the *Leopard* fired on the other vessel after which four men were taken from the *Chesapeake* as deserters from the British Navy. From that time the nations drifted rapidly towards war, for which the British Government made preparation. In New Brunswick as before stated THOMAS CARLETON was Lieutenant-Governor. He retained this position until his death in 1817, but in 1803 having gone to England, on leave, the administration of the government devolved on GABRIEL G. LUDLOW, who had been the first mayor of Saint John. In 1808 he was succeeded by EDWARD WINSLOW who occupied the office of administrator from February until May of that year. On May 24th Major-General MARTIN HUNTER assumed the administration, the home government having decided to appoint military officers over all the provinces. He continued in office until 9th April, 1812, with the exception of two short absences in 1808 and 1811, during which Lieutenant-Colonel GEORGE JOHNSTON and Major-General WILLIAM BALFOUR presided. In 1812 Major-General HUNTER was succeeded as President of His Majesty's Council by Major-General G. TRACEY SMYTHE.

On the 18th June of that year an act of Congress was passed declaring war against Great Britain. The necessity for a military governor and the advisability of such an appointment was now shown. On the intelligence being received in New Brunswick His Honor, the President, promptly communicated with the City of St. John on the subject of fortifying that place against the probable danger of invasion. At a meeting held on 1st July, 1812, the common council resolved, 'that they

'would lend every aid and assistance within their power to-
'wards the objects suggested, and would take steps forthwith to
'agree with the proprietors of the lots on and around the ruins
'of Fort Frederick to satisfy and compensate them for any
'damage that might be necessarily sustained by them in con-
'sequence of erecting the contemplated fortifications.'

They also resolved, 'that the members of the board would
'personally attend to aid and assist in the work, and do all
'within the compass of their power to induce the inhabitants
'of the city to volunteer their exertions and services in so
'necessary an undertaking.'

Aldermen SANCTON and SEELY and Assistant GARDNER were appointed a committee to see the proprietors of the lots on and surrounding the ruins of Fort Frederick and to enter into any arrangement with them that might be requisite, on the subject of the intended fortifications.

At the next meeting of the city council, held July 7th, 1812, a remarkable communication was laid before them by the mayor. It was a letter which had been received by him from 'the chair-
'man of a committee of public safety for the town of East Port,
'in the District of Maine, expressive of a determination of the
'inhabitants of that district to abstain from all depredations on
'the property or hostility against the persons of the inhabitants
'of this province during the present war declared by America
'against Great Britain so far as is consistent with the duty they
'owe to their country.' Upon the reading of this letter the council unanimously resolved that the mayor be requested to convey to the committee their approbation of the sentiments therein contained and to assure them that everything on the part of the city should be done to promote a reciprocal line of conduct.

Alderman CROOKSHANK, the captain of the artillery was present at these meetings. The government at that time took possession of Fort Frederick (old Fort LaTour) for the purposes of defence. Despite the danger of invasion the military force in the lower provinces was not strengthened until 1813. In the early months of that year SIR GEORGE PREVOST ordered that the 2nd battalion of the 8th regiment be sent to Quebec by the overland route. This was subsequently countermanded and the 104th, a provincial regiment which had been raised as the King's New Brunswick Regiment, mentioned in the first chapter, was selected for the duty which was nobly performed. These gallant fellows left St. John in the bitter cold of February, 1813, the inhabitants assisting them with sleighs and all other conveniences at their command. Their history does not form a part of this narrative as their services were rendered in other than local defence, but their record has added an imperishable lustre to the province of New Brunswick. It will be remembered that in the previous September, the great army of invasion had retired from the burning City of the North to perish on the frost bound steppes under the terrible breath of a Russian winter.

Early in 1813 SIR JOHN SHERBROOKE despatched to St. John ten 24-pr. guns for the batteries on Partridge Island at the entrance to the harbor. He also forwarded necessary ammunition and other requisites besides one thousand stand of muskets, but the ship *Diligence*, on which they were laden became separated from H. M. S. *Rattler*, her convoy, in a snow storm while near Cape Sable. The *Diligence* afterwards went ashore on Beale's Island, about twenty miles below Machias. The *Rattler* had four hundred of the muskets on board and this was all of the cargo that arrived at its destination. The poor *Diligence* with the remainder of the stores fell into the hands of the enemy. There was no means of replacing this loss and misfortune followed misfortune. A short time afterwards the *Lady Johnson*, a transport vessel fell into the hands of the French while on her way to Halifax with forty pieces of battering cannon, two thousand barrels of gunpowder and other stores on board.

With the exception of a list of officers in an almanac of 1812, not even the most meagre account of the artillery company during these stirring times can be obtained, but it is certain that no branch of the militia could have been exempt from the arduous duties which devolved upon the citizens at this period. The commerce of the provinces was exposed to the attacks of privateers, and the Royal Navy brought prize after prize into the colonial ports. There cannot, it would seem, be the slightest doubt but that the defence of his home was foremost in the mind of every subject, and that this, though unrecorded, was really the most eventful period of our military history.

Before the close of the period to which this chapter is devoted, two more references to military affairs are to be found in the common council records. On the 9th March, 1813, the freedom of the city was granted to Major DRUMMOND, lately the commandant of the troops in garrison at Fort Howe. He was probably of the 8th regiment.

H. FLEMING SENHOUSE, commanding H. M. S. *Martin* and senior officer on this station solicited the influence of the council among the proprietors of sleds, etc., to assist on their way a number of sailors destined for the lakes of Canada. The board took the matter up heartily at a meeting on 27th January, 1814, and employed the truckmen of the city to convey the men as far as Fredericton. For this service they received the sum of ten shillings per man conveyed which was paid by the city.

July 13th, 1813, witnessed the bringing of three prizes into the harbor of St. John by H. M. schooner *Breem*, under command of Lieutenant CHARLES HARE. This event and the wrecking of H. M. S. *Plumper* at Dipper Harbor are referred to in the late J. W. LAWRENCE'S 'Foot Prints.' In July, 1815, CROOKSHANK & JOHNSTON, as auctioneers, offered for sale the wreck and unrecovered part of $70.000 in specie which had been destined for the Commissariat, but had by accident got into the locker of Davy Jones.

News was brought to Halifax by the *Empress*, packet, which arrived there on Saturday, May 21st, 1814, after a passage of twenty-nine days from Falmouth, that the allied armies had entered Paris and restored the empire of the Bourbons. At St. John the tidings of the abdication of NAPOLEON and the restoration of the peace of Europe were hailed with delight. On the 23rd May an ox was roasted whole, in King square, and the city was illuminated. The eventful period in the history of St. John with which this chapter deals, is graphically described in the recollections of JAMES BUSTIN, who was born in the year 1800, and was a lad in the days which he recalls. The following extract is made from a copy of his reminiscences which he had prepared for his family, and for its reproduction here, as well as for much valuable assistance in the preparation of the entire work, the Battalion is deeply indebted to CLARENCE WARD, Esq., a gentleman whose gracefully written sketches of the early history of the city, are as accurate as they are delightful. Mr. BUSTIN says: 'The inmates of the almshouse, (then situated 'where the Dufferin hotel now stands) had, in 1808 to take 'other quarters for a short time there being an apprehension

'of a French invasion. All available places were taken for
'barracks, a general draft was made throughout the province and
'the city was filled with soldiers.   *   *   *   *   *

'In early years the troops garrisoned at Fort Howe marched
'in military order each Sunday to church, there was no filing
'off to other places of worship allowed without special permission.
'From Fort Howe the sound of the morning and evening gun
'was heard as notice of the opening and closing of each day
'until the troops moved to barracks at Lower Cove in 1824.
*   *   *   *   *   *

'War was declared by the United States against England in
'1812, this caused much excitement in the city, the old folks
'had not forgot the hard conflict they had passed through from
'1776 to 1783—business of all kinds was nearly suspended
'but this lasted for but a short time. The bustle of prepar-
'ation and the continual arrival of soldiers, and their passing
'through on their way to Canada, added to this warships,
'large and small, prize vessels sent in, etc., made things lively.
'I am doubtful whether our city ever had so much life or
'business (according to population) as she had during those
'three years. Our defences were small, the Tower in Carleton
'commenced building in 1812 with one or two block-houses and
'the remains of Fort LaTour of historic fame, with a few old
'broken down French batteries was all the defence on the west
'side. On this side the harbor there was not much Sabbath
'for some time as all who were capable of handling an axe or
'an auger were employed in fitting up gun carriages and other
'preparations. Our defences were from the heights on Fort
'Howe hill and out around the lower part of the city from
'Battery point to Reed's point. The artillery were stationed
'at the lower cove—the soldiers of the line stationed at Fort
'Howe. Our militia had at times to stand their draft.'

The war with the United States was ended by the Treaty of Ghent on 24th December, 1814, but the desperate battle of New Orleans had been fought before the people of Canada heard that peace had been proclaimed. It was not until the 3rd of March of the next year that the news reached Halifax. It had been proclaimed at Washington on 18th February. The contest had been bloody and exhaustive. The provinces had borne their burden manfully and the long roll of battles reflects even more credit upon the raw Canadian militia than upon the trained troops with whom they co-operated. It was a struggle marked by incompetency on both sides almost from beginning to end, but yet, when peace was signed, the Americans had not a foothold upon our soil. Annexation, the fad of a few demagogic politicians in the United States today, was a very dead thing then. Blood and treasure were expended in vain for the accomplishment of that purpose, and with the conclusion of the war of 1812 the opportunity passed away forever. For every man that Canada had then she has ten men today; for adhesion she has cohesion; for weakness she has strength. Day by day and year by year her attachment to the British Crown has grown and strengthened until today she stands the foremost among the colonies of Britain.

CHAPTER IV.

1816-1837.

Changes of Officers—Accession of George the Fourth—Arrival of Sir Howard Douglas—Recollections of John R. Marshall—Militia Records—Companies Outside of Saint John—New Companies Formed—Loyalist Jubilee.

AFTER the cessation of the war but little in the way of history must be expected from our organization until the time of the regimental formation. There are of course the records of promotions, a few salutes fired in commemoration of public events and the other trivial incidents which constitute the history even of a regiment of the line in a time of profound peace. The militia laws of this period did not require a great deal of service from the citizen soldiery. Generally one or two days drill by companies and one day's muster by battalions was considered sufficient, but little as it was this much was required until long after the formation of the regiment. To-day there are few incidents in the routine of any corps that are thought to be history. Inspections and reviews, drills and salutes are mostly a matter of course, and the writer of the next century will probably think that we have done as little to deserve perpetuation as some of the present day may think our predecessors have done. Yet they, as well as their successors, did all that there was to be done, and though the record may appear somewhat barren, yet it is one of which any soldier may well be proud, that of duty performed.

The second captain of the Artillery Company, Andrew CROOKSHANK, died February 13, 1815, at the age of 49 years. The succession to the captaincy occasioned considerable correspondence between Major JOHN WARD, (formerly second lieutenant in the company) then commanding the 1st battalion of the St. John County regiment, and Lieutenant-Colonel HARRIS WILLIAM HAILES, who was then administering the government of New Brunswick. Since 1812 SIR THOMAS SAUMAREZ and General SMYTHE had alternately presided over the council, no regular governor having been appointed. Major WARD'S first letter is dated August 10, 1816. In it he refers to Lieutenant-Colonel WETMORE having recommended CRAVEN CALVERLY for the command of the Artillery company, but which that gentleman had refused, as it would interfere very much with his private business.

'The company of Artillery,' he says, 'formerly the most 'respectable in the regiment, is now without an officer, and I 'am at a loss whom to recommend to your Honor. If it 'should meet your approbation to remove Captain JAMES 'POTTER from the Sea Fencibles to the Artillery company, the 'Sea Fencibles would then have Captain JAMES REED with 'them. They were allowed two captains on account of their 'numbers. DAVID WATERBURY, who has made application for 'leave to resign, is out of town. I think him a proper person 'to hold a commission and would wish an opportunity to 'speak to him on the subject before he is allowed to resign. 'If your Honor thinks proper to appoint MR. CALEB WARD 'second lieutenant in the Artillery I think the company will 'be well officered. In compliance with your Honor's recom-
'mendation to me, I have issued an order for the captains of 'companies to receive and take care of their respective com-
'panies' arms during the time of peace, which I trust will be 'the means of preventing any loss of arms in the future.'

The commander-in-chief replied approving of the recommendations, and on the same day a militia general order was issued transferring Capt. JAMES POTTER from the Sea Fencibles to the Artillery company *vice* CALVERLY, whose appointment was cancelled; promoting DAVID WATERBURY to be first lieutenant and appointing CALEB WARD, gentleman, to be second lieutenant.

On the 20th September, 1816, Major WARD issued an order requesting Captains HUMBERT, McKEE and POTTER to take charge of their several companies agreeably to the general order partly quoted above.

It is, however, doubtful whether Captain POTTER assumed command of the company, as on 18th April, 1821, Major WARD recommended the promotion of DAVID WATERBURY to the captaincy '*vice Crookshank deceased*.' It is not at all likely that this expression would have been used if Captain POTTER had been the officer retiring. At the same time he recommended the promotion of CALEB WARD to first lieutenant and the appointment of JOHN C. WATERBURY as second lieutenant. GEORGE SHORE, then adjutant-general, replied on May 1st, making the appointments as desired. The militia general orders of 10th August, 1821, of interest to the artillery, were as follows:

'Major WARD, commanding the St. John militia, having 'expressed a wish to retire with his rank, the corps is to be 'divided into two battalions, the first under CHARLES DRURY, 'ESQ., the second under command of CHARLES SIMONDS, ESQ., 'which gentlemen the commander-in-chief is pleased to appoint 'majors commandant of the same. The companies at present 'enrolled within the limits of the city, including the Artil-'lery, Sea Fencibles and African companies are to form the 'first battalion, the remaining companies are to form the second. 'The commandants will recommend officers to complete their 'corps agreeably to the proportion provided in the militia Act, 'as also their staff, paying every possible attention to the 'priority of claims for rank amongst the officers at present 'belonging to their respective battalions.'

GEORGE III, having died in 1820, the PRINCE REGENT ascended the throne as GEORGE IV. The "Courier" of 6th May, 1820, thus describes the proclamation of the new monarch:

'Yesterday the ceremony of proclaiming King GEORGE THE 'FOURTH took place in this town, and we are warranted in 'saying, that in no part of the provinces has it been conducted 'with more zeal, order or propriety. At half past ten o'clock 'the militia artillery company commenced firing minute guns 'which were continued until half past eleven. The colors were 'hoisted half mast high both ashore and on vessels in the harbour. 'The church bells commenced tolling at the same time. The 'procession moved from the Grammar school at half past 'eleven, and proceeded to the Court house in slow march with 'solemn music. It consisted of the sheriff, coroner, clergy, 'magistrates, inhabitants, garrison and militia artillery. After 'the proclamation was read at the Court house and signed by 'the magistrates and other principal persons, JAMES BARBER, 'Esquire, who was appointed herald, read it to the people, the 'whole of them being uncovered. They were the most num-'erous and respectable body we have ever seen collected together 'in this county. When the proclamation was concluded, three ' hearty cheers were given, the troops presented arms, and the 'band struck up "God Save the King," the people still re-'maining uncovered. At this time the colours were hoisted to 'the mast-head and the church-bell rang. A royal salute of ' twenty-one guns was fired and the cheering was repeated. The ' procession then marched from the court house (the sheriff 'and herald being on horseback) and proceeded to the church 'and other parts of the town, when the proclamation was read 'and the acclamations continued.'

The sheriff was JAMES WHITE; the mayor of the city, JOHN ROBINSON, and the coroner, JAMES C. F. BREMNER. The court house was then on Market square, and the only church bell was that in old TRINITY.

The coronation of the new sovereign which took place the following year was celebrated at St. John on 24th October, 1821. A ball was held in the Madras School-room, King square, which was attended by more than two hundred guests. The following day was the anniversary of the landing of the Loyalists' fall fleet. Tables were set on the King square and three oxen roasted whole to the great delight of the populace. In the evening there was a banquet, at which Colonel CHARLES DRURY presided, and Governor SMYTHE was present. A salute was fired by the artillery.

DAVID WATERBURY, the third captain, was born in Stamford, Conn., in 1758. He came to St. John with the Loyalists in 1783, and died 28th November, 1833. He lived on Dock street and kept a cooper shop on Nelson street. His tombstone in the Old Burying Ground has the simple record of his birth-place and death. He was often elected a vestryman of Trinity church, and for many years was chief of the Volunteer Fire Company. He was also a prominent Free Mason, being the second W. M. of St. John's Lodge, and the first of the Union Lodge of Portland. The engraving of Capt. WATERBURY is from an old daguerrotype given to the author by the late J. W. LAWRENCE, Esq.

JAMES POTTER, the predecessor of Captain WATERBURY died on Monday, 26th June, 1826, after a few hours illness. He was a retired ship-master and resided for many years on the east side of Prince William street.

Changes in command were frequent in those days. On September 3, 1822, JOHN C. WATERBURY was promoted to the captaincy, and THOMAS T. HANFORD and GEORGE WATERBURY were appointed first and second lieutenants respectively. The imperfect records of this period are assisted by an advertise-

CAPTAIN DAVID WATERBURY.

ment of the 1st Battalion St. John Militia regimental orders, under the date 19 July, 1823, which appears in the St. John "Courier." These orders refer to the four officers of the Artillery company who have just been mentioned, and also show that at that time there was a Grenadier company, of which BENJAMIN L. PETERS, father of the late Judge, was captain ; ALEXANDER EDMOND, uncle of the venerable JOHN WISHART, who died in 1893, JOHN R. PARTELOW, chamberlain and Mayor of St. John, and JAMES H. FOWLER were lieutenants. There were, besides these, six companies of the battalion, a company of light infantry, a rifle company and the African Staff company. The battalion was ordered to parade for drill on Friday the 5th and Saturday, 6th September, preparatory to its inspection ordered for the 8th of that month. The commanding officer requested that the men of all companies should appear in white trowsers, and the officers were also required to conform to this regulation.

The 74th Regiment, Lieutenant-Colonel MEIN commanding, was stationed in the city at this time. It left for Halifax in July or August, and an address was presented by the City corporation to the commanding and other officers.

The legislature was opened on 21st January, 1824, by the President of Council, the HON. WARD CHIPMAN, who was administering the government, pending the arrival of SIR HOWARD DOUGLAS. The President in his speech referred to the returns of the inspecting field officers of the militia which would be laid before the house, and from which additional proof would be derived of the expediency of a continued provision for the service. Shortly afterward His Honor died, his funeral taking place on February 16th. Preceding the hearse were the troops in garrison at Fredericton, and field pieces manned by the Royal Artillery and Captain MINCHIN'S company of militia Artillery, the whole being under the command of Major McNAIR of the 52nd Regiment, and forming the guard of honor and firing party.

April 23rd of that year was the anniversary of the tutelar Saint of England and of the birth of king GEORGE IV. In honor of His Majesty royal salutes were fired by the Royal Artillery at Fort Howe, and the militia artillery in Queen square. The firing of the latter was accompanied by a *feu de joie* from the 52nd Regiment and the Uniform companies of the 1st and 3rd battalions of the St. John Militia, under the command of Sir JOHN M. TILDEN. It was said they had a very fine effect.

On Tuesday, 24th August, Sir HOWARD DOUGLAS, the new governor, arrived at St. John in H. M. S. *Samarang*. At one o'clock the next afternoon he landed and proceeded through an avenue formed from the wharf to the Exchange Coffee House by two single ranks of soldiers, composed of a company of the 52nd Regiment, under Major McNAIR, and the Uniform companies of the 1st and 3rd battalions of the local militia under Major DRURY. When His Excellency left the ship the fact was announced by a salute from the *Samarang*, responded to from Fort Howe. On his landing the militia artillery fired a salute and the governor was cordially welcomed by Hon. JOHN MURRAY BLISS, who had administered the government since the death of JUDGE CHIPMAN. His Excellency was attended by the members of the executive council, the mayor, common council and magistrates of the city, and the heads of departments. The next day the corporation gave a dinner to Sir HOWARD and tendered an address to him. The population of St. John at this time was about eight thousand five hundred people. On 18th September Sir HOWARD reviewed about fifteen hundred men of the 1st, 2nd and 3rd battalions of militia under Major DRURY. In a general order published a few days afterwards His Excellency spoke of the great satisfaction which he had had in the review. He was 'very much pleased with 'the Artillery company under Capt. WATERBURY, who performed 'their firing and movements with celerity and precision and 'proved themselves deserving of all the encouragement which 'could be shown to them.' His Excellency held a levee in the city on 27th, in the Masonic hall, at which militia officers appeared in uniform.

By a general order of 29th March, 1825, the 2nd battalion was excepted from an order of the 24th October, 1824, which had constituted all the battalions in St. John city and county one regiment, of which the governor was colonel and Major DRURY lieutenant-colonel. The 2nd battalion now became the Regiment of St John County Militia, and Major CHARLES SIMONDS was appointed its colonel commandant. The annual inspection took place on 8th October, and was followed by a dinner, but the newspapers of the time do not give any details of the event. Colonel LOVE was the field officer inspecting.

Captain JOHN C. WATERBURY retired on 4th July, 1826, retaining his rank. He was afterwards County Treasurer, and died in the Parish of Portland on the 9th February, 1837, at the age of 47 years. THOMAS BARLOW, who had been appointed first lieutenant on September 8th, 1821, succeeded, on 9th January, 1827, to the command of the company, which he retained for upwards of eleven years.

The St. John "Courier," printed by HENRY CHUBB & Co., contains brief paragraphs referring to dinners following the annual musters of 1826 and 1827, but no particulars are given. It is of the time of Captain BARLOW that the earliest recollection can now be obtained from the lips of the living. JOHN R. MARSHALL, who, from 1862 to 1890, was chief of police of the City of St. John, joined BARLOW's company in 1830. He drilled with them for many years in an old fire engine house on Dock street. The company had two 3-pr. guns, which were kept in the battery at Lower Cove. Chief MARSHALL remembers, as sergeants, JAMES G. MELICK and LEWIS DURANT, afterwards officers of the company. In 1838 he assisted in firing a salute of 100 guns on the King Square in honor of the Queen's coronation. He ran through the steps of lance corporal, corporal and sergeant, to a second lieutenancy, which he obtained in 1848. His further promotions will be seen to have been of great importance to the present battalion in the way of establishing the continuity of its history with that of the old COLVILLE company.

From the year 1830 the first militia records, regularly kept as such, are available. In all matters previous to this old newspapers, almanacs and correspondence are the only sources of information. Through the kindness of Lieutenant-Colonel MAUNSELL, D. A. G., the records of his office from the date mentioned have been placed at the disposal of the writer, and have rendered possible a task which, even with this assistance, has been by no means an easy one. The tabular appendix to this book, showing the officers of the Artillery in all parts of the Province, is as complete and accurate as it is possible to make it, but the sources from which the information has been derived and the impossibility in a great many cases of testing the accuracy of a statement by comparison with official, or indeed any other records, render it impossible to claim that it is more than approximately correct. Considerable information has been obtained regarding the organization at St. John, but in the other parts of the Province it is absolutely impossible to do more than state the facts collected and the authority for them, leaving the reader to supplement them by conjecture.

In Charlotte County, as early as 1822, there appears to have been some artillery in connection with the infantry battalions. Attached to the 1st Battalion at St. Andrews there was a Lieutenant WILLIAM WHITLOCK, whose commission is dated 27 May, 1822. Lieutenants WM. GRAY and JOHN MESSINETT, date from 10th and 11th March, 1828, respectively, and on 19th May of the same year Captain JAMES MUIR appears. He was succeeded 4th February, 1829, by WILLIAM WHITLOCK, and at this time THOMAS BERRY appears as lieutenant. This company became a part of the regiment in 1838.

Some of the old almanacs shew a company attached to the 2nd battalion of Charlotte county. By reference to the names in the appendix it will be seen that, with the exception of Capt. JOHN MOWATT, 2nd July, 1829, they and the dates of commissions are the same as those of the 1st battalion. It is probable that lieutenants GRAY and MESSINETT were transferred to the company with the 2nd battalion when Capt. WHITLOCK took command of the one in connection with the 1st battalion. This company did not become a part of the regiment until 5th December, 1840.

There was still another company of artillery in Charlotte county with headquarters at St. Stephen. It was connected with the 1st battalion but on the 4th battalion being organized in 1835 it was transferred to the latter. The first captain on the list is T. or J ARMSTRONG who was succeeded by WILLIAM T. ROSE. While under Capt. ROSE the company came into the regiment. Though there could have been no battery for many years, yet Capt. ROSE retired as major on 13th June, 1866, and Lieutenant CLEWLY was promoted to the captaincy *vice* ROSE. The names of the officers are elsewhere stated.

Westmoreland county also appears to have had some men who could handle the rattling gun. When on August 3rd, 1825, Sir HOWARD DOUGLAS visited Sackville the Artillery company, under command of Capt. HARRIS, attached to the 2nd battalion, fired a salute of fifteen guns. In this county the artillery were attached to the 2nd and 3rd battalions, a departure from the usual course. The names of Westmoreland artillery officers, so far as known, are given in the appendix.

In 1825, on 11th July, when Sir HOWARD DOUGLAS visited Miramichi a salute of seventeen guns was fired, and later in the year troops were called out because of the great fire. It does not appear, however, that they were militia artillery.

York county, which prior to 31st March, 1831, included Carleton county, furnished considerable strength to the artillery of those times—but from inaccuracy in detail of available records it is difficult to determine the precise commands held by the officers named in connection with it. In 1824 Major GEORGE MINCHIN appears, his commission bearing date the 25th May of that year. In 1826 RICHARD DIBBLEE, then a merchant of Fredericton, was lieutenant. He subsequently removed to Woodstock and became a company officer there. On 10th September, 1827, Sergeant-major JAMES HOLBROOK was promoted to a lieutenantcy, and by orders of 20th March, 1832, he was appointed to the captaincy of a new company, probably infantry. ABRAHAM K. SMEDES WETMORE, a prominent lawyer, was on 22nd November, 1828, gazetted as lieutenant. He, too, afterwards removed to Woodstock, and succeeded on 17th September, 1833, to what was called the second captaincy, which appears really to have been the captaincy of a second company. His predecessor was GEORGE P. BLISS, who, on 10th September, 1827, had been appointed and now received a majority. There is also a reference in militia records to Capt. THOMAS JONES, artillery, 3rd York battalion. He was appointed on 3rd July, 1829, but of him there is no further trace.

JOHN 'SAUNDERS. SHORE was gazetted lieutenant on 25th August, 1834, and DONALD McLEOD on 2nd September in the same year. The former succeeded to a captaincy on the death of Major BLISS, 18th June, 1836, and GEORGE M. ODELL was appointed lieutenant on the same day. These officers came into the regimental formation in 1838.

In 1833 another St. John company was formed under Captain THOMAS L. NICHOLSON, with JOHN POLLOK, CHARTERS SIMONDS and WILLIAM ROSS as lieutenants. This was the Portland company. NICHOLSON was an auctioneer and commission merchant on the North wharf; POLLOK was in ROBERT RANKIN & Co., an old time firm of great repute; SIMONDS was in that employ and ROSS was a steamboat engineer. ROBERT REED, Esq., who died a few years ago, was afterwards an officer in this company, and as a private was largely instrumental in its organization. He was then a clerk with JAMES WHITNEY, the pioneer steamboat owner of St. John. Shortly before his death he mentioned JAMES ANDERSON and JOHN HOPKINS, of St. John, as the only survivors of the original company. In the same year Sergeant ROBERT ROBERTSON and CHARLES J. MELICK were appointed second lieutenants in the COLVILLE company.

St. John has always boasted of a 'Kid Glove' battery. One was formed in 1834 by the appointment on 26th April of WILLIAM PARKER RANNEY as captain, WILLIAM HUGHSON as lieutenant, and NEWTON WARD WALLOP, FREDERICK A. WIGGINS and STEPHEN KENT FOSTER as second lieutenants. This was a city battery.

The city artillery fired a salute from King Square on 18th May, 1833, being the Jubilee of the landing of the Loyalists. The event was celebrated by a corporation dinner given in the Masonic Hall at the head of King street.

An incident belonging to this period may here be told as its precise date can not be ascertained. GEORGE F. THOMPSON who, in 1859, was appointed to the RANNEY battery, was a son of MICHAEL THOMPSON, a petty officer in the Royal Navy who afterwards held a position in H. M. Customs. He was born in 1817 and joined the battery about 1835. Shortly before he was enrolled he was one day watching a sham fight in which BARLOW's and NICHOLSON's batteries participated on opposite sides. NICHOLSON was entrenched on the northward of Fort Howe holding the hill while BARLOW was attacking the position from the southward. The ammunition of the attacking party having run short, Capt. BARLOW came up to the enemy's lines and asked NICHOLSON for a supply 'to keep the fun going.' 'March these prisoners to the rear!' was the military response, and the valiant commander, foaming with rage, was obliged to submit to the carrying out of the order. He was soon released, however, and with the desired ammunition and a grudge to pay, renewed the attack.

In the last year with which this chapter deals, the cry 'The King is dead, long live the Queen!' was heard throughout the British dominions, and ever since the wish of length of days and happiness to her has echoed throughout the empire.

LIEUT.-COLONEL HAYNE.

CHAPTER V.

1838.

Formation of the New Brunswick Regiment of Artillery—Regimental Officers—Companies which formed the Regiment—Sketches of their Officers—Celebration of the Queen's Coronation.

UNDER the system prevailing at the time, the companies of artillery mentioned in the previous chapter were not available for concerted action. There is no doubt but that they must have been very meagrely supplied with outfits, for in those days the burden of clothing himself in some sort of military garb was thrown entirely upon the volunteer. The few guns which could be spared to the outlying districts were, however, probably far less obsolete than are those at present supplied to the militia artillery. But the great deficiency of the time was method. The companies being attached to infantry battalions, and there being no system of inspection at all similar to that of the present time, it was well nigh impossible that uniformity of drill could be maintained. Nor was this the worst feature of the administration. If the services of the militia should at any time have been required the artillery could not have been commanded advantageously by the infantry colonels, nor had they any officers of their own arm who had active experience of the duties of any rank above that of captain. Had they been put in the field there was no officer qualified for the work of looking after the issue of those supplies which are specially required for artillery. But happily for this important branch of the service, both the hour and the man had arrived for a change which resulted in the uniting of all the scattered companies into one body, and in giving to New Brunswick a regiment which for upwards of fifty years has maintained an existence, sometimes precarious indeed, but always continuous. The step which was then taken was probably accelerated by the events of 1837, which are familiar to all students of Canadian history. While the battle of responsible government was being fought in this province, on the floors of the assembly, hundreds of excited and reckless men were gathering around the standard of rebellion raised in Upper and Lower Canada by McKenzie and Papineau. The militia forces of the Upper Provinces proved quite adequate to avert the danger, but troops of the line were hurried forward to the scene of civil war. Those stationed in New Brunswick were ordered to the front, and during their absence the militia were called on to garrison the posts at Fredericton and St. John. In November, 1837, the 11th, 43rd and 83rd Regiments of the line were sent forward on sleds, and the militia called out for garrison duty were not relieved until the general order of 27th January, 1838, which mentions the 1st Battalion, York Co., and the St. John City militia as having taken part in this service.

On 28th February, 1838, the following general order was issued constituting the regiment:

"His Excellency the Lieutenant Governor and Commander-
"in-chief, considering it important to render the militia artillery
"of the Province efficient and available with as little delay as
"possible, has been pleased to appoint Captain Richard
"Hayne, on the half pay of the Royal Staff Corps and for-
"merly of the Royal Artillery, to be Lieutenant Colonel com-
"mandant of the said militia artillery. His Excellency has
"been further pleased to direct that this arm of the service
"be increased to ten companies and formed into a regiment,

"entitled 'The New Brunswick Regiment of Artillery,' the "distribution of which to be as follows, viz. :

At Fredericton,	2 Companies.
At St. John,	2 "
At St. Andrews,	1 Company.
At St. Stephen,	1 "
County of Westmoreland,	1 "
County of Northumberland,	1 "
County of Kent (Richibucto),	1 "
County of Carleton, (Woodstock),	1 "
Total,	10 companies.

"Each company to consist of one captain, one first and one "second lieutenant, four non-commissioned officers and thirty- "two privates. The officers belonging to the companies already "formed will consider themselves respectively attached to the "same until further orders. The uniform of the corps to be "blue and red facings, and similar to that now worn by the "Royal Artillery, the button to be struck with three guns, "surmounted by a crown and encircled by the words, 'New "Brunswick Regiment of Artillery.'"

By an order of 8th May, 1838, Major GEORGE F. STREET (unattached) was appointed major ; EDWARD PICK, gentleman, to be adjutant, and J. W. BOYD, Esq., to be paymaster. On 25th June of the same year DR. J. TOLDERVY, surgeon of the 3rd Battalion of York County was transferred to the regiment as surgeon. There was no quartermaster until 30th March, 1841, when E. B. PETERS was appointed to that position.

The following were the officers of the companies which in 1838 constituted the regiment :

At Fredericton :

Captain, - - JOHN S. SHORE.
Lieutenants, - - DONALD MCLEOD,
GEORGE M. ODELL.

Captain THOMAS BARLOW of the COLVILLE company was permitted to retire with rank by the general order which established the regiment.

At St. John:

1st (Colville) Company.

Lieutenant Comd'g, GEORGE WATERBURY.
Second Lieutenants, ROBERT ROBERTSON,
CHARLES J. MELICK.

2nd Company.

Captain, - - WILLIAM PARKER RANNEY.
Lieutenants, - - WILLIAM HUGHSON,
NEWTON WARD WALLOP,
STEPHEN KENT FOSTER,
FREDERICK A. WIGGINS.

At St. Andrews:

1st Company.

Captain, - - WILLIAM WHITLOCK.
Lieutenant, - - THOMAS BERRY.

At St. Stephen:

1st Company.

Captain, - - WILLIAM T. ROSE.
Lieutenant, - - J. CAMPBELL.
Second Lieutenants, J. MAXWELL,
W. ANDREWS.

At Woodstock:

Captain, - - A. K. SMEDES WETMORE.
Lieutenant, - - R. DIBBLEE.

No companies from Westmoreland, Northumberland or Kent were enrolled or became part of the regiment.

Soon after the formation of the regiment a second company was raised at Fredericton with the following officers and was accepted by general order of 8th May, 1838 :—

Captain, - - GEORGE F. BERTON.
Lieutenant, - - JAMES F. BERTON.
Second Lieutenant, EDWARD B. PETERS.

and on 25th June of the same year Captain NICHOLSON'S company at St. John was also included:—

Captain, - - THOMAS L. NICHOLSON.
Lieutenants, - - JOHN POLLOCK,
CHARTERS SIMONDS,
WILLIAM ROSS.

During the year JOHN C. ALLEN was appointed second lieutenant in Captain SHORE'S company, and lieutenant GEORGE WATERBURY of the COLVILLE company retired with his rank. On 12th November the volunteers were again called out for duty, the regulars having been sent forward on the second outbreak of the PAPINEAU rebellion. This service lasted for a week but it is not known what portion of the militia was employed.

A brief sketch of some of the first officers of the regiment will be appropriate at this stage. Others will be dealt with on the occasion of their promotion when a fuller record can be given. Of some, nothing can be said, for though the names have a familiar sound yet their histories have apparently perished.

Captain HAYNE, R. A., the first lieutenant-colonel of the regiment, was born in Devonshire, England, in 1804, and was educated at the Royal Academy, Woolwich. In 1820, as second lieutenant, R. A., he went with Sir HUDSON LOWE to St. Helena, where NAPOLEON was at that time confined, and remained there until the ex-emperor's death. In 1831 he came to Canada with Colonel BY, having been appointed to the Royal Staff corps, and was there employed on the Rideau canal and other engineering works. He went to England in 1836 and came to New Brunswick in the following year as commissioner to the New Brunswick and Nova Scotia Land company. He returned to England in 1870, and died at Dittesham, Devonshire, in 1874.

A daughter of Lieutenant-Colonel HAYNE became the

wife of the late WARD CHIPMAN DRURY, the late well known registrar of deeds for the city and county of St. John. His son, Major C. W. DRURY, of the Regiment of Canadian Artillery, served for some time in the present corps before receiving his permanent appointment.

GEORGE F. STREET, the first major, was a prominent figure in the politics of New Brunswick at this time. As a member of the 'Family Compact' he was strenuously opposed to Responsible Government, and in 1837, while a member of the Executive Council, was entrusted by his colleagues with a secret mission to the Colonial office, having for its object the frustration of the schemes of the Reform Party. In this, most fortunately for the future good government of the province, he was unsuccessful. He was a son of SAMUEL DENNY STREET, who in 1781 was on service at Fort Howe, and afterwards settled in Sunbury County. Major STREET was one of the principals in a celebrated duel fought on October 2nd, 1821. On leaving court at Fredericton an altercation occurred between him and GEORGE LUDLOW WETMORE, father of the late Mr. JUSTICE WETMORE. A challenge followed, and the parties, accompanied by Lieutenant R. DAVIS of the 74th Regiment and JOHN H. WINSLOW, met at Maryland Hill. The result was fatal to Mr WETMORE, and the surviving principal with the seconds fled from justice. They afterwards surrendered themselves and were tried on the 22nd February following before Judge SAUNDERS, when they were acquitted for want of sufficient proof of identity.

JOHN SAUNDERS SHORE was a son of GEORGE SHORE, the adjutant-general. He afterwards went into the 24th Regiment, and on 13th January, 1849, was killed at Chillianwalla, a town of British India in the Punjab situated on the left bank of the river Jhelum, in a conflict between the British forces commanded by Lord GOUGH and an army of Sikhs under SHERE SINGH. An obelisk was erected at the place bearing the names of the officers and men who fell in the action.

Of the St. John officers GEORGE WATERBURY was a merchant on Nelson Street; ROBERT ROBERTSON was a sailmaker, and CHARLES J. MELICK a tanner. The sword of lieutenant, afterwards Major MELICK, was in the possession of the late ROBERT REED, Esq.

WILLIAM PARKER RANNEY was of the firm of RANNEY & STURDEE, wholesale wine merchants; WILLIAM HUGHSON was a merchant, and FRED A. WIGGINS was a son of the benevolent founder of the WIGGINS' Orphan Institution of St. John. The life of STEPHEN KENT FOSTER was so largely identified with the corps that it must be dealt with elsewhere. NEWTON WARD WALLOP was a grandson of the veteran Major JOHN WARD and son of BARTON WALLOP, a naval officer, grandson of the second EARL of PORTSMOUTH. NEWTON WALLOP and his brother BARTON had a thrilling experience in their boyhood to which an allusion was previously made. They accidentally caused the death of DANIEL DEVOE, one of the signers of the first muster roll of the Artillery company. DEVOE had been in a company which served on the Royalist side in the American Revolution, and was commanded by JOHN WARD, the grandfather of the boys. On the 13th June, 1818, DEVOE, then an old man, was going to his home on King street, and in doing so had to pass the residence of CHARLES WARD where the lads were playing. They had discovered their uncle's horse pistols which he had left upon a table on returning from militia training. Not knowing that they were loaded they pointed them at each other and snapped the flints without effect. BARTON, seeing the old man coming up the street, aimed at him and pulled the trigger, when the pistol went off and DEVOE fell dead. The lads were taken into custody and an inquest was held, which exonerated them.

Captain NICHOLSON of the company which was long afterwards known by his name, was, to use the words of Mr. ROBERT REED, 'a sterling man.' His daughter is Lady RITCHIE, widow of the late Sir WILLIAM J. RITCHIE, who was Chief Justice of the Supreme Court of Canada. Lieutenant JOHN C. ALLEN, who afterwards became adjutant of the regiment, is now Sir JOHN C. ALLEN, the honored Chief Justice of New Brunswick. He was born October 1, 1817, of Loyalist descent, his grandfather having been ISAAC ALLEN of Trenton, New Jersey, who was a judge of the Supreme Court of New Brunswick from its erection until his death in 1806. Sir JOHN's life has been an active one. He was admitted to the bar of his native province in 1838, and rose rapidly, filling the offices of solicitor and attorney general, and eventually obtaining a seat on the bench in 1865. Ten years later, on the promotion of Sir WILLIAM J. RITCHIE to the Chief Justiceship of Canada, he became Chief Justice of New Brunswick, and in 1889 was knighted. At the time of the Papineau rebellion he was a bombardier and did garrison duty with his company.

The annual dinner of St. George's Society at St. John in 1838, held on the day of the patron Saint, was an event of unusual importance, as it was the first since the accession of HER MAJESTY to the throne. On the president rising to propose the Sovereign's health a royal salute was fired by Captain RANNEY's company from the King square. It was received with enthusiastic applause by the guests at the banquet which

SIR JOHN C. ALLEN,
(Chief Justice of New Brunswick.)

was given in the St. John Hotel, then on the corner of King and Charlotte streets.

A contemporary account of the celebration of the Queen's coronation, 28 June, 1838, says that 'a volunteer company of artillery under the command of Lieutenants FOSTER and WIGGINS paraded the streets with their field pieces, preceded by a band, and at nine o'clock went through their exercises on King square. At eleven o'clock the 11th Regiment, then in garrison at St. John, under command of Colonel GOLDIE, and the Royal Artillery, under command of Captain ARMSTRONG, turned out in parade upon the Barrack Square, where, at the cordial invitation of Colonel GOLDIE, they were joined by the militia companies. At noon a royal salute was fired, and a *feu de joie* given in fine style; and then the soldiers went through various evolutions admirably, while the regiment's excellent band played delightfully. There was a corporation dinner at six o'clock in the City Hall and a ball and supper at night in the St. John Hotel, which was well attended. On the Carleton side of the river royal salutes were fired in good style during the day.'

CHAPTER VI.

1839.

The Aroostook War—Militia Called Out--The Nova Scotia Legislature and the City of St. John vote Assistance--A Peaceful Solution—Recollections of George F. Thompson—Story of a Sham Fight.

WE have now arrived at a period in the history of this province when the maintenance of the rights of its inhabitants endangered the peace of the empire. Since the war of 1812 a gradual change had taken place in the relations between New Brunswick and the neighboring State of Maine. At that time the influence of the New England States had been exerted against a rupture with Great Britain because of the kindly feelings which prevailed between the colonies and those states, but during the quarter of a century which followed that effusive protestation of friendship the aspect of affairs had materially changed. Our warmest neighbors had become our bitterest foes, while in Washington, where the Capitol had been burned by British soldiers, a more moderate and pacific tone prevailed. The cause of the rupture was one of the commonest in country districts—it was the old trouble about a line fence. In this case it was not, of course, the division line between farms, but states. For many years the State of Maine had claimed that their boundary lay further eastward than that admitted by the British government. The treaty of Paris, made in 1783, had divided the territories by a line drawn from the source of the St. Croix river to the " highlands dividing the waters falling into the Atlantic from those emptying themselves into the St. Lawrence." In 1798 a decision had been given favorable to the contention of Great Britain—that the Schoodiac river was the St. Croix of the treaty, but the situation of the highlands remained undetermined. Upon the settlement of this question depended the ownership of a large tract of valuable timber land. For many years the matter was debated in the Maine legislature, and session after session the feeling ran high. In 1831 the King of the Netherlands had, as arbitrator, given a decision, but the United States refused to be bound by the award. When the PAPINEAU insurrection broke out, that rebel had the sympathy and support of many on the American side of the line, and nothing was asked but the most trivial pretext to warrant the people of Maine commencing hostilities. A community does not usually have long to wait for such a chance, and the 'Disputed Boundary' question, as it was called, was precipitated into the 'Aroostook war' by a small event. In January, 1839, about 150 men from Maine made a raid into the debatable country and seized some timber which had been cut by New Brunswick lumbermen. Instantly both countries were ablaze with a desire for war. McINTYRE, the Maine land agent, and two men who were with him were seized and carried to the gaol at Fredericton. Governor FAIRFIELD, of Maine, ordered the State militia to march forward. Major-General Sir JOHN HARVEY, governor of New Brunswick, issued a proclamation asserting the rights of Great Britain to occupy and preserve order in the territory until the dispute should be settled by some international arbitration. In moderate but earnest language he requested Governor FAIRFIELD to withdraw his troops. This gentleman who seems to have been anxious to have a war a any cost answered Governor HARVEY's demand by calling for more troops to the number of ten thousand men. Sir JOHN acted promptly. He despatched ninety men of the 36th regiment then at Fredericton, under Colonel MAXWELL, to Woodstock. On 13th February a draft was ordered from the 1st and 2nd battalions of the Carleton county militia. A request for troops was sent to Sir JOHN COLBORNE, the commander in Upper Canada. The militia of St. John volunteered; the first to come forward being fifty men of the Highland company under Captain, afterwards the Hon. JOHN ROBERTSON. A draft was made on the militia in that city, one company of seventy-five men being taken from the 1st battalion and another of equal strength from the rifle battalion. These men did garrison duty during the absence of the regulars from the city. The regiment of Artillery volunteered its services which were accepted by the following order:—

HEADQUARTERS, FREDERICTON,
19th March, 1839.

Militia General Order :—

His Excellency the Lieutenant Governor and Commander-in chief, having accepted the voluntary offer of service of the New Brunswick Regiment of Artillery, has been pleased to order into actual service one officer, two non-commissioned officers and nine gunners per company (together with the adjutant) at each of the following stations, viz. : Fredericton, Woodstock, Saint John and Saint Andrews.

Lieutenant-Colonel HAYNE will be pleased to take immediate steps for carrying this arrangement into effect.

By command,

(Signed)   GEORGE SHORE,
Adjutant.

Next day this order was rescinded and a much larger number called out, as follows:

	Officers.	N. C. O's.	Men.
At Fredericton,	1	3	16
At Woodstock,	2	8	24
At St. John,	1	6	33
At St. Andrews,	1	2	12
The adjutant at headquarters,	1	..	...
	6	19	85

On the 23rd March a detachment of the Artillery consisting of one officer, five non-commissioned officers and sixteen gunners with two light 3-pr. militia guns and sufficient ammunition were ordered to proceed to Woodstock on the following Monday. This detachment was placed under the command of Major STOW, R. A.

In this time of danger the people of New Brunswick had the hearty support of the legislature of Nova Scotia, which voted £100,000 for assistance if needed. The assembly chamber resounded with cheers when this vote was given, which were re-echoed in the parliament buildings at Fredericton when the news of the generous act was received there. New Brunswick placed all her revenues at the disposal of the governor. The City of St. John voted £1,000 for the maintenance of the families of the volunteers while the militia were at their posts. Sir JOHN COLBORNE responded promptly sending the 11th Regiment under Colonel GOLDIE. The troops were drawn up on the frontier awaiting the signal for combat. But SIR JOHN HARVEY was a diplomat as well as a soldier, and despite the blusterings of the great DANIEL WEBSTER, the representations of the British minister at Washington swayed the policy of the administration toward peace. General WINFIELD

Scott, who had fought against Sir John Harvey at Lundy's Lane, was sent to the border to take command of the state troops. The two old opponents met, talked the matter over quietly, and as a result Governor Fairfield was compelled to withdraw his troops.

The following order was issued upon the settlement of the dispute and the consequent withdrawal of the American forces:

Woodstock, March 27th, 1839.

Militia General Order :—

The governor of the State of Maine having issued his orders for the immediate withdrawal of the armed militia force from the disputed territory, Major-General Sir John Harvey is happy to permit their return to their homes of the militia and volunteer force of this province, of whose services he had felt it proper to avail himself during the late border differences; the arrangements for their disbandment will be promulgated in a militia general order.

In making this communication the Major-General and Lieutenant-Governor desires to express to the whole of the provincial force now on duty the highest degree of satisfaction which he has derived from the reports which have been made to His Excellency of the general exemplary conduct, and particularly of the desire which has been very generally manifested by them to avail themselves of the opportunities which have been afforded to them of gaining a knowledge of their military duties, under the instruction of officers and non-commissioned officers of Her Majesty's service —whose willing attention and unwearied patience in affording that instruction will, the Lieutenant-Governor is persuaded, be gratefully recognized by the militia of that province.

To Her Majesty's regular troops the Major-General tenders his sincere thanks for their general excellent conduct, and for the cheerfulness with which they have met the discomforts and inconveniences inseparable from military movements in such a climate and in such a season of the year; and the fact of their having continued in so perfectly healthy a state, the Major-General is justified in imparting wholly to their uniform steadiness, sobriety and good conduct, and to their unshaken determination to do their duty to their Queen and country.

The zeal, judgment and ability evinced by Lieutenant-Colonel MAXWELL claim the Major-General's warmest thanks which he likewise begs to offer to the officers commanding corps and detachments—to the several officers in command of detached posts—to the staff and departmental officers, and to all who by their zealous exertions and excellent arrangements have contributed to the soldiers' comfort and efficiency, and subsequently to the promotion of the objects of the service for which the troops have been assembled.

The Major-General cannot allow the force under Colonel GOLDIE to return to Canada without tendering to the Colonel and the officers and soldiers of the 11th Regiment and Royal Artillery under his command, his cordial thanks for their zealous co-operation in a service which has subjected them to a long and arduous winter movement.

By command,
(Signed) SAMUEL TRYON,
A. D. C.

Thus by the prompt action and wise judgment of one man a war was averted which would have entailed much distress upon both countries; and whose results would, in all probability, have affected the present generation. Mr. GEORGE F. THOMPSON, of Saint John, who had joined BARLOW's company about 1834 or 1835, recalls the time when he was on duty on this occasion. The detachment from this company did three days garrison duty and was held ready for orders for a week afterwards. The three companies, BARLOW's, NICHOLSON's and RANNEY's were very strong, numbering at this time about four hundred men, all uniformed at their own expense. Mr. ROBERT REED, another old artilleryman, also remembers that the three St. John companies agreed to do a fortnight's duty alternately. His, the NICHOLSON company, were marching down St. James street, on their way to the barracks, when a messenger brought the word that 'the war was over.' They continued doing duty until the next day when they were discharged.

At Fredericton both companies contributed to the service. Captain BERTON, with twenty-five or thirty men, was sent forward to Woodstock, where he remained for about two months, while Captain SHORE's company did garrison duty in the barracks at Fredericton. The Woodstock company was, of course, on duty. By an order of 30th March, 1839, all the volunteers were relieved from further duty, and this brief and bloodless campaign was closed.

In closing the record of this year the following sketch of a sham fight, taken from the "Weekly Observer," a St. John newspaper of that period, may be considered appropriate and interesting.

The following is the programme of the sham fight which took place on Tuesday last (12th November):

The troops were formed in column of companies in King's square. The enemy was represented by three divisions of the 69th Regiment, three companies of militia and two companies of militia artillery—the whole under the immediate command of Captain O'HALLORAN, 69th Regiment. In continuation of the manœuvres performed on the 1st instant, it was supposed that the right of the enemy's rear guard was in position covering their retreat and passage over the river on pontoons at Indiantown. The position taken up with this object was as follows: The right resting upon the heights rising in rear of the road passing by the ship yard to the short ferry, and flanked by the river; their centre on the continuation of the ridge extending across the high road to Indiantown, occupying the vicinity of the church on the left of it in force; their left resting on the small fir wood and ravine flanked by the morass which extends from the rear of Fort Howe in that direction. The enemy having an outpost on the heights of Fort Howe, and also a detached picquet in advance of their centre to watch the bridge of Portland and the roads leading thence to the city, and also having videttes on the high ground above Portland to give information of any movement in their front ; a picquet was also sent a little in advance of the left to watch that part of the ravine which debouches on the morass.

The attacking force, under the command of Major BROOKES of the 69th Regiment, advanced in two columns, the right by the road in rear of the Attorney General's house, to the pass leading to Fort Howe After possessing itself of this, and leaving a division to attack the heights in front, it proceeded under cover of the broken ground and the wood to the left of the Kennebeccasis road, to gain a passage at the head of the morass. This having been effected, it continued to skirt the opposite side of the morass till it arrived where the Indiantown mill-stream empties itself, when it halted. The left column proceeded by Union street to the head of Portland Bridge. When the skirmishers of the right column commenced their attack on the enemy's outposts on the heights, the left passed the bridge, driving back the enemy's picquet, which, after exchanging a few shots with the skirmishers, retired. The column then proceeded up the main street of Portland until it arrived at the point where it is intersected by the road leading to the river and that leading up to Fort Howe, where it divided, one division of it being detached and posted on the lower road running parallel with the river, near the shipyards, the others remaining in rear of the buildings to the left of the high road to Indiantown. When the skirmishers of the right column had possessed themselves of the heights of Fort Howe, captured the guns planted there, and turned them on the enemy, the left commenced a sharp skirmish with the enemy, and drove them back from the shipyards and buildings in front of their position. Having succeeded in this, it then attempted to force the right and centre of the position, but this attack, from the heavy fire of the Artillery and musquetry and the natural strength of the ground, did not succeed ; the attacking party falling back followed by the enemy to the ground they occupied previous to the attack, which they maintained. The attack on the right and centre having failed, the right column (which had now arrived on the extreme left of the enemy), after crossing the mill-stream commenced a vigorous attack upon it, and having gained possession of the fir wood and crossed the head of the ravine, turned the position, and continued the attack by echelon movement to their right, gained the high road and cut off the retreat of the enemy from their supposed pontoon bridge at Indiantown. In the meantime the left column having made dispositions preparatory to a renewed attack upon the centre and right, which it commenced as soon as it was perceived that the enemy's left had been turned, and after a severe contest it gained the heights and captured the enemy's guns, who being thus defeated and cut off from the main body fell back on the ridge in rear of the grave yard, and their whole force being thrown on the peninsula formed by the bend of the river, and without the means of escape, surrendered.

CHAPTER VII.

1840-1843.

Decline of the Old Militia System—Celebration of the Queen's Marriage—Opening of the Mechanics' Institute—Jubilee of the Artillery—Address to Major Ward—His Reply—Sketch of his Life.

THIS chapter opens with the year in which began the decadence of the old militia system of the province—a system which had few merits and almost innumerable defects. Yet it served the necessity of the times fairly well, and for many years after its growing inadequacy had been recognized it kept a place in the affairs of the country for want of a better substitute. Like all things which become obsolete its decline was gradual, and the history of the transition from it to the succeeding system must be postponed to a later chapter. Suffice it to say here that the end had begun.

The year 1840 witnessed the promotion of Lieutenant JOHN C. ALLEN to the adjutancy, and the addition to the regiment of Captain MOWATT's company of Charlotte county artillery. In July of this year an almost triumphal reception was accorded to the new governor-general, Right Hon. C. P. THOMPSON. He was received with a salute of nineteen guns from the Royal Artillery, and passed through the assembled trades on Prince William street. A portion of the New Brunswick Regiment of Artillery was stationed on the King square, and fired a salute as His Excellency entered the court house. He afterwards reviewed the militia from the St. John Hotel, then kept by the Messrs. SCAMMELL. On February 10th of the succeeding year a splendid ball was given by the officers of the several battalions of the militia of the city and county of St. John. It was held at the St. John Hotel in honor of the anniversary of Her Majesty's marriage, which was also the day fixed for the christening of the Princess Royal. The band of the 69th Regiment furnished music on this occasion.

A second major was appointed to the artillery in this year in the person of THOMAS L. NICHOLSON who has been mentioned before in connection with the formation of his company. Capt. RANNEY resigned about the same time and the vacancy so caused was filled by the promotion of Lieutenant S. K. FOSTER. By some oversight no quartermaster had yet been appointed to the new regiment but E. B. PETERS was gazetted to the position on 26th April. Lieutenant-Colonel HAYNE was appointed provincial A. D. C. to His Excellency on 7th May, and JAMES F. BERTON succeeded G. F. S. BERTON, deceased, in the captaincy of the company at Fredericton.

On Thursday, 12th August, the 1st Battalion of city militia under Lieutenant-Colonel PETERS, and the three St. John companies of the Regiment of Artillery commenced the annual training. On the following Tuesday the inspection took place, and a set of handsome colors was presented to the 1st Battalion. The drill served as good preparation for the pleasing duty which a portion of the artillery had next to perform. His Excellency Sir WILLIAM COLEBROOKE and suite landed at Indiantown about eight o'clock on the 16th August, and were received by Captain FOSTER's Artillery company and the Irish Royals, under Captain DRURY, as a guard of honor. As the governor left the steamer the Portland militia band struck up the National Anthem and the artillery fired the customary salute. On arriving at the St. John hotel His Excellency was received by a guard of honor of the 36th Regiment, and another salute was fired by Captain ROBERTSON's Artillery company which was stationed on the King square.

The birth of the PRINCE OF WALES was celebrated on the 8th December by the Royal troops firing a salute, but the newspapers do not state whether there was any demonstration by the militia.

On the 17th August of the next year a bazaar and exhibition was held in the Mechanics' Institute under the patronage of Lady COLEBROOKE. Upon the opening an address was read by Vice-President JACK and Sir WILLIAM read an answer on behalf of Lady COLEBROOKE. As Her Ladysh'p entered the hall a royal salute was fired by a detachment of the artillery under Major NICHOLSON, and the National Anthem was played by the band of the 30th Regiment. It is interesting to note that among the articles exhibited were working models of a steam engine projected by LEWIS W. DURANT and manufactured by him and JAMES G. MELICK. The exhibition was on quite a large scale for those days. It aspired to the dignity of a picture gallery in which the place of honor was assigned to the portrait of Major WARD.

In September of this year Major LOCK's company of Royal Artillery, then at St. John, was relieved by a detachment under Captain TUITE. On the 12th of the month the St. John division of militia artillery assembled for drill.

The next year's militia orders show CHARLES J. MELICK to have succeeded to the command of the old company of 1793, which was about to celebrate its jubilee. The orders also note that in August the New Brunswick Regiment of Artillery subscribed the sum of £9 toward the rebuilding of the monument to Sir ISAAC BROCK. This year was destined to be ever memorable in the history of our corps. Though since that time the records of its early history have been almost entirely destroyed by the many terrible fires which have devastated the City of St. John, yet the celebration of the 18th of May of that year has put beyond all doubt the fact that the original company had maintained a continuous existence. For some time previous to that loyal anniversary paragraphs appeared in the St. John newspapers intimating that the day would be especially commemorated in connexion with the Artillery company and its only surviving officer, Major WARD. The events of the day can better be related by the following extract from the St. John "Courier" of the 20th May, than by any paraphrase made by one who has no other knowledge of the time:

LANDING OF THE LOYALISTS.

THE FIFTIETH ANNIVERSARY OF THE FORMATION OF THE FIRST ARTILLERY COMPANY.

Thursday, the 18th May, being the day appointed by our good and loyal citizens for celebrating the above anniversary—the morn was ushered in by a salute on King square, and by the displaying of the "Union and Cross" on the various buildings and shipping in the harbor, the sun shone forth in unclouded splendor—not a cloud intervened to darken the approaching festivities—every heart beat high in anticipation of the events, and all seemed to hail the commemoration of so memorable an occasion with feelings of pleasure, satisfaction and enjoyment.

The uniform companies of our gallant militia were on the field at eleven o'clock precisely, under the command of their respective officers, who seemed to vie with each other in the neatness of their military costumes and the regularity and correctness of the movements of their men.

At twelve o'clock an address was delivered by Major NICHOLSON, of the New Brunswick Artillery, to Major WARD, the Father of the city, and who is now the oldest of that "noble band" who, with others, sacrificed all for their principles, their king and country—which address was nobly responded to by the gallant major. From thence the troops proceeded to the Queen square where a salute of fifty guns was fired with admirable precision by the artillery companies—after which they proceeded on their march round the city—thence to King square, where a royal salute was fired and the troops dismissed, after conducting themselves with credit to their commanders and with honor to the day.

Immediately after the conclusion of the above ceremonies, by invitation of the venerable gentleman addressed, the officers of the New Brunswick Regiment of Artillery partook of a very handsome luncheon at his residence.

In the evening a splendid ball took place at the St. John hotel, where all the pride, beauty and loyalty of the city were assembled, and where the youth of both sexes amused themselves till a late hour. We must not omit to mention the brilliant display of "fireworks" which was exhibited to the admiring spectators on King's square during the evening, and which reflects great credit on the projectors.

The following is a copy of the address alluded to above with Major WARD's reply:

SAINT JOHN, May 18th, 1843.

Sir :—

Assembled for the purpose of celebrating the Sixtieth Anniversary of the Landing of the Loyalists in this province, and the fiftieth of the formation of the first (or Loyal) Company of Artillery, now embodied in the New Brunswick Regiment of Artillery, we, the officers of that corps in St. John, gladly avail ourselves of the occasion to express the sentiments of high respect entertained towards you by our regiment and in which we feel assured every member of this community participates.

Deservedly beloved and esteemed as you have ever been by all round you throughout the course of a life already extended beyond the ordinary span allotted to mortals, we claim you with pride as one of the first officers of the corps to which we have now the honor to belong; and we hail you at the same time as one of the few survivors of that gallant band, who—surrendering all save the undying honor of their sacrifice—followed the standard of their Sovereign to these shores, and whose landing we this day commemorate.

That health and prosperity may yet long be yours, and h at the evening of your days may be as free from a cloud as your past life has been unspotted is the sincere desire of the corps in whose behalf we have the honor to subscribe ourselves.

With great respect, Sir,.

Your obedient servants,

T. L. NICHOLSON,
    Major N. B. R. A.
JAMES WILLIAM BOYD,
    Captain and Paymaster.
STEPHEN K. FOSTER,
    Captain.
EDW. B. PETERS,
    Lieut. and Quartermaster.
CHAS. C. STEWART,
    1st Lieutenant.

WILLIAM HUGHSON,
    Captain.
CHARLES J. MELICK,
    Captain.
WM. WRIGHT,
    1st Lieutenant.
N. W. WALLOP,
    Lieutenant.
LEWIS W. DURANT,
    Lieutenant.

To JOHN WARD, Esquire, J. P., Major, etc.

[Reply].

To Major Nicholson and the officers at St. John of the New Brunswick Regiment of Artillery:

GENTLEMEN—

Your address revives early recollections of a most thrilling nature. Nearly seventy years now have passed since first I joined the standard of my country as a British soldier. I most cheerfully consented to every sacrifice to maintain the rights of my Sovereign, the being of the Constitution—and when it pleased that Sovereign to suspend the struggle, I yielded to the event, retaining my allegiance—and sixty years have now elapsed since we first erected the standard of loyalty in this place, and the corps that you now represent was soon after embodied,— a corps whose high character for efficiency and discipline is so

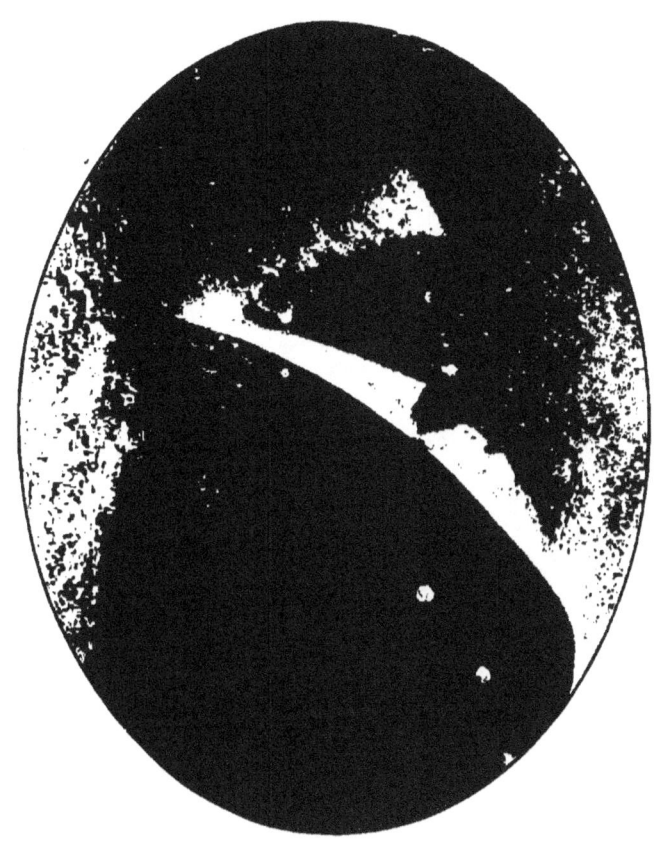

MAJOR JOHN WARD.

well supported by your present New Brunswick Regiment of Artillery.

It has pleased the Almighty to prolong my days beyond the period usually allotted to man, and many blessings have attended me, and mingled with the greatest is the esteem of my fellow citizens, and this additional mark of your regard will be fondly cherished by me during the few short hours I may yet be with you.

Gentlemen—I thank you for your address as one of the few surviving Loyalists—as an early member of your corps—and as a citizen proud of your esteem, I thank you—accept the blessings of an old man.

Yours affectionately,
May 18.   JOHN WARD.

Another paragraph records the ball as follows:

'The ball on Thursday evening, given by the St. John 'division of the New Brunswick Regiment of Artillery, was far 'more numerously attended than any during the season. Over 'sixty public guests were invited on the occasion, a large num- 'ber of whom, including Lieutenant-Colonel ORMOND, Major 'POYNTZ, and the officers of the 30th and 52nd Regiments; 'His Worship the Mayor, colonels of militia and heads of 'departments generally, with their families, honored the com- 'pany with their presence. We also particularly noticed Mr. 'HENRY ANTHONY, one of three only survivors of the ninety- 'seven good and loyal men who fifty years ago established the 'first Artillery company in this city, the formation of which 'they were invited to celebrate in connection with the sixtieth 'anniversary of the landing of the Loyalists on these shores. 'The other two survivors are Major JOHN WARD, who was a 'lieutenant in the corps, and Mr. DANIEL BELDING, of Dipper 'Harbor. The company is now attached to the New Bruns- 'wick Regiment of Artillery, and under the command of 'Captain CHARLES J. MELICK.'

To do full justice to the memory of Major JOHN WARD, whose name and person were so honored by our predecessors of half a century ago, would require a volume at least as large as the present, and might profitably be written if the regimental history permitted of biography in detail. But we must content ourselves with a few of the more prominent events in his remarkable career. Major JOHN WARD was born at Peekskill, Westchester County, in the Province of New York, in 1752. His family were all loyal, and three brothers served the crown during the Revolutionary war. He joined the "Loyal American Regiment," with the rank of ensign; from which he was promoted to a lieutenancy on 7th October, 1777, when he was twenty five years of age. He served with his regiment through the war, being frequently in action and was once wounded. He had a friendly intimacy with the unfortunate Major ANDRE, and when the latter started up the Hudson in the *Vulture* sloop of war, on his ill-fated mission to General BENEDICT ARNOLD, Lieutenant WARD was in command of the escort which accompanied him.

At the peace of 1783 he came to Parrtown with the rear guard of his regiment and many women and children. No accommodations had been provided for them and they lived in tents thatched with spruce boughs, erected on the Barrack grounds, Lower Cove. The winter was rigorous and many women and children died. Lieutenant WARD'S son, JOHN WARD, jr., was born in one of these tents on the 18th December, 1783.

Lieutenant WARD removed to Sussex Valley in the spring of 1784, but only remained there a short time, as in 1785 he entered into business in St. John with his brothers BENJAMIN and MOSES. This firm was the pioneer in the West India business, which brought so much prosperity to St John in the early days. The subject of our sketch was a man of more than ordinary enterprise. In company with the late Hon.

HUGH JOHNSTON, he put the first steamboat on the St. John river. It was called the *General Smythe*, and made the first trip to Fredericton on May 10th, 1816. The *General Smythe* was followed by the *St. George*, *John Ward* and *Fredericton*. Naturally he took much interest in military matters and until his resignation in 1816 was for many years in the command of the militia of the city and county of Saint John. In 1809, 1816 and 1819 he represented the county of Saint John in the House of Assembly. His name, for many years, stood first in the commission of the Peace for the city and county, until on 5th November, 1846, he died at his residence, corner of King and Germain streets, in the 94th year of his age. The following is an extract from the obituary notice which appeared in the St. John "Courier" upon his demise :—

"Thus full of years and honors has departed one who has led an unblemished life, and who carries with him to the grave the highest esteem and most profound respect of the community to whom his noble and venerable appearance, his strict integrity and amiable disposition have long been familiar."

So with the life story of a good and noble man whose youh was brilliant with courage and whose multitude of years taught wisdom, closes the first half century of the corps of which he was a founder and which venerates his memory today as that of a hero and a patriarch.

CHAPTER VIII.

1844-1859.

Muster Days—Drilling on the Flats—Major Foster—Colonel Hayne becomes Adjutant-General—Debate on Militia Law—Its Former Provisions—Uniform Companies—Beginning of Re-organization.

THIS was an era of profound peace, and for years it seemed unnecessary to many persons that militia training should be kept up. But despite the lack of encouragement from the government, which year by year withdrew its support from the militia system, and despite the growing indifference of the people to its welfare, the regiment kept its ranks fairly well recruited. It is true that the artillery did not drill many days in each year, but it is equally true that whenever their services were required for the celebration of an anniversary, especially that of their Loyalist forefathers, they were ready and willing to respond. That the corps of which we are so proud has a century of history to which we can point to-day, is the best possible tribute to that officer by whose exertions it was kept alive. To Lieutenant-Colonel FOSTER is due the credit of having by his personal influence and example, at a time when regiment after regiment of militia was dying out, maintained in some efficiency a portion of the old regiment, sufficiently strong to preserve the organizations of 1793 and 1838 until they were placed upon a firmer basis in 1860. The reader must expect but little from these days, and be surprised rather because there is a record at all, than at the meagreness of the one which is presented.

On 5th July, 1844, Captain JOHN C. ALLEN was appointed a provincial aid-de-camp. In these times the Fredericton company always fired a salute at the opening and closing of the legislature, and in dealing with this period it is to be particularly remembered that during the whole of it, and for years afterwards, a company was available for this purpose. In September of the following year Colonel HAYNE left Fredericton *en route* to England whither he was called on business connected with the Nova Scotia and New Brunswick Land Company. On the same morning (29th September) Captain POULDEN's detachment of the Royal Artillery also left Fredericton and Captain BERTON's company of the N. B. Regiment turned out and gave them a farewell salute.

In 1846 there was quite a number of promotions and appointments. Among them was that of ROBERT REED, of St. John, who became second lieutenant in the NICHOLSON company, then under command of Captain WILLIAM HUGHSON. Mr. REED had been in the corps for many years and up to his death had a vivid recollection of the old days. He recalled the times in the early '40's when the companies used to cross over to the Carleton shore in scows and go down to the Manawagonish road for their training. In 1839, as before stated, he was on garrison duty in St. John during the Aroostook war. At this time the artillery had two light 6-pr. guns. They drilled in the open air, generally about King square, which was then a common of very uninviting appearance. This drill would continue for three days after which the muster took place on the sands at Courtenay Bay. The selection of the day for the muster was always governed by the tide, it being arranged that the militia should leave King square about the time that the tide began to ebb. When the soldiery reached their parade the flats were quite dry and in beautiful condition for marching. Training day was in the nature of a fete to the people of the little city. The country people drove in and the city people drove out. Booths were erected and a thriving business done in all kinds of refreshments. Old women with shrivelled faces set up their apple stands, old men whose days of training were long past extolled the attractions of their wares in quavering voices. Boys rushed about pell-mell, and tumbled over everybody in their anxiety to get the best possible view of all that was going on. Wives, sisters, mothers and sweethearts, sought the sandy slopes beyond the Marsh, each believing that her representative in the ranks was the finest soldier of them all. They were merry, merry days, and we cannot but feel a touch of sadness when the old men of to-day relate these bright experiences of their boyhood. The sun seems to have shone more brightly, the grass was greener, the waters were more careless, and the world was happier in those days of old than it is in this more progressive but sterner age of terrible reality.

There were no World's Fairs then, but when the stock of provisions had been consumed, the bugles had sounded and the boys in blue and scarlet were marching home again, the stimulus of liquid refreshment raised many a volunteer and many a spectator to the summit of human bliss. There were no more worlds to conquer, and when the crowd returned to the city which had been unguarded in their absence, a night of jollification ensued. Such were the Muster Days.

The annual inspection of 1846 was held on 20th May. In the next year Captain THOMAS B. WILSON was appointed provincial aid-de-camp. On the laying of the corner stone of the Provincial Lunatic Asylum at St. John, in 1847, a salute was fired by a company of artillery under Major NICHOLSON. In 1848 Colonel HAYNE became assistant adjutant-general in the place of Lieutenant-Colonel W. H. ROBINSON, who had died shortly before. The death of Major THOMAS L. NICHOLSON occurred in this year, and the vacancy thus caused was filled by the promotion of Captain S. K. FOSTER to the majority. Mr. G. SIDNEY SMITH, of St. John, remembers the funeral of Major NICHOLSON, at which he says the artillery was present under Captains FOSTER, MELICK, WRIGHT and STEWART.

The "Courier" of 19th May, 1849, contains the following account of the celebration of the sixty-sixth anniversary of the landing of the Loyalists, which had been observed on the previous day :—

"The anniversary of the landing of the Loyalists in this city in 1783 was celebrated yesterday. Flags were to be seen floating from the dwellings of many of the descendants of the loyalists and from other conspicuous situations, and some of the vessels in the harbor were bedecked with their colors. The St. John companies of the New Brunswick Regiment of Artillery fired a royal salute at noon and marched through the streets preceded by one of the amateur bands playing some lively airs. In the evening Queen's square and its environs were crowded by a dense mass of people to witness a display of fireworks. The exhibition exceeded anything of the kind ever seen here, and was grand and beautiful in the extreme, and reflected great credit upon all concerned in getting it up. The committee of management were Major S. K. FOSTER, of the Artillery; Captain T. E. G. TISDALE, City Rifles, and Mr. JOHN SEARS, all descendants of the first settlers of St. John."

The annual muster of this year was held on the 9th October. The 18th of May of the next year was observed by the firing of a salute and a display of fire works on the Queen's square similar to that of the previous year.

There were several promotions in 1849, among them that

of Lieutenant FRED A. WIGGINS to be paymaster *vice* BOYD, resigned. Much dissatisfaction was afterwards caused by the granting of rank to this officer, which, it was claimed, was unjust to those who had done more work than he. The matter was adjusted, but not until the interest of several officers in the regiment was destroyed.

In 1851 Colonel HAYNE became adjutant-general of the province upon the death of Lieutenant-Colonel the ·Honorable GEORGE SHORE, which occurred on 18th May. Though not an officer of our regiment, yet the record of Lieutenant-Colonel SHORE is so thoroughly identified with the militia system of New Brunswick that a slight digression may be pardoned, in extracting from the "Courier" of May 24th of that year the notice of his death. It is as follows:

"On the afternoon of Sunday last Lieutenant-Colonel the Hon. GEORGE SHORE expired at his residence in this city (Fredericton) after an illness of three days duration. Colonel SHORE came to this province in 1804—was an officer in the 104th Regiment, and marched at the head of the light company of that corps to Canada in 1813, where he served during the continuance of the last American war. After returning from Canada, Colonel SHORE was appointed A. D. C. and private secretary to the late General SMYTHE, then governor of the province, and subsequently, at different periods, filled the offices of auditor-general and surveyor-general.

In 1825 Colonel SHORE was permanently appointed to the office of clerk of the pleas in the Supreme Court, which office he continued to hold up to the time of his death. The deceased was also at one time inspecting officer of militia, and was afterwards appointed adjutant-general, which office he held at the time of his decease. Besides filling in turn, with credit to himself and satisfaction to the country, the offices which we have already enumerated, the deceased was more than once an executive adviser of the crown, and for many years had a seat in the legislative council of the province." * * * *

The funeral of Colonel SHORE was strictly private.

The 29th September, 1852, was an eventful day in the history of New Brunswick, being the occasion of the signing of the contract for the building of the line of railway from St. John to Amherst, and also from St. John to the American frontier. The contract was signed at St. John at 12 o'clock, noon, of that day, and the volunteer artillery, under command of Major FOSTER, fired a salute from Chipman's Hill.

There was a somewhat acrimonious debate over the introduction of a new militia bill in the House of Assembly on the 24th March, 1853. Though the bill was offered in compliance with royal instructions, yet it was ridiculed by some of the members, and apparently misunderstood. The House had no sympathy with a militia system. But one branch of that system had still some life in it, for we find that the 18th of May of that year, being the seventieth anniversary of the landing of the loyalists, was observed in the usual manner by a salute from the New Brunswick Regiment of Artillery. On the 14th September there was a great demonstration in the city of Saint John in honor of the turning of the sod of the European and North American Railway, for the building of which the contract had been signed in the previous year. The day was ushered in by a salute from the artillery, and at ten o'clock the streets were crowded by a throng of people. Half an hour later one of the great old time trades processions began to move through the city. First came a body of citizens on horseback, then a company of the New Brunswick Artillery; the marshals; the president and directors of the Mechanics' Institute; the trades; Common Council; fire companies; justices of the peace; millmen; men of the Black Ball Line of Liverpool Packets; pilots; Freemasons and many others; in all upwards of 5,000 persons. The procession was nearly a mile in length.

The artillery fired a salute when the first sod was raised by Lady HEAD, wife of the Lieutenant-Governor, and deposited in an elegant wheelbarrow.

At this, the transition period from the old to the new systems of organization of the militia, it may be well to briefly review the provisions of the militia laws of the time. Reference has previously been made to the law in force at the time of the formation of the COLVILLE company, which, however, was changed from time to time. There seemed for many years to be a feeling against having a permanent militia law on the principle which has always been urged against standing armies. Whether or not that was the true reason, it is a fact that the law was frequently enacted, the provisions of the acts varying but very little. At length, in 1825, acts relating to the militia were consolidated. All male residents of the province from sixteen to sixty years of age were rendered liable to militia service in battalions to be formed in each county. Where the counties were sufficiently populous more than one battalion might be formed. The company was the unit, and each was to consist of not more than sixty rank and file under one captain and two subalterns. The exemptions were members of the Legislative Council and House of Assembly, established clergymen, licensed ministers of the gospel, all persons exercising civil or military commissions under the crown; officers on half pay, supernumerary militia officers then in commission; officers of customs, revenue and naval officers; physicians and surgeons, licensed to practice as such; one miller to each grist mill, and one ferryman to each established ferry, and Quakers who had been members of that sect for one year. Nearly all of these exempts were liable to service in case of actual invasion. Provision was made for drilling regiments or battalions one day in each year, and battalions were to be drilled by companies twice during that period. To assist in the administration adjutants and sergeant-majors of battalions received a small money grant annually. Exempts, except ferrymen, had to pay a tax of ten shillings per year, and there was also a license upon aliens. When drafts for actual service were made they were confined to persons between eighteen and fifty years of age and volunteers were to be accepted without draft. The commander-in-chief was given power to establish artillery and sea fencible companies, and to direct the mode of drilling them. In cases of emergency which might render the services of the artillery more necessary than others, the officer commanding any regiment or battalion in which there might be an artillery company was authorized to call out the whole or part of such company though the number so called out might exceed the proportion of men which the company was liable to furnish.

As stated before the Artillery company at St. John was always uniformed. In 1827 an act was passed for the encouragement of this and other uniform companies. In after years membership in these companies became quite a privilege as they kept up regular drill and the members were fairly well instructed. All who did not join the companies were called out for one or two days drill each year, and from their ignorance of squad drill were termed the 'flat feet.' Those belonging to uniform companies acted as instructors of the others and always had much fun with the amusing blunders of the raw recruits.

In 1839 provision was made for the establishment of battalions of Artillery and Sea Fencibles, but in the case of the Artillery a regiment had been formed in the previous year.

In 1851 owing to great opposition on the part of the people who were drilled as 'flat feet' many provisions of the militia law were suspended for that year. When the statutes were revised in 1854 the whole militia law was consolidated without alteration, and the sections of the old acts which had been suspended were further suspended until 1856, it being provided that the Commander-in-Chief might by proclamation revive these sections or any portion of them. The suspended portions of the law, however, applied only to that branch of the militia which is now designated as the 'Reserve.' Chapter 82 of the Revised Statutes which dealt exclusively with the Artillery and Sea Fencible companies was not suspended, and the keeping of a militia force was always sanctioned. The portions of the acts suspended dealt with the imposition of penalties for non-attendance at drill and similar vindicatory provisions of the law. That this construction of the law is correct is amply proved by the act of the Lieutenant-Governor, Hon. J. H. T. MANNERS SUTTON, who, in 1859, without issuing a proclamation accepted the services of several volunteer companies. During the period of suspension some commissions were issued and among them one dated 18th April, 1855, to Sergeant-Major THOMAS PAISLEY as second lieutenant in the Artillery company at Fredericton. As before stated the Fredericton company always fired a salute at the opening and closing of the legislative session. Of course, it is not pretended for one moment that there was a thoroughly organized and well disciplined body of men continuously existing as the New Brunswick Regiment of Artillery, but what can be successfully proved is, that one or more companies had an existence during this period of inactivity; that on many public occasions they assisted in their capacity of an artillery force, and that, when vigorous recruiting began again in 1859, some of the old officers retained command of their companies while the appointment of new officers was, in many cases, recognized in general orders as being in substitution for others who retired.

One of the last incidents in which the St. John Artillery took part, during the period with which this chapter deals, was the celebration on September 1st, 1858, consequent on the successful laying of the Atlantic cable.

After the Crimean war there was a very enthusiastic volunteer movement in England which has continued with increasing strength to the present time, resulting in one of the finest forces of modern times. The inception of the system seems to have attracted the attention of Major-General Sir FENWICK WILLIAMS, who, on leaving England in 1859 to assume command of the forces in the North American provinces, suggested a scheme of defence for the colonies based on similar principles. The DUKE OF NEWCASTLE, then Colonial Secretary, wrote to the Lieutenant-Governor of New Brunswick expressing a desire that he might confer with General WILLIAMS whose views had the sanction and concurrence of the home government. In consequence of this request it was intimated that the services would be accepted of such companies as might volunteer, and in the summer of 1859 the work of instructing the militia was recommended, and has been continued to the present time.

CHAPTER IX.

1859.

*Offers of Service Accepted—Many New Officers—Captain Mount's Work
—The Colville Company Continued—New Companies in Carleton
and Portland—Other Companies—A New Uniform Adopted—A
Review—The Prince of Wales Expected.*

IN his despatch to the DUKE OF NEWCASTLE, dated 9th December, 1859, Lieutenant-Governor MANNERS-SUTTON stated that the revival of the militia acts by proclamation would have necessitated the calling out of the whole able-bodied population of the province, which would be an unnecessary interference with industry. No such objection could be urged against his acceptance of the spontaneous offer of any portion of the several regiments of militia to volunteer in companies for drill and exercise, under command of the officers of their respective regiments. He had applied for and received from Lieutenant-Governor Sir FENWICK WILLIAMS, in command at Quebec, three thousand stand of rifles with accoutrements, which were stored at St. John. In that city four companies of the artillery had volunteered; their services had been accepted, and they would be instructed in rifle practice and drill. Adjutant-General HAYNE's report, dated 12th January, 1860, a copy of which was also transmitted, showed the state of the artillery to be as follows:

Counties.	No. of Companies completely formed.	No. in course of formation.
York,	...	1
Queens,	..	1
St. John,	3	3

The companies in St. John and Fredericton were then being drilled by their own officers and non-commissioned officers. A subsequent report of 10th March showed that the company was still being formed at Fredericton; that five companies consisting of two hundred and eighty men had been enrolled at St. John and that another company was in process of formation, while one of thirty-eight men had been enrolled at Woodstock. Two light guns at St. John and two at Woodstock were in use, and the artillery were also being drilled with rifles.

When active work ceased Colonel HAYNE was in command of the regiment; S. K. FOSTER, major; JOHN C. ALLEN, adjutant; E. B. PETERS, quarter master; FRED. A. WIGGINS, paymaster; J. TOLDERVY, M. D., surgeon, and LEB. BOTSFORD, M. D., assistant surgeon. In St. John the officers were:

Colville Company.

Captain,	CHARLES J. MELICK,	10 April,	1843.
Lieutenant,	LEWIS DURANT,	12 April,	1843.
Second Lieutenant,	JAMES G. MELICK,	10 August,	1848.

Nicholson's Company.

Captain,	C. C. STEWART,	12 August,	1848.
Lieutenant,	ROBERT REED,	10 October,	1845.
Second Lieutenant,	ROBERT SWEET,	13 August,	1848.

Ranney's Company.

Captain,	WILLIAM WRIGHT,	11 August,	1848.
Lieutenant,	JOHN R. MARSHALL,	12 August,	1848.

At Fredericton:

Captain,	JAMES F. BERTON,	23 July,	1841.
Lieutenant,	THOMAS PAISLEY,	18 April,	1855.

At Woodstock:

Captain,	A. K. S. WETMORE,	8 March,	1839.
Lieutenant,	WALTER D. BEDELL,	30 October,	1845.
Second Lieutenant,	CHARLES H. CONNELL,	10 August,	1848.

At St. Stephen:

Captain,	WILLIAM T. ROSE,	8 April,	1834.
Lieutenants,	J. CAMPBELL,	9 April,	1834.
	J. MAXWELL,	26 March,	1827.
	W. ANDREWS,	9 April,	1834.
	PETER BROWN,	9 April,	1884.

It is difficult to place any other officers with accuracy, but an attempt has been made to do so in the appendix to this work.

The active work of re-organization in St. John was done by JAMES MOUNT, who had been a sergeant in a company of the Royal Artillery. He was appointed captain in the militia artillery about June, 1859, and set to work enrolling a volunteer company. Success attended his efforts, and in a few weeks the roll was signed by one hundred and twenty of the brightest and most active young men of the city. The first name was that of GEORGE H. PICK, whose connection with the artillery will be many times referred to in these pages.

Militia general orders of 20th September, 1859, contain the appointment of Captain MOUNT to the adjutancy *vice* JOHN C. ALLEN, who resigned that office only and retained his rank of captain in the regiment. On the 14th November GEORGE H. PICK, ROBERT SNEDEN and GEORGE THOMAS were gazetted lieutenants. These were officers of MOUNT'S company, which was afterwards designated as 'No. 1.' On an evening in the summer of 1859 the company met in an old building on the corner of Duke and Prince William streets, St. John, afterwards used as a dance hall and bowling alley, and elected officers, a proceeding which would seem strange in these days. Besides the lieutenants just mentioned, FRANK LANSDOWNE and JAMES F. ROBERTSON were chosen sergeants. The latter is now a member of the well-known firm of MANCHESTER,

ROBERTSON & ALLISON. On December 6th of that year Major FOSTER attained the rank of brevet lieutenant-colonel, and Captain CHARLES J. MELICK, of the old COLVILLE company was gazetted major *vice* Hon. G. F. STREET, deceased, thus filling up the regimental establishment of two majors. The RANNEY company was also filled up by the promotion of Lieutenant JOHN R. MARSHALL to the captaincy and the appointment of GEORGE F. THOMPSON, ROBERT J. LEONARD and FRANCIS SMITH as lieutenants. On the same day a new company was accepted with JOSIAH ADAMS, captain, JOSEPH CORAM, EDWIN J. WETMORE and GEORGE J. STACKHOUSE, lieutenants, which was subsequently designated as 'No. 2,' and is now the Carleton company. They drilled in the upper rooms of a store on South Rodney wharf and exercised on the wharf with their guns. The superintendent of ferries of St. John, Mr. H. ADAM GLASGOW, was one of the first sergeants of the company. In January, 1860, Lieutenant PICK became captain of No. 1 and FRANCIS LANSDOWNE succeeded to a lieutenancy, while in Portland HURD PETERS as captain, with ALEXANDER RANKIN and JAMES KIRK, raised a new company which is still in existence as 'No. 3.' They organized in the fire engine house on Simonds street, and from thence removed to the Madras school building where St. Peter's church now stands. The company afterwards occupied the Portland temperance hall. They had two 3-pr. guns from the barracks and were supplied with Enfield Snider rifles. Another company was also formed in Portland under Captain RICHARD SIMONDS and Lieutenant W. ROGERS, principally from the men of Protector No. 2 Engine Company. They drilled for some time, but eventually most of the members went into one of the infantry companies then being raised, and Captain SIMONDS' company ceased to exist.

In the same month LEWIS DURANT of the COLVILLE company became its captain; second lieutenant JAMES G. MELICK was promoted to the first lieutenancy and THOMAS COKE HUMBERT was also gazetted as lieutenant. In February the Woodstock company, known as No. 5, was re-organized with JAMES EDGAR, captain; WILLIAM SKILLEN and EDWARD D. WATTS lieutenants. Another company, afterwards known as No. 7, at Chatham, Northumberland County, was organized in March with JAMES C. E. CARMICHAEL, captain, ELIJAH PARSONS and THOMAS F. GILLESPIE, lieutenants; while at Gagetown J. WARREN TRAVIS, captain, FRED. LUNDRINE KNOX and WILLIAM J. FROST, lieutenants, added another to the roll.

Yet another company was formed in the next month of this year. It was a second company in Carleton, St. John, with JOHN McLAUCHLAN, captain, RICHARD NEWELL KNIGHT and THOMAS MITCHELL McLACHLAN, lieutenants. The numbers by which these companies are referred to were not given at the time of formation and do not appear in any official list In fact the question of priority was one of considerable doubt and may in some sense be even yet considered an open question. As stated previously, the commissions of all the regimental and many of the company officers remained in force though active work had not been carried on for a few years. In Fredericton a company always fired a salute at the opening and closing of the legislature and in St. John any public celebration was generally accompanied by a salute. Yet the COLVILLE company was not in a position to take up drill without recruiting and it does not appear that Captain CHARLES J. MELICK made any active effort to begin the work. His accession to the majority afforded an opportunity for younger blood to make the necessary effort but time was thereby lost, and Captain PICK'S company was undoubtedly in an efficient state before any other. But even then the claim was made by Captain DURANT and his successor, Captain JAMES G. MELICK, that they were the heirs of the COLVILLE company, and though the authorities at a subsequent time chose to designate Captain PICK's company as No. 1 and that of Captain DURANT as No. 3, their decision does not appear to have been based upon historical claims but rather upon the order in which the rolls were forwarded. It is to be noted that the numbering is not used in any official reports. The result of a great deal of investigation given to this subject shows that the DURANT company was beyond doubt the lineal successor of the COLVILLE company.

The guns of the St. John artillery at this time were 3-prs. and were kept in a barn on King street east about opposite to the gymnasium. They were under the charge of Major MELICK. The use of these guns by the older organizations is recalled by JOHN R. MARSHALL, still living, who from 1862 to 1890 was chief of the St. John police force. About 1830 he joined Captain BARLOW's company when GEORGE WATERBURY, ROBERT ROBERTSON and CHARLES J. MELICK were lieutenants, and rose through the ranks of bombardier, corporal and sergeant to a lieutenantcy in 1848. When he joined the company JAMES G. MELICK and LEWIS DURANT were sergeants. Drill was carried on in the old fire engine house then on Dock street, and the two 3-pr. guns were kept in the battery at Lower Cove. On his appointment to a lieutenantcy he was transferred to WRIGHT's company of which, as we have seen, he afterwards became captain. They drilled principally on the King square and afterwards in the Mechanics' Institute, and had sixty stand of rifles which were kept in Captain MARSHALL's house, in rear of St. John's (Stone) Church. In 1862 the rifles were sent away and the company did not re-enrol under the new militia act of that year. Captain MARSHALL took part in the coronation salute of one hundred guns in 1838, which was fired from King square.

A meeting of the officers of the regiment was held on the evening of the 26th April, 1860, at No. 3 Engine house, Lieutenant-Colonel FOSTER in the chair, at which the question of uniform was discussed. That originally agreed upon for officers and men was the shell jacket and trousers similar to the undress of the Royal Artillery, but some of the officers were opposed to this, contending that for the officers, at least, the uniform should be a tunic or frock coat. After a long discussion the first idea prevailed, and the dress chosen was a dark blue jacket trimmed red; trousers with red stripe down the side; forage cap with red band for privates and non-commissioned officers, and a gold band for officers. It was voted that the regiment should fire salutes on the 18th and 24th of May of that year should they be then in possession of their guns. The boys must have got their guns in time, for the salutes were duly fired, and a newspaper item states that there was a muster of one of the companies on the 24th, the members of which looked very well in their new uniforms.

The recollections of Mr. GEORGE F. THOMPSON, of MARSHALL'S company, on the subject of uniforms are quite interesting. He purchased his uniform cap; shell jacket and gold laced trousers for £25 from MCKENZIE, the King street tailor, who was afterwards cruelly murdered in the Little River tragedy. His sword and belts cost him £15 more. The uniform previously worn, said Mr. THOMPSON, consisted of a jacket with two short tails. Underneath the jacket there was a hook with a curve slightly protruding to hold the belts, which were two inches wide. The sea fencibles used artillery guns. Their uniform was a blue cloth round-about jacket with white duck trousers and a glazed cap. The rank of officers in those days was distinguished by epaulets, the lieutenants wearing one and captains two.

One or two items gleaned from the newspapers of the day must bring this chapter to a close:

"On the evening of May 31st several companies of the New Brunswick Regiment of Artillery belonging to the city and Portland were inspected on the Barrack Square by Major-General TROLLOPE. The companies were drawn up in line by Captain and Adjutant MOUNT. The lieutenant-colonel commanding the district placed himself in front, and on the arrival of the general and his suite, received him with the customary honors. The general, after reviewing the companies, addressed the colonel, officers and men in a pleasant and appropriate manner, concluding with the hope that on the arrival of the PRINCE OF WALES the part which the artillery should bear in his reception would not only do credit to themselves and their noble province, but to this city."

"On the evening of May 30th two companies of artillery on the West Side, under the command of Captains ADAMS and McLAUCHLAN, turned out and paraded through the various streets in Carleton, the men made an excellent appearance, and marched with a precision and regularity that would have been creditable to a body of soldiers of the line. Previous to their marching they were inspected by Lieutenant-Colonel FOSTER. After considerable marching and counter marching they escorted the Lieutenant-Colonel to the ferry boat where they were drawn up in line and addressed by the Colonel,—who complimented them on the appearance they made, and upon the proficiency they had made in their drill. The men then marched back to the armory and soon after dispersed."

There was also an inspection at the Barrack square on June 1st, by Major-General TROLLOPE, at which the artillery and city volunteer companies were present.

So began the later history of the New Brunswick Regiment of Artillery, bright with earnestness and full of endeavor, and though the incidents which follow may be less thrilling than those which precede them, yet credit must be given for the motives which gave rise to this activity. For, strange to say, while a threatened war with France in the early days of our province evoked the military ardor of her inhabitants, to the same cause may be ascribed the great volunteer movement in the mother country which spread to our land with the result which has been related.

CHAPTER X.

1860.

Visit of the Prince of Wales—Reception at Saint John—The Artillery under Captains Durant, Pick, Peters, McLauchlan, Adams and Travis take Part—Major Carter in Command—An Inspection.

THREE signal guns rapidly fired from the Fort at Partridge Island about half-past nine o'clock on the evening of Thursday, 2nd August, 1860, announced the arrival of H. M. S. *Styx* in the outer harbor, and opened the greatest *fete* ever held in St. John. The vessel bore HIS ROYAL HIGHNESS THE PRINCE OF WALES, and an eager multitude anticipated with loyal interest the first welcome to the Province of an heir apparent to the British throne. Not since the visit of the DUKE OF KENT in 1794 had a scion of royalty been seen in the city. Those who recalled that event were few, but nowhere could the PRINCE have been more welcome than in that city which had been erected in the wilderness by the enthusiastic loyalty of its devoted founders. The ship with her royal passenger moored near Reed's Point and was visited by the Lieutenant-Governor and Colonel HAYNE. The militia artillery slept little that night and when the morning broke, in the most beautiful of Queen's weather, the men were at their posts. A salute from all the forts, joined by our regiment of artillery rang out at sunrise, and long before the hour of landing the batteries of Captain PICK and Captain HURD PETERS were on duty at the Ballast Wharf. The wharves and Prince William street were thronged by the whole population of the city reinforced by thousands of visitors, joy and music adding to the zest of the occasion. Captain DURANT's company was stationed at the entrance to the Chipman House, where the grand-father of the PRINCE had lodged, and under their guns was the house of Captain COLVILLE, the first commander of their company. Captain MCLAUCHLAN's (Carleton) company was also stationed there. Next came the rifles and infantry companies, the national societies, the cartmen mounted, the Sons of Temperance, firemen and trades, so that the line extended from the Chipman House to the place of landing at Reed's Point. Each company of the artillery and other volunteers contributed eighteen men to a guard of honor which was under command of Colonel THURGAR.

At half past ten o'clock the PRINCE, accompanied by the DUKE OF NEWCASTLE, EARL ST. GERMAIN and *suite* was rowed to the landing stage at Reed's point, the yards of the war vessel being manned and a salute fired. The National Anthem was played by the band of the 63rd Regiment, and as the PRINCE stepped on shore the volunteers presented arms. A large procession of escort was formed consisting of provincial and corporation officers, the judges, members of legislative council and house of assembly, and office bearers of the national societies. Triumphal arches had been erected along the route. That at Reed's point was styled a grand Reception Pavilion and was beautifully decorated. The interior of the Pavilion seated sixteen hundred people. Opposite the old city building which then stood just below the COLVILLE house, near the present warehouse of W. H. THORNE & Co., the civic arch, a magnificent fabric, had been constructed. It was fifty feet in height from the ground to the inside of the upper arch so that persons standing in the CHIPMAN grounds could look under it to Reed's point. Its panels were suggestive of the early history of the Province and the date "1783" was conspicuously displayed. . Five thousand Sunday school children gathered in the CHIPMAN grounds greeted H. R. H. with the national anthem, special words having been adapted to the music for the occasion. The procession then retired and reformed. It was reviewed by the PRINCE from the porch of the Court House on Sidney street. First came the band of the 63rd Regiment, then Captain PICK's company of the N. B. R. A. followed by the other companies under Captains DURANT, ADAMS, HURD PETERS, and MCLAUCHLAN. It is noteworthy that in the newspaper accounts of this event Captain PICK's is referred to as the 'Prince of Wales' company, a designation which is still retained by No. 1. After the artillery came other volunteer companies to the number of about 350 men. The temperance bodies, firemen, cordwainers, millmen, shipbuilders and caulkers, founders, St. George's, St. Patrick's and St. Andrew's societies, mounted draymen and others completed the pageant. The officers of volunteers, among others, attended the levee in the Court House at which addresses were presented. The PRINCE was expected in Carleton in the afternoon but owing to some misunderstanding as to arrangements did not arrive. Captain ADAMS' company, however, was on hand and fired a salute. On Saturday morning the PRINCE went to Rothesay by special train and was received by a salute from the artillery under Captain DURANT, and a guard of honor from the artillery and rifle companies. Leaving Rothesay by the steamer *Forest Queen* the royal party arrived at Fredericton by 6 o'clock and was received by a guard of honor from the militia companies including the artillery under Captains BERTON and TRAVIS. On Sunday H. R. H. attended the cathedral and on

Monday there was a levee. A ball was held in the evening at which the PRINCE remained until three in the morning. On Thursday at two o'clock he arrived· at Indiantown, and was received with presented arms by companies of the Infantry volunteers under Captains CROOKSHANK, MACFARLANE and STOCKTON. There was no artillery salute as Captains PICK's and PETERS' companies, which had gone to Fredericton, had not been able to return in time. All the other artillery companies were in Carleton. At the Suspension Bridge the troops were drawn up and a royal salute was fired from Carleton heights. At the city line, Carleton, the PRINCE was received by the firemen of Nos. 7 and 8 Engine companies, who took the horses from the carriage, which was drawn by hand through the streets and under an arch on King street. Here the party was received by school children, the militia artillery and Wellington Bay ship builders. The PRINCE visited the saw mill of Hon. JOHN ROBERTSON and witnessed the manufacture of a log into lumber. Entering a barge from the *Styx* at Rodney Wharf the PRINCE took farewell of the city, DURANT's, ADAMS' and MCLAUCHLAN's companies firing a salute. At a quarter to five the *Styx* weighed anchor, the batteries and the artillery companies fired their parting salutes and the visit of England's future King was ended.

Though time and the official programme did not admit of the PRINCE visiting other points of interest in the province yet the enthusiam was none the less in Bathurst where, on the day that the PRINCE arrived in St. John a salute was fired as soon as the news came, nine o'clock at night.

In connection with the reception of the PRINCE militia general orders had been issued calling out, amongst others, Captain BERTON'S company at Fredericton, Captains DURANT,

PICK, PETERS, MCLAUCHLAN and ADAMS, at St. John, and Captain TRAVIS, at Gagetown. The whole force, including one troop of cavalry and sixteen infantry and rifle companies, was placed under the command of Major CARTER, then in command of H. M. 63rd Regiment. Major CARTER, who very soon afterwards became Lieutenant-Colonel, on assuming command of the militia promulgated the following order:

FREDERICTON, N. B., July 24th, 1860.

Having in accordance with a militia general order, of this day's date, assumed command of the several companies called out by His Excellency the Commander-in-Chief, I undertake the duty with which His Excellency has honored me in the fullest confidence that I shall receive such support as will enable me to perform the services with which I have been entrusted with every credit to the militia of New Brunswick.

(Signed)   W. F. CARTER, Major
63rd Reg't,
Commanding H. M. Troops in New Brunswick.

On retiring from the command after its services had been performed he issued the following general order, conveying his appreciation of the service of the force under his command:—

FREDERICTON, N. B., August 11, 1860.

His Excellency the Commander-in-chief no longer requiring my services with the militia force which was called out for the purpose of doing all honor to H. R. H. THE PRINCE OF WALES, I cannot resign this command without thanking the whole of the officers, non-commissioned officers and men for the able and zealous manner in which they performed their different duties during that period. I have also to return my best acknowledgments to Lieutenant-Colonel HAYNE, adjutant-general of militia, and other field officers who gave me their valuable assistance on that occasion. My connection with the militia of New Brunswick will ever be remembered by me with feelings of pleasure, and I shall always continue to take a deep interest in the welfare and efficiency of this important force.

   (Sgd) W. F. CARTER, Major 63rd Regt.,
       Commanding H. M. troops in New Brunswick.

Major CARTER was assisted in the performance of his duties by Lieutenant-Colonel THURGAR, Lieutenant-Colonel GRAY, Lieutenant-Colonel FOSTER, N. B. R. A.; Lieutenant-Colonel ROBERTSON, Major MELICK, N. B. R. A., and Captain MOUNT, adjutant N. B. R. A., and also by Lieutenant-Colonel HAYNE, adjutant-general; Lieutenant-Colonel DRURY, deputy quarter master general, and Captain MINCHIN, deputy adjutant-general.

The following general order was also issued upon Major CARTER transferring his command :—

       FREDERICTON, August 13th, 1860.

Major CARTER, 63rd Regiment, commanding Her Majesty's troops in New Brunswick, has submitted to His Excellency the Commander-in-chief a highly satisfactory report of the conduct of the whole of the militia force, cavalry, artillery and infantry recently under his command, not only while they were under arms, but also during the whole period for which they were called out.

His Excellency has had an opportunity of personally observing their appearance and the manner in which they performed their duties during the visit of H. R. H. the PRINCE OF WALES, and he gladly avails himself of this occasion to express his warm approbation of their steady and soldier-like behaviour.

His Excellency the Commander-in-chief has received from H. R. H. THE PRINCE OF WALES permission to announce that it is the intention of H. R. H. to present a "Challenge Cup" (to be competed for every year) as a prize for the best marksman among the companies of militia, in uniform, which have volunteered or may volunteer for drill and exercise. His Excellency is sure that this announcement will be received as a most gratifying recognition on the part of H. R. H.

of the soldier-like and steady conduct of the militia force called out by His Excellency's proclamation of the 25th ult., and of the zeal which induced them to volunteer for drill and exercise; and he has no doubt that the same spirit which assembled together so large a force of militia of all arms (uniformed at their own expense) during H. R. H. visit, will continue to animate them and extend to every battalion of militia in the Province. The officer in command of every company of militia volunteering for drill and exercise may apply to His Excellency the Commander-in-Chief for service ammunition for practice, (at the rate of five rounds per man in uniform) on shewing that a suitable and safe practice ground has been marked and secured for the company.

(Sgd) R. HAYNE, Lieutenant-Colonel,
Adjutant-General Militia.

There are yet a few more incidents to be noted in this eventful year, and though they naturally attracted much less attention than those just related, yet some of them are by no means devoid of interest. On 30th May, 1860, ISAAC NAISH was gazetted first, and ALEXANDER MITCHELL second, lieutenant. There is nothing to show to which company these gentlemen were attached, but as on 25th March, 1861, MITCHELL was promoted to the first lieutenantcy *vice* NAISH, deceased, and is remembered by Sir JOHN C. ALLEN as having been in Fredericton, it is probable that both were in Captain JOHN ALLEN'S company which was then being formed.

In Captain ADAMS' company JOSEPH CORAM resigned his commission and was succeeded by Lieutenant JAMES QUINTON, from St. John County militia.; while in Captain DURANT'S company THOMAS C. HUMBERT gave way to ALEXANDER RANKINE.

Another officer was appointed to Captain MCLAUCHLAN'S company in the person of GEORGE HUNTER CLARK as a second lieutenant.

A meeting of the officers of militia of the city of Saint John was held on August 11th in the parlor of No. 2 Fire Engine house, at which Lieutenant-Colonel FOSTER, Captains MOUNT, PICK, DURANT and ADAMS, Lieutenants MELICK, SNEDEN, THOMAS, QUINTON, MCLACHLAN, TAYLOR and RANKINE of the artillery were present with quite a large number of others. Lieutenant-Colonel FOSTER occupied the chair and stated that the object of the meeting was to enable officers to become personally acquainted and for the cultivation of the unanimity of sentiment essential to the success of the volunteer movement. As an outcome of his suggestions it was resolved that the militia companies of St. John should assemble for a general inspection on 26th September and that Colonel THURGAR be invited to act as inspecting officer. A request was also sent to the Lieutenant-Governor for a supply of artillery and rifle ammunition to enable practice to be carried on.

The "Morning News" of September 28th says that the general appearance of the men at this inspection was excellent. 'The Carleton artillery excelled in their marching with small 'arms and in their manual exercise, while Captain PETERS' '(Portland) artillery with field pieces went through their march-'ing in very good order. The other bodies on the ground 'were the Prince of Wales (PICK'S), Captain DURANT'S and 'Captain ADAMS' artillery companies, Captain CROOKSHANK'S 'rifles—these represented the city; Captain STOCKTON'S Port-'land rifles; also companies of rifles from Pisarinco, Golden 'Grove and Milkish, (Captain MACFARLANE's Scottish company 'were not out)—the whole force being under the command of 'Lieutenant-Colonel FOSTER. After the review the 'troops, ac-'companied by the Courtenay Bay band, marched through 'several of the streets, and in the evening Colonel THURGAR 'gave the officers a luncheon at the Waverley House.'

The report of the adjutant-general, Colonel HAYNE, for 1860 expressed a high appreciation of the work which had been done. He advocated greater encouragement to rifle shooting by increasing the allowance of ammunition, and pointed out that the Canadian government allowed one hundred and forty rounds of ammunition annually to each company of artillery. Without such assistance as this they could not acquire a practical knowledge of gunnery. During the year drill instructors had been loaned by the colonel of the 63rd regiment and a great deal had been achieved with their assistance, but he emphasized the necessity of officers qualifying themselves to instruct their men. The report also shows the existence of the Woodstock company still under Captain WETMORE, one at Northumberland under Captain CARMICHAEL, and one at St. John under Captain RICHARD SIMONDS. The latter as before stated scarcely had any potential existence as artillery.

CHAPTER XI.

1861.

Lecture by Captain Hurd Peters—New Officers—Prince Albert's Visit—Disobedience of Orders—Presentation of Colors—An Imposing Ceremony—B. Lester Peters' Battery—The Muster Rolls—The 'Nippers'—The end of the Story.

THE first event of 1861 was the assembly of Captain McLAUCHLAN's (Carleton) company to the number of thirty-four, on January 21st for the purpose of making a presentation to their instructor, Corporal JAMES ANDERSON of the R. A. The company was then styled 'Havelock Battery No. 6.' They went through the manual and firing exercises and formed in square when the presentation was made. An address was read by Sergeant WILLIAM J. McCORDOCK, and was signed by himself, WM. BROWNE, FRED. R. LINDE and GEORGE F. HARDING. The former is now an official of the public works department of Canada and the latter is an officer in the treasury department of the city of St. John. JOHN A. CHESLEY, now M. P. for St. John, was then one of the bombardiers.

A lecture was delivered in the Mechanics' Institute on February 18th by Captain HURD PETERS upon "Our Volunteers." The subjects of the lecture attended in uniform, there being present the City, Carleton and Portland artillery companies, Pisarinco, Golden Grove and Milkish rifles, besides the city rifle companies of Captains MACFARLANE, CROOKSHANK and TRAVIS. Lieutenant-Colonel FOSTER and other officers occupied the platform. Captain PETERS, among other things, referred to the establishment of the 1793 company, and read the names from the original roll, remarking that 'every year since the 'thunder of their guns might be heard on some national 'holiday.'

Changes were rapid in the COLVILLE company. Captain LEWIS DURANT retired retaining his rank on 18th March, and on 13th April was succeeded by Lieutenant JAMES G. MELICK, who also retired with rank on the same day. This was followed by the promotion of Lieutenant ALEX. RANKINE, who had joined in the previous year. WM. FREDERICK DEACON and ROGER HUNTER were also posted to the company as lieutenants. This company, says Captain RANKINE, originally drilled in the Barrack Square, afterwards on King street (east), near St. John Presbyterian church. The guns were kept by Major MELICK. Lieutenant DEACON had been in the British army and had served in the Crimea. He was very active in an important event, the procuring of the regimental colors, which is elsewhere recorded.

The Queen's birthday was celebrated in much the usual manner, there being a review of the volunteers and a salute fired by the artillery. All the St. John companies turned out on this occasion, and for the first time appeared the company commanded by Captain B. LESTER PETERS, long known as the 'Kid Glove battery.'

On the 29th May H. R. H. PRINCE ALFRED arrived at St. John from Halifax and spent a day in the city. On his departure on the morning of the 31st two companies of artillery fired a salute. The boys in blue apparently thought that some want of respect was evinced toward the PRINCE by their not being called out to do him honor and endeavored in their own way to supply the omission. The reason was, however, the recent death of the DUCHESS OF KENT, mother of HER MAJESTY. A general order issued shortly afterwards informed the militia of St. John that HIS ROYAL HIGHNESS was fully aware that the rest of the force only abstained from a demonstration because of the order of the Commander in-Chief, and while His Excellency attributed to the excitement of the moment the partial disobedience of the order, evinced by the salute just mentioned, he assured the companies by whom the order was obeyed that their absence was attributable only to their sense of discipline and to their desire to show that in their military capacity they could be trusted to obey orders. The rebuke was rather caustic, and it may safely be assumed that the artillery never again disobeyed a general order. The punishment was moderate, however, compared with that which in later years was meted out to another St. John corps which disobeyed orders calling them out for duty.

The annual inspection on 29th August was a very creditable affair. Colonel THURGAR commanded the parade and the volunteers were inspected by Major RVND of H. M. 62nd Regiment. Captains PICK'S and HURD PETERS' companies were put through their field gun drill by Lieutenant MACARTNEY of the R. A., and are said to have acquitted themselves to his entire satisfaction. Captain B. LESTER PETERS' company also performed garrison gun drill on that occasion in a manner reflecting great credit upon themselves.

Hon. ARTHUR HAMILTON GORDON, C. M. G., assumed office as Lieutenant-Governor of the province on 26th October, and among the gentlemen appointed as his aides-de-camp was Lieutenant-Colonel HAYNE.

In this year, on 2nd September, MARTIN HUNTER PETERS,

M. D., was gazetted lieutenant of Captain ADAMS' company, *vice* GEO. J. STACKHOUSE, resigned, and thus began the militia career of an accurate and enthusiastic officer.

During the year the efforts of Lieutenant DEACON to obtain for the corps a set of colors had been very successful, and in December the silken trophies arrived from England. Their presentation to the regiment was an interesting and imposing event. The following is an account taken from a newspaper of the time :—

The Colors recently procured in England for the New Brunswick Regiment of Artillery were presented at the Institute last evening (18th December). The hall was filled to overflowing shortly after seven o'clock, and hundreds of people retired unable to procure admittance. Large numbers of those present remained standing during the whole of the evening, it being impossible to obtain seats for all who gained admittance.

The volunteers in and about the city attended in large force and made quite an interesting appearance. About eight o'clock Captain RANKINE's company, carrying the colors furled, entered the hall and marched upon the platform, the City Band playing "British Grenadiers." The colors were then unfurled, the band playing " Rule Brittania."

Lieutenant-Colonel THURGAR informed the audience that the colors were now to be presented in the name of the ladies of St. John, and he called upon Rev. Dr. GRAY to consecrate them.

The address of presentation was delivered, extempore, by Lieutenant-Colonel GRAY. He spoke (an unusual thing for him) so low as to be heard quite indistinctly in the further part of the house. Addressing himself to the officers and men of the artillery he said that he was honored by the command of the ladies of the City and County to represent them on this occasion. What, he asked, is the purpose that has brought us together? This banner (pointing to the dark blue banner) beautiful as it is, is but the product of the worm ; the work upon it is that of frail, though, perhaps, young and beautiful hands. Yet it lives, it moves, it is the embodiment of the triumphs and glories of the arms of England. This unstained banner of your country's honor is about to be committed to your care, are you prepared to receive it and maintain the purity of its unsullied character? It has waved triumphantly in Spain and France and India, in every quarter of the globe, and whether carried forward to glorious victory or borne back in honorable retreat, it has never been stained—on its folds no bar sinister shows it to have been disgraced. You, volunteers, are not asked to carry this flag beyond the confines of your own province; you are asked to stand by your own homes, to defend, if need be, those dear ones who look to you for support and protection. In the heart of every truly brave man there will be, I am sure, a warm response to the prayer made this evening, that the dark cloud which now hovers over our country may be averted; but, if called upon, not one of you would hesitate to discharge your duties as becomes men, in the face of danger, difficulty and death. In you are embodied the three great nations from which our forefathers came. Each of them has its peculiar characters. The Irishman is quick, fearless, joyous and obedient. He fights with a light heart for he loves it; his joyous temperament sustains him in many a trying situation, while his ready obedience to command impels him forward at the call of duty.

The Scotchman fights for the love of home, one of the strongest feelings of his breast, and no matter what beautiful country or sunny land he may be in, no kindred appears to him like his own, no clan like his, and his heart ever recurs with warm feeling to the mossy heaths and barren moors of his native land, and for that land he sheds his blood with ready willingness. The Englishman fights because it is a duty he has to do. Gloomy, savage, almost relentless when face to face with the foe, he knows no shrinking and whether victorious or beaten, to him it is the same, he perseveres with equal determination. All are ready, as you should be, to maintain the integrity of that flag, under which he who seeks protection is sure to find it or a nation to avenge his wrongs. Mr. GRAY then alluded to the date, 1793, on the flags, commending the principles of the loyalists, and ended by asking the volunteers if they were prepared faithfully, manfully and fearlessly to preserve the colors which were to be presented to them.

THE COLORS AND TROPHIES OF THE CORPS.
JONES CUP.   BOTSFORD CUP.   SHOEBURYNESS CUP.
The three smaller Cups were the gift of G. J. PINE Esq., of London, Eng.

In response Lieutenant-Colonel FOSTER replied as follows :—

Colonel GRAY,—In the absence of Colonel HAYNE, our commanding officer, who was invited by the committee of arrangements to take his part in the ceremonies on this occasion, it becomes my duty, on behalf of the officers, non-commissioned officers and gunners of the New Brunswick Regiment of Artillery, to return their warmest thanks for the magnificent gift which they have this night received at the hands of Miss GRAY from the ladies of the City and County of St. John.

These colors come to our hands unstained. In their virgin purity, fresh from the hands of youth and innocence, we receive them ; most faithfully will we defend them, and whatever difficulties may arise, in consequence of the present most unhappy condition of political affairs on this continent, we shall endeavor with the blessing of Almighty God to transmit them to our successors untarnished.

The nucleus of our regiment dates its organization from the 4th day of May, 1793, ten short years subsequent to the landing of the loyalists, and was known as the Loyal Artillery. Its ranks, to the number of ninety-four, were filled by a body of Englishmen, Irishmen, Scotchmen and British Americans, comprising the principal merchants and ship owners of the city at that period ; men of whose moral worth any community in the world might feel justly proud. Its first captain was JOHN COLVILLE, founder of the commercial firm of CROOKSHANK & JOHNSTON. Its first sergeant was the venerable and highly esteemed JOHN WARD.

Our vocations are those of peace. Our several duties and positions in life preclude that close application to the study of military affairs which is expected and required from those whose lives are devoted to the profession of arms, consequently, we should not be expected to possess that thorough knowledge of all those little niceties of military etiquette which are by some considered so essentially necessary. We are all willing and desirous to learn, and ready at all times to give a cheerful response to the order of our superior officer ;—none, other than weak minds, would smile at our imperfections ; and none but imbeciles would, under our peculiar circumstances, jeeringly apply to us the term unmilitary.

When the honor of our QUEEN or the interests of our country

demand our active services, under the guiding hand of the Most High, those services will be rendered. The sacredness of our homes and the purity of our families must be preserved from the polluting touch of an invading foe. From our progenitors we inherit those principles of loyalty and patriotism by which they were governed. As the descendants of Englishmen, Irishmen, Scotchmen, and British American Loyalists, we are proud of our nationality, and thank that merciful Providence who has made us the subjects of a Sovereign whose manifold virtues as daughter, wife, mother and queen, entitle her to the fullest confidence of all her subjects, as well as to the respect and admiration of the whole civilized world.

Miss GRAY then presented the flags to Lieutenant HUNTER and Lieutenant M. H. PETERS, the juniors of the regiment, simply saying that she made the presentation.

The colors were then marched into the ranks, the band playing "God Save the Queen," after which three rousing cheers were given for the Queen, three for the Lieutenant-Governor, and three for the New Brunswick Regiment of Artillery.

Lieutenant-Colonel THURGAR thanked the Rev. Dr. GRAY for his attendance and assistance.

The "Queen's Color" is a Union Jack with the crown worked in floss, and 1793 beneath worked in figures of gold.

The "Regimental Color" is a blue ensign—in the centre is a figure with the letters "New Brunswick" encircled by a wreath and surmounted with the crown, all beautifully wrought in floss, with 1793 in figures of gold beneath. Both colors are made of the heaviest and most costly description of silk, and as there is a total absence of paint of either color, they are calculated to do service for many years.

An incidental reference has been made to Captain B. LESTER PETERS' battery. The history of this fine organization, of the memory of which the artillery and citizens are still proud, begins with an order of 25th March, 1861, transferring Lieutenant B. LESTER PETERS from the St. John City Militia to the N. B. R. A. as captain, for garrison gun duty. Previous to this, and in fact until the Fenian trouble, there was practically no garrison gun drill done by the regiment. Captain PETERS' battery generally used the field pieces, but was the pioneer in the use of the heavier ordnance. The formation of the battery was accomplished under circumstances which need not be narrated. Suffice it to say that a number of men from Captain PICK'S battery withdrew and became members of the new battery, and after approaching several other gentlemen, obtained B. LESTER PETERS as their commanding officer. It was a wise choice, and whatever may have been the feeling engendered at the time by what was termed the 'revolt,' it was productive of good to the N. B. R. A., which for nearly eight years had two splendid batteries whose efficiency was increased by rivalry. While Captain PETERS' battery existed, it, as well as Captain PICK'S, received deserved commendation from all quarters, military as well as civil, and the praise of one is no disparagement of the other. The rivalry, not friendly at first, which existed between the organizations was productive of a higher state of efficiency in both, and probably to-day the old members of the Prince of Wales battery are as proud as the survivors of the 'Kid Glove battery' of the successes of the latter. With Captain PETERS were associated Lieutenants R. R. SNEDEN, GEORGE E. THOMAS and F. G. W. LANSDOWNE, all from Captain PICK'S battery. The roll shows during its history the names of scores of young men, many of whom have made a reputation in after life. There was much about the personality of the captain to attract men. Tall, of commanding presence, with a regal air which seems to belong almost exclusively to a generation that has passed away, he appeared to men of the present day the embodiment of dignity and reserve. And yet his old comrades after pointing out the strictness of the discipline which he enforced, relate with fondness incidents of the social meetings at which the 'Captain' unbent, and the zest with which he entered into the sport and merriment of the hour. After serving for upwards of a quarter of a century as Common Clerk of the city of St. John, an office for which he made traditions, he was elevated to the post of County Court Judge, which office he held until his death in 1894.

Through great good fortune the rolls of his battery and the minute books of their meetings have been preserved. All bear the emphasis of his character. Exactness characterizes every entry and the records form a history. Among the secretaries of the battery is found I. ALLEN JACK, Esq., who, until a year ago, filled the important office of Recorder of St. John and left upon the history of that office an abiding influence and power that will, like his captain's record, remain long after the memory of his day has faded.

The meetings of which such a record was kept are from 1862 to 1864 when the new militia law removed the self governing feature of the organization. The minutes of that period, however, breathe in their brief chronicle of events a reverence which amounts to affection for the 'captain.' It was well that Captain B. LESTER PETERS never had a successor, for those qualities which marked his leadership are rare among men.

There are humorous incidents, too, which are told by old members who are now no longer 'the boys.' One in particular is well worth relating. The captain's thoroughness in discipline had caused him to lecture the battery on the unsoldierliness of turning out of the way to avoid a bad spot on the street. The boys treasured the lecture and waited an opportunity to show their appreciation of it. It soon came. Ordered down to the Barracks for drill one day the leading files noticed a trench cut more than half way across the road, and directly

HON. B. LESTER PETERS,
(Late Judge St. John County Court.)

in the line of march. A man was in it plying the pick and shovel vigorously, and had piled up large mounds of stiff brick clay on either side of the excavation. The battery was in charge of Lieutenant SNEDEN, and the captain was at a distance walking with some friends, and for once not paying any attention to his battery. One of the leading men was the late paymaster of our corps, GEORGE F. SMITH. He and his comrades kept their direction perfectly and leaped over the trench causing the loose clay to fall in on the poor laborer, who got out as quickly as possible. File after file leaped over tumbling the clay in until the trench was nearly full. Not a man was so unsoldierly as to turn out of the way. The captain's lecture was duly heeded, and probably no one better enjoyed the joke than he.

The following is a transcript of the roll book. It appears from the minutes that there must have been an earlier roll in 1861, but it can not be found. A footnote gives the additions so far as they can be gathered.

19th May, 1862:

Captain—B. Lester Peters, barrister-at-law.
First Lieutenants—Robert R. Sneden, merchant.
George E. Thomas, accountant.
Second Lieutenant—Frank G. Lansdowne, clerk.
Sergeant-Major—W. Albert Lockhart, merchant.
Sergeants—P. Robertson Inches, druggist.
G. Lawrence Foster, merchant.
James F. Robertson, merchant's clerk.
Corporals—F. Gallagher, clerk.
F. A. W. Davidson, attorney's clerk. Resigned 13th April, 1863.
S. K. Foster, jr., merchant.
Bombardier—W. Street Berton, accountant. Resigned 13th April, 1863.

Gunners—Robert D. Davis, clerk. Resigned 1863.
C. G. Berryman, merchant.
John C. Miles, manufacturer.
R. V. Bonnell, clerk. Resigned 12th Oct., 1863.
Matthew Stead, jr., architect.
Joseph Allison, clerk.
William H. Crozier, clerk.
Andrew W. Davis, clerk.
G. DuVernett Lee, clerk. Died Feb'y 16th, 1863.
Bombardier Jno. H. Morehouse, clerk. Struck off roll 12th October, 1863.
Gunners—Charles R. Reed, clerk.
G. F. Ring, clerk.
W. Colebrooke Perley, student-at-law.
John Cameron, clerk.
Charles H. Whittaker, clerk.
Edward Jones, student-at-law. Resigned—promoted to commission Portland battery.
Dawson Hayward, printer.
T. R. Wheelock, clerk. Left province.
John C. McKean, civil engineer. Resigned. Commissioned in Engineer corps.
W. H. Carman, merchant.
A. Chamberlain, accountant. Resigned 8th February, 1864. Left province.
Bombardier—George F. Smith, clerk.
Gunners- A. W. Peters, clerk. Resigned.
Charles Campbell, accountant. Resigned. Commissioned in Volunteer Battalion.
F. Whelpley, clerk. Left province.
H. E. Stickney, agent.
Charles U. Hanford, agent
J. Fred. Seely, gentleman.
G. Clowes Carman, accountant.
S. J. King, clerk.
Charles H. Chandler, student-at-law. Struck off roll 12th October, 1863.
John H. Parks, civil engineer. Resigned. Promoted to commission Engineer Corps.
A. M. Saunders, photographer. Left Province.

N. B. GARRISON ARTILLERY.　111

Gunners—J. Fred Lawton, mechanic.
　　　　W. P. Ritchie, student-at-law.
　　　　H. Machattie, clerk. Left Province.
　　　　W. E. Vroom, clerk.
　　　　Robert S. Besnard, clerk. Left Province.
　　　　R. Poyntz, merchant's clerk. Left Province.
　　　　J. R. Smith, clerk.
　　　　A. Cowie, clerk. Died 4th April, 1864.
　　　　James W. Milledge, clerk.

9th June, 1862 :
　　Gunner—R. Brooks Peters, student-at-law.

11th August :
　　Gunners—C. Fred Langan, mechanic.
　　　　I. Allen Jack, gentleman.
　　　　A. Winniett Peters, clerk.
　　　　J. L. Bunting, clerk.

16th October, 1862 :
　　Gunners—W. H. Merritt, clerk.
　　　　W. W. Jones, merchant's clerk.
　　　　F. W. Wisdom, clerk.
　　　　George Johnston, clerk. Struck off roll 12th October, 1863.
　　　　H. W. Baldwin, agent.
　　　　Stanley Boyd, student-at-law.
　　　　——— Robertson, ———

8th December, 1862 :
　　Gunner—Robert Matthew.

9th February, 1863 :
　　Gunners—John Simonds, gentleman.
　　　　Vernon Nicholson, customs house clerk.

8th June, :
　　Gunners—Wm. Lee,
　　　　Hamilton Hazlewood.

12th October, :
　　Gunner—Henry Stewart, merchant's clerk.

11th January, 1864 :
　　Gunner—David D. Robertson, merchant's clerk.

8th February:
  Gunners—John J. Daley, law student.
  Joseph B. Stubbs, clerk.
  James Sullivan, musician.
  Albert S. Hay, silversmith.

January, 1866:
  Gunners—John T. C. McKean, architect.
  Samuel K. Wilson, surveyor.
  R. H. Arnold, clerk.

26th March:
  Gunners—Thomas Lister, clerk.
  M. Chamberlain, clerk.
  W. M. Burns, clerk.
  James J. Grahame, clerk.
  Barclay Boyd, clerk.
  Alfred B. Sheraton, clerk.
  Arthur B. Perley, student.
  Chas. McLauchlan, jr., clerk.
  P. Reid Disbrow, clerk.
  J. Russell Armstrong.
  H. D. Troop, clerk.
  Daniel Jordan, jr., law student.
  J. M. Kinnear, gentleman.
  J. M. Robinson, jr., clerk.
  Joseph S. Fairweather, clerk.
  F. V. McLaughlin, clerk.
  Peter P. Clarke, clerk.
  Lewis D. Millidge, clerk.
  Thomas Millidge, student-at-law.
  James Beveridge, student-at-law.
  John McLauchlan, clerk.

31st March:
  Gunners—Fred H. Barteaux, druggist's clerk.
  Geo. N. Robinson, jr., druggist's clerk.

2nd April:
  Gunners—John H. Thomson, clerk.
  Fred M. Robinson, student.
  A. R. Ferguson, clerk.
  W. S. Livingstone.

9th April:
    Gunners—Andrew D. Robertson, clerk.
              Arthur W. Lovett.
13th April:
    Gunner—Gideon K. Wetmore, clerk.
16th April:
    Gunners—G. L. Robinson.
              F. O. Allison, clerk.
18th April:
    Gunner—Geo. K. Berton.
19th April:
    Gunners—Edwin Berton.
              Richard Tremaine, merchant. Resigned and discharged. Left the Province 1866.
1st May:
    Gunner—Warwick Street, clerk.
19th May:
    Gunner—Robert P. Wetmore, clerk.
29th June:
    Gunner—B. O. Kinnear, clerk.
8th May, 1867:
    Gunner—J. B. Gregory, clerk.
9th July:
    Gunner—J. M. Dick, clerk.
24th July:
    Gunner—Geo. F. Anderson.
26th July:
    Gunner—R. R. Cunningham, dentist.
9th September:
    Gunner—George B. Hegan, clerk.
6th April, 1868:
    Gunner—Thos. A. Chipman, clerk.
26th June:
    Gunner—Jas. S. Kaye.

From the minutes the following appear to have been members anterior to the making up of the 1862 roll: Gunners, E. G. SCOVIL, —— HAMMOND, W. L. MAGEE, Z. R. EVERETT, C. A. HOLSTEAD; Corporal, J. P. PERKINS; Gunners, J. R.

CALHOUN, G. F. MUNROE, G. E. THORNE, GEO. N. ROBINSON, G. FRED SANCTON, H. D. TROOP (Mr. TROOP joined later on), H. HANSELPECKER, HENRY RAINNIE, C. D. THOMPSON, SIMEON PHILLIPS, GEO. MASON, jr., and GEO. McDONALD.

The names of JOHN TAYLOR, E. N. STEWART, GEORGE FLEWELLING, SIDNEY PATTERSON, JAMES MANCHESTER, S. W. LEE, WM. FLEMING, HENRY F. PERLEY, INGERSOLL BROWN, F. S. HANFORD, JER. DRAKE and HENRY KENDALL were accepted. They are not on the roll and do not appear to have been struck off any previous roll. The inference is that they were accepted as members but never joined the battery.

The meeting for organization was held January 4, 1861, in the parlor of No 5 Engine house, Germain street. RICHARD D. DAVIS was secretary and W. A. LOCKHART, treasurer. In March they changed to Union Hall, Horsfield street and elected W. A. LOCKHART, 1st, PETER R. INCHES, 2nd, and GEO. L. FOSTER, 3rd sergeant. S. K. FOSTER, jr., was also chosen third bombardier. On the 18th May they fired a salute of nineteen guns with the Royal Artillery ordnance at the barracks. At the 24th May parade of that year they fell in on the right of the rifle companies, forty-two strong; 'having,' says the record, 'no rifles to carry or cannon to use.' Captain PETERS gave a dinner at the Waverley hotel in the evening.

The men got their rifles on 1st July. In the next March Bombardier GALLAGHER became corporal and W. S. BERTON bombardier. On the 9th of that month the battery was visited at its drill room, then in the Wiggins building, Johnston's wharf, by Lieutenant-Colonel FOSTER and Major MELICK. Gunner Edward Jones was called to the front and presented with the Prince of Wales medal by Lieutenant-Colonel FOSTER.

On 14th July, 1862, Sergeant LOCKHART became sergeant-major; Corporal ROBINSON, sergeant; Bombardiers DAVIDSON and S. K. FOSTER, corporals; GEORGE F. SMITH and JOHN MOREHOUSE became bombardiers.

The battery, at a meeting on September 9th, passed resolutions of regret upon the death of an honorary member who had befriended them, Mr. MOSES H. PERLEY, H. M. Commissioner of British North American Fisheries, who had died on 17th August at Forteau, Labrador. On May 11th, 1863, the thanks of the battery were returned to the captain for the presentation of a bugle and trumpet to them, and on the succeeding 18th royal salutes were fired at King Square at 6 a. m. and at Reed's point at noon. A little later in the month, at request of Judge WILMOT, two detachments drilled for his inspection. In this year J. FRED SEELY and W. C. PERLEY became bombardiers: Bombardier CHAMBERLAIN, corporal, was succeeded on his leaving the city by Bombardier SEELY, and we read on 14th March, 1864, that the "Captain had much pleasure in accepting the picture of the 'Nippers' presented to him by No. 1 detachment." The 'Nippers' were a gun detachment famous for their celerity and precision, and their efficiency has never been excelled by any detachment of the regiment or brigade.

On 18th April Sergeant INCHES became sergeant-major; Corporal FOSTER, a sergeant; Bombardier PERLEY, corporal, Gunners REED and CAMERON, bombardiers. Then on 13th June, we read that, proposed by Gunner LANGAN, JOSEPH B. STUBBS was accepted as a member, and the pleasant record told by secretaries R. D. DAVIS, A. CHAMBERLAIN, I. ALLEN JACK and R. BROOKS PETERS comes to a close.

Years afterwards, on the 2nd July, 1869, the 'members and friends of No. 2 Battery St. John Volunteer Artillery,' to the number of forty, sat down to dine at Stubb's Hotel. Captain, then

Brevet Lieutenant-Colonel B. LESTER PETERS was presented with a handsome silver cup, engraved with his arms and motto, 'Sans Dieu Rien,' and bearing this inscription : "Presented to Captain BENJAMIN LESTER PETERS by the officers, non-commissioned officers and gunners of late No. 2 Battery New Brunswick Regiment of Artillery of St. John, New Brunswick, 1869." GEORGE F. SMITH presided and I. ALLEN JACK filled the vice chair. An address was read by the latter to which the captain responded, and after which, in the early morning, the old battery fell into marching order and escorted the captain home. And thus the record ends.

A. CHAMBERLAIN, G. I. FOSTER, J. FRED SEELY, JOHN CAMERON,
S. K. FOSTER, Jr. J. L. BUNTING, F. W. WISDOM, WILLIAM C. LEE, J. FRED LAWTON.

'THE NIPPERS.'

CHAPTER XII.

1862-1864.

The Trent Affair—Arrival of Troops at Saint John—Service of the Artillery—The New Militia Act—Changes in Officers—Prince of Wales' Cup Won by Gunner Jones—Roll of Portland Battery.

IN the latter days of 1861 there was a change of governors in New Brunswick, Hon. Mr. MANNERS-SUTTON being replaced by Hon. ARTHUR GORDON. The departing governor received a salute from the guns of RANKINE's company on the 22nd October, and his successor was received by a full militia display in which the Rothesay, Renfrew, Queen's Own Rifles and City Guards took part on behalf of the infantry, while HURD PETERS, RANKINE and B. LESTER PETERS' batteries fired a salute. At the Court House the troops were drawn up in a square and Lieutenant-Colonel THURGAR read an address from the volunteers to His Excellency. The governor was in the uniform of a Scotch volunteer company, having been quite prominent in that movement in Scotland.

A despatch from Boston on the 12th December threw the province into a state of great excitement. It announced the now historic news of the stopping of the British mail steamer *Trent* by the U. S. S. *San Jacinto* under Captain WILKES, and the taking from her of MASON and SLIDELL, the commissioners of the Southern confederacy. The *Trent* was on her way from Havana to St. Thomas and was stopped by force on 8th November, searched, and the commissioners seized. British indignation was at the fever point. The provincial sympathy had largely been with the Southerners, and this made the feeling more intense. By the middle of December a royal messenger, bearing a demand for the return of the commissioners, reached Washington. Troops were despatched to Canada as rapidly as they could be got on board the ships, and by New Year's, 1862, were landing at Halifax and St. John. At that season of the year the St. Lawrence was frozen and the regiments had to be sent to Upper Canada through New Brunswick. The new governor issued a proclamation on 28th December, requesting members of the volunteer companies to offer their services as a fatigue party available for duty on the arrival of H. M. troops. From fifty to eighty men were required. His Excellency assured the volunteers of the importance which would be attached to this service and thanked those who had that day been on duty at the Barracks. These were from the artillery under Captains PETERS and RANKINE. The same newspaper which contained the proclamation had also a despatch stating that the United States had agreed to surrender MASON and SLIDELL, and this, of course, was an assurance that peace would be preserved. In the meantime the north wing of the Custom House, the Temperance Hall on Sidney street, Railway Car Shed, Madras School, Varley School, Lower Cove Market House, new Police Office and Watch House, Cudlip's Building, on Princess street, and Trinity Church Sunday-school, were being fitted up as sleeping shelters for the troops which were daily expected by the steamers *Cleopatra, Adriatic, Parana and Australasian.*

The volunteers readily assumed the work of fatigue duty. The whole force was addressed on January 3rd, in the Mechanics' Institute, by Governor GORDON, who pointed out the necessity and advantage of a well organized militia and made a most fervent and patriotic appeal to the people. By the 10th February the troops were all *en route* from St. John, having been dined and lionized most heartily by an enthusiastic people. All danger was over and the ordinary duties of life were resumed by our artillerymen who had learned much of practical value by their intercourse with the troops and their fatigue duty. All who assisted in the debarkation and reception of the troops were thanked by a general order.

On February 10th despite very cold weather Captain PICK's company met at the rifle range, Gunner HENRY BOULTON winning a medal offered by the captain.

In this year Lieutenant-Colonel HAYNE became quartermaster-general, his term of office as adjutant-general having expired, and the following general order was issued under date of 1st January:—

"His Excellency the Commander-in-Chief cannot permit Lieu-
"tenant-Colonel HAYNE to retire from the office of adjutant-
"general, which he has so long filled, without expressing his
"thanks for the zeal and assiduity with which he has discharged
"the onerous duties of that office. His unremitting attention
"to the welfare and discipline of the militia calls for His Ex-
"cellency's warmest approbation, and the sincere gratitude of
"all those who desire the efficiency of that force.

" His Excellency feels certain that Lieutenant-Colonel HAYNE
"will carry to the discharge of the duties of the responsible
"office he now holds, the same zealous devotedness and single-
"ness of purpose which he has always shown as adjutant-
"general."

A new militia act was passed this year which provided for the organization of a force on principles which are embodied in the present Militia and Defence Act of Canada. By it the male population between eighteen and sixty years of age liable to bear arms was divided into two classes, the active and the sedentary militia. The latter was not required to drill in time of peace. The active militia was further divided into three classes: class A, consisting of volunteers; class B, unmarried men and widowers without children; class C, married men and widowers with children.

There were to be drilled annually one thousand men for a period of six days, and should that number not be filled by volunteers it was to be made up by a draft from the next class. Volunteers could not quit their companies without two months' notice, and their engagement required two years'. service, though, as at present, under ordinary circumstances a discharge could always be obtained.

Previous to the passing of the act, as has been shown the associations for drill were purely voluntary, and though they had the sanction of the law, yet were without its compulsion. A system of company internal government had grown up, no doubt in part adopted from the English volunteer model and in part an evolution of local requirements. To preserve this spirit of self-government a number of rules were collected and published with a view to their adoption, so far as might be expedient by the organizations then to be formed. They provided for the classification of company members into enrolled members, sub-divided into effectives and non-effectives, and honorary members who contributed to the funds of a company but were not enrolled for service. The companies voted on the admission of members subject to the veto of the commanding officer. There was a secretary and treasurer, the captain always acting as president. The secretary was generally required to call a meeting of the company upon the requisition of five members, but the company could not deal with any question of discipline. In recommending the appointment of officers the commanding officer was to recommend as far as possible such persons as would be agreeable to the company, but the responsibility rested with him. This was a departure from the old system of electing officers. It is apparent that there was much of merit in such an organization, as it recognized distinctly the social life of the volunteer and combined it with his military services. No better reason can be assigned for the remarkable *esprit de corps* which characterized the provincial forces at this period, and as time runs on the old idea seems again to be gaining ground, so that before many years we may again, in city corps at least, have a revival of the volunteer system and the voluntary spirit.

Owing to the legal change in the status of the militia, the commander-in-chief directed circulars to be forwarded to all militia bodies, asking whether or not they desired the acceptance of their services under the new act. The companies commanded by Captains HURD PETERS, JOHN McLAUCHLAN, B. LESTER PETERS and GEORGE H. PICK were accepted on 23rd June, and Captain ADAMS' company, then under Lieutenant MARTIN HUNTER PETERS on 8th July, the latter officer being promoted to a captaincy on 11th July. Captain ADAMS remained unattached until 1863, when he retired retaining rank. Captain and Adjutant MOUNT was appointed enrolling officer for the eastern district of St. John city. In Captain McLAUCHLAN'S company Lieutenant KNIGHT retired, being succeeded by Second Lieutenant McLACHLAN, and Sergeant McCORDOCK was promoted to the vacancy. In October Captain TRAVIS was transferred to the Queen's Co. militia infantry, and promotions were made in his artillery company, the services of which, under Captain F. L.' KNOX, were accepted in December. At the same time a Fredericton company, under Captain E. W. CHESTNUT, was enrolled. In the previous month the company at St. John under Lieutenant DEACON was accepted, SAMUEL R. THOMSON having become captain. This gentleman was one of the most celebrated members of the New Brunswick bar, and was induced to command the company for his social prestige and influence. Lieutenant DEACON remained in the service.

Owing to the recent death, 1861, of the PRINCE CONSORT, HER MAJESTY directed that there should be no public observation of her birthday, so by proclamation the 20th June was substituted as a public holiday.

Six batteries, under Lieutenant-Colonel FOSTER, were inspected on 24th October by the Lieutenant-Governor, Colonel COLE, 15th Regiment, and Captain SMYTH, R. A. They were those of Captains PICK, HURD PETERS, McLAUCHLAN, B. LESTER PETERS, M. H. PETERS, and THOMSON (then commanded by Lieutenant DEACON). Those of Captain PICK and B. L. PETERS were very highly commended in the report which states that the gun drill of the regiment was good, though company movements were deficient. Some members of almost every battery were not in uniform. By general order the pattern of artillery uniform previously in use was retained. Dress regulations, in detail, were issued in the following year.

During 1862 Governor GORDON visited many parts of the province and received numerous addresses. Volunteers of the present day may take warning from the experience of the companies at Richibucto, who followed the prevailing custom and tendered the governor a parchment scroll of eulogistic character. He told them that as this was their first offence he would overlook it and accept the address, but warned them and all other militia men not to pursue the custom. The right to praise, he said, implied the right to blame, and as discipline forbade the censure of an officer by those under his command, the right to praise was impliedly taken away. It must be remembered that the Lieutenant-Governor was, in those days, Commander-in-Chief of the militia.

It does not seem clear that the Woodstock company enrolled under the new act, but the commissions of the officers remained in force and promotions at a later date were founded upon them. Captain A. K. S. WETMORE retired with the rank of major after long and useful service.

In the rifle competitions of this year Gunner EDWARD JONES, of Captain B. LESTER PETERS' company won the Prince of Wales cup. Gunner W. MORGAN, of Captain HURD PETERS' and Gunner J. L. BUNTING of Captain B. LESTER PETERS', each won government silver medals. Gunner JONES was a son of the sheriff of Charlotte county. On the return of the winner from Fredericton he was royally received at Indiantown by the battery and with Captain PETERS driven in a barouche to his home.

March 10th, 1863, the day of the wedding of the PRINCE OF WALES, was observed by salutes fired by Captain PICK's battery from King Square ; Captain THOMSON's, from Queen Square ; Captain B. L. PETERS,' Reed's Point ; Captain M. H. PETERS,' flagstaff, Brooks Ward, Carleton ; Captain McLAUCHLAN's, flagstaff, Guys Ward, Carleton ; Captain HURD PETERS,' Fort Howe. The usual salutes were fired on the Queen's birthday, and on 24th June, Captain M. H. PETERS' battery fired a salute at the laying of the corner stone of Carleton City Hall.

The Prince of Wales cup did not come to the artillery in this year, but Gunner JONES won the second prize, a gold watch, while in a local competion Gunner BUNTING, of

B. L. PETERS', and G. J. COSTER, of Captain MCLAUCHLAN'S battery, each won a silver medal. There was a grand review at Torryburn on 25th September at which the artillery and all other forces acquitted themselves creditably They were accompanied on this occasion by Captain MORRIS' battery of Royal Artillery.

There was not the same *ecla,* attending the reviews of that portion of the active militia which was not enrolled in the volunteer companies. By an absurd provision in the law they were called out for one day's drill in each year. Of course they formed the butt for all who chose to jeer, and the descriptions in the newspapers of the time are most ludicrous. No training was given or could be attempted and these farces served simply for the enrolment of the men.

During the year Captain HURD PETERS retired from the command of the Portland battery, which he had brought into existence and which had been very successful under his charge. He was succeeded in command by Lieutenant SIMONDS, who had been gazetted 27th April. Lieutenants KIRK and RANKIN also retired and Gunner Edward JONES, of B. L. PETERS' battery and RICHARD FARMER obtained commissions in the battery.

Captain KNOX's battery at Gagetown went out of service. Captain CHESTNUT's at Fredericton was strengthened by the appointment of GEO. C. PETERS and JOHN M. STRATTON as lieutenants. The latter was drowned in the Saxby gale of 1869. Lieutenant Quinton was also transferred from Captain M. H. PETERS' battery to the county militia.

The remarks of Lieutenant JAGO, R. A., who inspected the artillery at St. John on September 10th, were very complimentary. Without underrating the other batteries he particularly commended B. LESTER PETERS' battery both for their smart and soldier-like appearance on parade, and also for their general efficiency in their duties.

The first militia order of 1864 appointed Captain B. LESTER PETERS provincial aid-de-camp *vice* Lieutenant-Colonel HAYNE, resigned. The following extract from the minutes of that officer's battery at a meeting held 11th January is interesting:

"On motion of Gunner JACK, seconded by Sergeant GEO. "FOSTER, Corporal CHAMBERLAIN was called to the chair, who "conveyed to Captain B. LESTER PETERS the congratulations "of the battery on occasion of His Excellency the Commander- "in-Chief having been pleased to appoint him to be provincial "aid-de-camp *vice* Lieutenant-Colonel R. HAYNE, resigned.

"The Captain then thanked the battery for their congratu- "lations, stating among other things 'that his duties as provincial "aid-de-camp would not interfere with his position as their "captain.' This announcement was received with reiterated "cheering."

Let the minutes of 18th April tell of another promotion:

"Captain announced that Sergeant-Major LOCKHART had "been appointed quartermaster of the New Brunswick Regi- "ment of Artillery. Captain promoted Sergeant INCHES to be "sergeant-major of the battery, Corporal FOSTER to be sergeant, "and Bombardier PERLEY to be corporal. On motion of "Sergeant-Major INCHES, seconded by Gunner VROOM,—It was "resolved that while this battery have heard with pleasure of "the promotion of their former sergeant-major, W. ALBERT "LOCKHART, to the post of quartermaster of the regiment, they "regret the loss of his immediate connection with the battery. "His long association with it, dating from its first formation, "the interest which he has always shown in its affairs and the "volunteer movement generally, as well as the high qualities "as a companion and associate which he has shown have "gained him their esteem and respect, and they therefore here- "by unanimously elect him an honorary member of this "battery."

The new sergeant-major is now Dr. P. R. INCHES of Saint John, and W. A. LOCKHART was from 1889 to 1891 mayor of that city. Dr. INCHES' brother, KEIR INCHES, was in 1838 a member of Captain, now Sir JOHN C. ALLEN's company at Fredericton, and was drowned on 19th July of that year while on duty. The regiment erected a tombstone to his memory.

In 1864 Captain JOHN MCLAUCHLAN was succeeded by THOMAS M. MCLACHLAN; Captain E. W. CHESTNUT and JOHN SIMONDS also retired. The Portland battery's officers became, captain, RICHARD FARMER; lieutenant, WM. CUNARD, and second lieutenant, GEORGE GARBY. Second Lieutenant F. G. W. LANSDOWNE of Captain B. L. PETERS' battery was given the rank of first lieutenant, practically a brevet rank. JACOB D. UNDERHILL was appointed second lieutenant in Captain PICK's battery, and Lieutenants SHANNON and TAYLOR retired. CHRISTOPHER MURRAY came into Captain S. R. THOMSON's battery as first lieutenant, and ROGER HUNTER was promoted to the same rank. W. W. STREET was also appointed second lieutenant.

Captain PICK's battery exhibited a great deal of social activity during the year. In February they had a 'tea soiree' in Smith's building, which was apparently a very enjoyable affair, and in November held an assembly in Ritchie's building, an event which seems to have given a great deal of pleasure.

The Portland battery held a ball in the old Temperance Hall on 25th February. The advertisement shows the committee to have been EDWARD JONES, RICHARD FARMER, THOMAS SCOTT, WM. MCKENZIE, GEO. KENNEDY, P. M. PARKINSON, WM. BARRON, WM. EWING, THOS. CLARK, JOHN LORD, JAMES MCCONNELL, MATTHEW MITCHELL, GEO. CARR, JAMES MCINTYRE. WM. CATHCART was secretary.

The muster roll of Captain FARMER's battery for 1864 is still extant. The following are the names:

Thos. Scott,	Tobias Armstrong,	Jas. Dunlop,
Wm. McKenzie,	John Andrews,	Joseph Lee,
Geo. Kennedy,	William Laughery,	John Vincent,
Jas. Napier,	John Young,	James Elliott,
P. M. Parkinson,	Benj. Logan,	James Boyd,
Wm. Hamilton,	Henry Buchanan,	Thomas Sullivan,
Wm. Morgan,	Robt. McClintock,	James McKenzie,
Wm. Court,	Richard Gillespie,	William Campbell,
Thos. E. Andrews,	John Cunningham,	Joseph McIntire,
James McConnell,	Jas. S. Morgan,	Thos. Morgan,
William Cathcart,	William Barron,	James M. Powers,
John Reed,	William Taylor,	Samuel Murphy,
Caleb Belyea,	George Tabor,	Henry J. Pratt,
John B. Riley,	Robt. Scott,	Oliver A. Boles,
Abel Hieben,	Andrew Johnston,	Thos. Nixon,
Frederick McKenzie,	Robt. J. Patterson,	J. Ewing,
Chas. Napier,	John Stratton,	William Allan,
Walter Starkie,	Alex. McDougall,	Joseph Saunders,
John Y. Lord,	William Farrell,	John A. Ruddock,
Geo. Sturks,	Herman Tapley,	Thos. Godsoe,
Jas. McIntyre,	Geo. Young,	Uriah Belyea,
Wm. Connor,	John Y. McDermott,	John F. Case,
Matthew Mitchell,	Henry Thos. Godsoe,	William Logan.

On the visit of the delegates from Upper Canada, who were viewing the land previous to confederation, a salute was fired at Fredericton by Captain BERTON's battery. In August Lieutenant-Colonel CROWDER, adjutant-general, resigned and was succeeded by Colonel THOMAS ANDERSON, of St. John Volunteer Battalion, who was formerly a captain in the 78th Highlanders.

The artillery of St. John to the number of one hundred and fifty, under Captains PICK, B. L. PETERS, MCLACHLAN and FARMER, were reviewed on September 22nd, at King square, by the new adjutant-general who presented to Gunner BUNTING the medal for rifle shooting which he had won in 1863.

In general orders of 12th October His Excellency thanked Captain SAUNDERS, of Hampton Troop of Cavalry, Lieutenant MURRAY, of N. B. R. A., and Captain BEER, Kings County Militia, for the tenders of service of their respective commands for camp duty during the annual rifle competition, which had been accepted. He also congratulated Lieutenant-Colonel FOSTER on having under his command a battery so admirable in drill and discipline as that of Captain PICKS, and regretted that circumstances did not permit his acceptance of the offer of Captain FARMER to bring his men to camp for duty at their own expense.

LIEUT. COLONEL S. K. FOSTER.

CHAPTER XIII.

1865-1868.

Rumors of a Fenian Invasion—A Run on the Savings Bank—Measures for Defence—Artillery Under Arms—An Alarm—'Court Martialed and Shot'—Thanks from the Governor—Confederation —End of the Colville Company.

A FEW changes of subordinate officers occurred in 1865, which are noted in the appendix of battery succession lists, and one battery, that of Captain MCLACHLAN, Carleton, was disbanded for non-attendance at drill. In this year Lieutenant-Colonel HAYNE, who had since 1838 had the title of command, though the more active duties were performed by Brevet Lieutenant-Colonel FOSTER, was promoted to the rank of colonel commandant, and STEPHEN KENT FOSTER attained to the subtantive rank of lieutenant-colonel. In this year, too, Captain GEORGE J. MAUNSELL, 15th Regiment, became adjutant-general of the province, a gentleman who for nearly a third of a century has been in close connection with our forces, and whose soldierly qualities combined with affability and kindness have endeared him to all who have sought his counsel or obeyed his commands. Besides an inspection of Captain PICK'S battery in January by Major MELICK, the holding of some quadrille assemblies by the men, at one of which Gunner WILLIAM MCAFEE was presented with a medal won for rifle shooting, and the usual 24th of May salute, there is nothing of local incident to chronicle in this year. The whole regiment was ordered into camp in July at Fredericton, and though the report is satisfactory no details are given. St. John was visited in May by General Sir F. WILLIAMS, the hero of KARS, who, on his departure, received a farewell salute from B. LESTER PETERS' battery.

The year 1866 was destined to try the mettle of the volunteer force throughout Canada. For some months rumors of a Fenian rising had been current, and as this year approached they seemed to take more definite shape. The first two months, however, were quiet enough. Under the new militia act of 1865 Captain THOMSON's battery was once more re-organized, Lieutenant CHRISTOPHER MURRAY becoming captain, with Sergeant STEPHEN KENT FOSTER, jr., as lieutenant. At Saint Andrews, where the artillery had died out, a new battery was formed in January under

Captain,   HENRY OSBURN,
Lieutenant,   THOS. T. ODELL,
Second Lieutenant, WALTER B. MORRIS.

This battery performed some interesting service a few months later. JOHN R. SMITH, of Captain B. L. PETERS' battery, obtained a commission as second lieutenant in Captain PICK's battery, which he resigned later in the year. Early in March newspaper items that the bonds of 'The Irish Republic' were being offered for sale in New York and other cities of the United States began to excite alarm. Agitators known as 'Head Centres' addressed largely attended meetings across the border, and the feeling grew that the descent of the troops which they were gathering would be upon the coast of New Brunswick. Popular imagination fixed the probable date for invasion as St. Patrick's day, and so great was the excitement that there was a run on the Savings Bank at St. John. Circulars, purporting to come from a republican committee in the city, were twice secretly distributed about the streets, calling on the citizens to rise, and assuring them that these 'republicans' had the sympathy of the Fenians and a part of the militia. The British and local governments made preparation and the drill rooms were closed to all but volunteers. On the 10th March in the House of Assembly Mr. WILMOT asked the attorney-general if the government intended sending volunteers to Campobello, intelligence having been received that a Fenian demonstration was expected in that quarter. No information was vouchsafed except that the government was adopting energetic measures for the safety of the country. In a few days despatches from New York stated that the organization was formed under experienced officers and that 15,000 uniforms and 2,000 rifles were stored in Burlington, Vt.

The measures for defence began by the appointment of Captain THOMAS ANDERSON, late H. M. 78th, as colonel in charge of the western military district of New Brunswick, and Lieutenant DARRELL R. JAGO, R. A., was appointed captain and assistant adjutant-general of artillery. On 14th March one captain, one first and one second lieutenant with eighty-three men of the N. B. R. A. were called out for actual service, together with the St. John Volunteer Battalion. The whole force was placed under command of Brevet Colonel JOHN AMBER COLE, H. M. 15th Regiment. The artillery called out were Captain PICK's battery with Lieutenant S. K. FOSTER, jr., and Lieutenant GEO. GARBY, of Portland battery. They were stationed on Partridge Island at the entrance to St. John harbor, and also at Reed's Point. On 4th April Captain M. H. PETERS, with Lieutenant E. J. WETMORE and twenty men, were called out and stationed at the Martello Tower, Negrotown Point battery (now Fort Dufferin), and at Sand

Cove, near St. John. Captain OSBURN, with one lieutenant and twenty men, was also placed on duty at St. Andrews. Major CUTHBERT WILLIS was made commandant at the latter place. Ensign NICHOLAS T. GREATHEAD was transferred from Charlotte County militia to Captain OSBURN'S battery and went on duty at St. Andrews. The St. John Volunteer Battalion was despatched to St. Andrews and served on the frontier with Captain OSBURN'S battery.

At Carleton, St. John, the old roof was removed from the Martello Tower and guns were mounted. Earthworks were thrown up on the adjacent hill and guns mounted at Fort Dufferin. On April 11th there was a rumor in the city that two hundred armed men had endeavored to take passage on the American boat at Portland for Eastport, but had been refused unless they left their arms behind them. Captain HOOD, of H. M. S. *Pylades*, telegraphed recommending a call of the volunteers. The St. John men had patrols out, that of the Carleton battery extending down the coast to Sand Cove. A system of signals was arranged by Major JAGO, and Captain PICK directed to have one sentry at the battery on Partridge Island and such others at look-out points as might be needed. An attempt at landing was to be announced by two guns, and very suspicious circumstances at night by three rockets at three minute intervals. Rockets sent up from Sand Cove were to be repeated at the Island, Lower Cove and at Carleton, Two guns at any one of the latter places were to be repeated by the others. Captain M. H. PETERS' force was increased to forty men, and afterwards four were taken from Captain PICK's and added to his.

On April 15th there was a landing at Indian Island, a small island near Campobello. The house of the collector of customs,

DIXON, was visited and the British flag seized. It was found a few days afterwards, and there has always been some doubt as to the real character of the persons who committed the depredation. But the province was in a blaze. There was another landing later on at the same place when the boat was challenged by an outpost under command of Lieutenant JOHN B. WILMOT, of the St. John Volunteer Battalion. Receiving no reply they fired, and the party left hurriedly. A few nights after, at a late hour, H. M. S. *Cordelia* in the harbor of St. Andrews beat to quarters and despatched rockets. Captain OSBURN'S battery fired from the guns of Fort Tipperary and the whole force turned out. It was only a 'scare' to test the efficiency of the men but it worked well. Nothing more serious occurred, and the Fenians after a repulse at Niagara disbanded. During the excitement General MEADE and staff, of the U. S. A., was stationed at Calais, on the frontier, with sixty-five men of the 1st U. S. Heavy Artillery. Generals MEADE and DOYLE exchanged civilities and took precautions for the safety of the province.

S. KENT FOSTER, jr, then lieutenant of MURRAY'S battery, says that part of Captain PICK'S force were from that battery. The only uniform most of them had was a great-coat. The men, except those on the island, went home at night and did about five hours work per day mostly garrison gun drill in which they became very proficient. Of course the other forces kept up sentries by night at their outposts. During the service Captain PICK reported two men, Gunners JAMES DEVEREAUX and BENJAMIN LOGAN, for having deserted their posts while on duty, and asked if there should be a court martial. Lieutenant FOSTER says that the men went into a shed and played a game of cards. The official correspondence does not go so far, simply stating that they were in a shed a short distance, not more than one hundred yards, beyond their beats, and that they stopped in there to light their pipes. Smoking on the beat was of course forbidden, and when the news got about it was currently reported that the men would be shot! The affair ended by Major JAGO, who heartily wished that his attention had never been called to the occurrence, delivering an impressive caution. In a letter on the subject he says, 'My own 'idea of volunteers is that you ought not to look too closely 'into their way of doing the work as long as it is done.' The exercise of such good common sense got over a difficulty which might have been very serious if formalities had been observed and affords a practical suggestion on the subject of discipline.

The whole force, consisting of Captain PICK with Lieutenant GARBY and forty-six men, Captain M. H. PETERS with Lieutenant WETMORE and forty-four men, and Lieutenant FOSTER with thirty men, was paid off on the 2nd June and the bloodless campaign was at an end. Three additional batteries had been formed as a result of the scare, that under Captain OSBURN at St. Andrews, already mentioned; one under Captain EDGAR at Woodstock, and a third under Captain WM. T. ROSE at St. Stephen. Captain ROSE had years before been in command of a battery which was now reorganized for service. He retired as major and was succeeded by Captain W. T. CLEWLEY.

Under these circumstances it may be imagined that the celebration of the Queen's birthday was more than an ordinary affair. At St. Andrews a dinner was given by Captain STEVENSON and the officers of the 'Gordon Rifles,' at which St. John officers were guests. On behalf of the St. Andrews battery, in response to that toast, Lieutenant GREATHEAD is reported as returning thanks. The whole force was inspected and the day was a great one for St. Andrews.

As B. LESTER PETERS' battery was largely composed of clerks in banks and other institutions it was impossible for them to go into service which would interfere with the discharge of their duties unless in case of such emergency as the actual commencement of hostilities. They, however, volunteered to a man to put in four hours drill daily at the garrison guns, and did so during the whole time that the force was under arms. This service was spontaneous and gratuitous and received the warmest thanks of His Excellency. During the winter, too, lectures were delivered by Hon. JOHN BOYD, Rev. G. W. M. CAREY, GEO. E. FENETY and Hon. WM. WEDDERBURN, the proceeds being in aid of uniforming MURRAY'S battery. Upon the disbandment of the forces a general order was issued dated 20th June, from which the following extracts are made:

'His Excellency desires in a special manner to acknowledge 'the services rendered by the batteries and detachments of the 'New Brunswick Regiment of Artillery. The officers and men 'of this branch of the militia force have shown a remarkable 'aptitude for acquiring a knowledge of their more difficult 'duties, which has called forth the marked commendation of 'the Major-General commanding in the Lower Provinces, and 'His Excellency has received the most satisfactory reports as 'to their general good conduct and efficiency.' * * * * 'To the forces generally employed on the frontier His Excel-'lency desires to express the gratification he has experienced 'in finding the officers, non-commissioned officers and men 'composing the force engaged in protecting those points of 'the frontier most threatened by attack, deserving of his entire 'confidence. His Excellency is fully aware that upon them 'devolved duties of a peculiarly difficult nature, the discharge 'of which was occasionally attended with a greater degee of 'hardship than His Excellency had anticipated or desired, but 'which have been accomplished to His Excellency's full satis-'faction.'

'Had it been the fortune of the militia volunteers of this

'province, as it was of those in Canada, to meet in conflict
'the armed invaders of our soil, His Excellency is certain that
'their conduct would have been such as to merit yet warmer
'commendation ; and they may take a pride in reflecting that
'the attitude assumed by the local force was among the causes
'which frustrated the projected invasion of this province.'

During the year Surgeon LEB. BOTSFORD, M. D., retired with the rank of major, and was succeeded by JOHN BERRYMAN, M. D., with Dr. JOSEPH L. BUNTING assistant surgeon. Captain B. LESTER PETERS received the brevet rank of lieutenant-colonel ; Lieutenant INCHES that of captain, and Sergeant JAMES F. ROBERTSON obtained a lieutenant's commission.

Captain PICK became a major by brevet and JAMES MCNICHOL, jr., was appointed a lieutenant in PICK's battery.

In 1867 there were many promotions and brevet rank was liberally granted. The raising of a new battery at Chatham, which had been undertaken in the previous year, was completed and the following officers gazetted :

Captain, THOMAS F. GILLESPIE,
First Lieutenant, FRANCIS J. LETSON,
Second Lieutenant, JOHN F. GEMMILL.

Major BERTON's battery at Fredericton having become noneffective was struck off the list. Major BERTON had been regimental major since Lieutenant-Colonel FOSTER's promotion He now retired and was succeeded by Major MOUNT on 19th June, 1867. Lieutenant S. K. FOSTER, of MURRAY's battery, became paymaster on the same day *vice* Captain WIGGINS, who retired with the rank of major. As Major MOUNT had vacated the adjutancy he was succeeded by Captain JACOB D. UNDERHILL on 17th July. Captain EDWARD H. CLARKE replaced Captain CLEWLEY in command of the battery at St. Stephen on 15th July of the following year. The minor promotions are all noted in the appendix.

The day appointed for the confederation of the provinces, July 1st, 1867, ushering into life the Dominion of Canada, was duly celebrated by our artillery corps. At noon royal salutes were fired from King Square by Captain MURRAY's battery, and from Fort Howe by Captain FARMER's. Captain B. L. PETERS' battery was at the guns at REED's Point to salute also, but only two guns were fired owing to a mistake in making up the cartridges, which were for 6-pr. instead of 3-pr. guns.

Under the new *regime* militia and defence were subjects placed under the exclusive control of the Federal government, and the provincial force was drilled in 1868 under regulations from Ottawa prior to another re-organization. Dominion Day was celebrated this year by three salutes fired at 6, 8, and 9 a. m. by PICK's and FARMER's batteries from King Square and Fort Howe. On the swearing in of Hon. L. A. WILMOT as Lieutenant-Governor of the province, July 23, three salutes of thirteen guns each were fired from Fort Howe by Captain FARMER's battery. On 10th September the regiment assembled for eight days drill, and on the 16th range practice was commenced with 32-pr. S. B. guns at the barracks. The target, a flour barrel, was twice carried away, once by Mr. JOHN KERR of the 'new battery recently organized,' and the second time by Sergeant FRODSHAM of Major M. H. PETERS' battery.

In October of this year notification was received that provision had been made for a class in gunnery at the school at Montreal. Companies were required to enrol in compliance with the new law. The year closed with the ninth anniversary of Portland battery which was celebrated by a ball and supper in the Temperance Hall, on December 23rd. Lieutenant-

Colonel FOSTER presented a gold medal to Sergeant NAPIER which he had won in the September competition.

This year, the last of the provincial organization, unfortunately brings to an end the historical continuity of the COLVILLE company. Though by a very slender thread at times, yet still by one that holds, succession can be traced to Captain MURRAY, but on 20th March, 1868, a militia order states that this battery having completed the term of engagement its services are dispensed with. It is probably better to withold the reasons which led to this step as they involve the charge of extremely disrespectful conduct by the captain of the battery to Major JAGO. There was no lack of efficiency on the part of the battery, however, and by July 14th of the same year there was a correspondence between Major JAGO and the D. A. G. as to the appointment of Sergeant-Major JOHN KERR of Captain PICK's battery as lieutenant of a new company which was composed of a number of Captain MURRAY's men together with recruits. Even before this Sergeant-Major KERR had been acting as lieutenant. Drill for this year was authorized though not by orders in the 'Gazette' as the Dominion government pending the enactment of a militia law dealt only with corps and companies in existence. Acting Lieutenant KERR's battery was so treated and the question of practical succession to the COLVILLE company becomes an open one for the reader. From 1865 Lieutenant Colonel WETMORE of the 2nd battalion Charlotte County militia had maintained Captain JAMES BOLTON's company at St. George as artillery. It was not in the regiment but was attached to the battalion for administrative purposes.

At the close of the provincial administration, then, there were at St. John five batteries under Brevet Major PICK, Brevet

Major M H. PETERS, Brevet Major FARMER, acting Lieutenant KERR, and Brevet Lieutenant-Colonel B. LESTER PETERS.

At Woodstock :   - -   Captain EDGAR'S battery.
At St. Stephen : - -   Captain CLARKE'S battery.
At St. Andrews : - -   Captain OSBURN'S battery.
At Chatham :   - -   Captain GILLESPIE'S battery.
At St. George :   - -   Captain BOLTON'S company.
The latter was not in the regiment.

And thus we leave the old 'N. B. R. A.' which had been in existence for thirty years and in whose ranks had been found some of the foremost men of the province. While we must all be glad that a new era of activity had opened before the old organization, yet the change must cause deep and lasting regret to all who care for the preservation of our regiments' story. For by an act of wanton vandalism almost every paper was destroyed which belonged to the records of the New Brunswick militia, and was not required to be transmitted to headquarters at Ottawa in connection with current business. Thus valuable material for accurate compilation is in many cases wanting, and this generation must depend upon the fragmentary details which in one form and another have been transmitted from the past. In Ontario and Quebec all militia records were transferred and the result is that to-day their forces are regarded as a continuation of those existing anterior to confederation, while ours has been in some quarters erroneously believed to have been of a much later creation. But it is submitted that these pages show conclusively that the company of JOHN COLVILLE, founded in 1793, lived to become a part of the regiment formed in 1838, the record of which under that designation is now brought to a close. Its future history will be told in the succeeding chapters under other titles. As a further evidence of continuity it may here be stated that in 1868 the regimental officers were:

Lieutenant-Colonel, S. KENT FOSTER, 29 March, 1865.
Brevet Lieut.-Col. 6 December, 1859.
Majors, { CHARLES J. MELICK, 6 December, 1859.
Brevet Lieut.-Col., 10 January, 1866.
J. MOUNT, 19 June, 1867.
Adjutant, JACOB D. UNDERHILL, 17 July, 1867.
Captain, 2 January, 1867.
Paymaster, S. KENT FOSTER (captain), 19 June, 1867.
Quartermaster, W. A. LOCKHART, 28 March, 1864.
Surgeon, JOHN BERRYMAN, M. D., 18 April, 1866.
Assistant { STEPHEN SMITH, M. D., 7 February, 1860.
Surgeons, { JOSEPH L. BUNTING, M. D., 18 April, 1866.

CHAPTER XIV.

1869-1876.

The 'New Brunswick Brigade of Garrison Artillery'—Visits of Lord Lisgar and Prince Arthur—Camp Barrack Square—Visit of Lord Dufferin—A Sad Accident—Formation of Dominion Artillery Association—A Gratifying Inspection.

ON the 7th January there was an assembly in the old drill shed, MERRITT's building, Princess St., of PICK's, FARMER's and KERR's batteries, at which a medal for shooting was presented to a gunner of Major PICK's battery whose name is not recorded in the brief chronicles of the time. This was probably the last occasion on which the batteries assembled as component parts of the old regiment. Early in February Lieutenant-Colonel FOSTER sent his service rolls to Lieutenant-Colonel MAUNSELL to get some difficulties straightened out. In some cases, such as the batteries at Chatham and Portland, every officer and man had re-enrolled and the number of lieutenants was greater than the regulations allowed. These officers had commissions under the old law and the subject was a difficult one to deal with. Happily, through the assistance and kind endeavors of Major JAGO, then assistant adjutant-general of artillery for the province, matters were brought into a state of harmony. It is, indeed, difficult to realize the extent of the obligations of our corps to Lieutenant-Colonels MAUNSELL and JAGO. At the time there was great uncertainty as to the positions these gentlemen would occupy. The latter had not for some years after confederation a regular appointment, but was continued in his position as if by sufferance and without that authority which his ability and the importance of his post demanded. It was also currently rumored that there were many applicants for the post of D. A. G., but fortunately for the service in New Brunswick no changes were made and the new militia organizations throughout the province had the care and assistance which was so greatly needed at the critical period of adaptation to a new order of things.

The continuity upon which our corps justly lays so much stress is evidenced by the following general order issued from the new headquarters under date of 6th February, 1869:

"The following corps enrolled under 31 Vic., c. 40, as well as those organized prior to 1st October, 1868, which have within three months after the act coming into force, re-enrolled as volunteers, are declared to be existing and continued as such.

* * * * * * * * * *

PROVINCE OF NEW BRUNSWICK.
NO. 8 MILITARY DISTRICT.
ARTILLERY.

Garrison Battery,	-	-	St. John.
do.	-	-	do.
do.	-	-	St. George.
do.	-	-	do.
do.	-	-	Chatham."

and by order of 5th March the batteries at Carleton and St. Andrews were declared to have been omitted from the order and were recognized, and a similar acceptance of the battery at St. Stephen was given by general order of 27th March. The order of 6th February also authorized the formation of a battery at St. George with the following officers:

Captain, CHARLES McGEE,
First Lieutenant, ROBERT A. STEWART,
Second Lieutenant, JOSEPH MEATING.

and the order of 5th March also authorized another battery at St. John, with

Captain, JOHN KERR,
First Lieutenant, JOHN A. KANE,
Second Lieutenant, JOHN EVANS DALEY.

As before explained, this battery was raised at a time when there was no authority to accept its services, and consequently it does not appear on the official records until this date.

The general order constituting the brigade bears date 26th May, 1869, and is as follows:

"The formation of a Brigade of Garrison Artillery is hereby authorized, to be designated as the 'New Brunswick Brigade of Garrison Artillery,' and will be composed of the following batteries, viz.:

No. 1, - St. John.
No. 2, - Carleton.
No. 3, - Portland.
No 4, - - St. Andrews.
No. 5, - - Woodstock.
No. 6, - - St. George.
No. 7, - - Chatham.
No. 8, - - St Stephen.
No. 9, - - St. George.
No. 10, - - St. John.

To be Lieutenant-Colonel, S. K. FOSTER.
" *Majors,* Lieut.-Col. CHARLES J. MELICK. Major J. MOUNT.
" *Paymaster,* Captain S. KENT FOSTER, jr.
" *Adjutant,* Captain J. D. UNDERHILL.
" *Quartermaster,* Quartermaster W. A. LOCKHART.
" *Surgeon,* Surgeon JOHN BERRYMAN, M. D."

The headquarters of the brigade were not ascertained until 17th December, when a general order fixed them at St. John. During the year the common council offered land at the

Ballast wharf for the erection of a drill shed but nothing was done towards providing the needed accommodation. In fact the complaint was frequent then, as it is in some respects yet, that the favors of the militia department are reserved for other localities than the Maritime Provinces.

The usual salutes were fired on the 18th and 24th of May, and on the former day the band of the 60th Rifles played. This was one of the last occasions in which the Imperial troops participated in a local event in the province. With confederation the garrison was removed from St. John and the defence of the port was left to the local forces. Under the new *regime* a school of instruction was opened of which many officers availéd themselves, the new regulations making the possession of a certificate requisite for promotion.

During the year the Governor-General, Sir JOHN YOUNG (Lord LISGAR) visited the Province. At Fredericton, on 31st August, he was received with due honors by the artillery under Lieutenant STRATTON, and on his arrival at Indiantown on the 3rd September Major FARMER's battery fired a salute. A large and enthusiastic crowd greeted His Excellency on his debarkation from the steamer *David Weston*, and when the carriage containing the vice-regal party arrived at the head of Portland another salute was fired by Major M. H. PETERS' battery from Carleton Heights. Salutes by Captain KERR's from Market Square, and Major PICK's from King Square announced the further progress of the party, and a guard of honor from the 78th Highlanders was drawn up at the Waverley Hotel. Next day a levee was held in the Court House, the 78th again furnishing the guard of honor. In the evening a firemen's parade enlivened the scene.

St. John received a royal visitor on the 7th of the month

in the person of H. R. H. PRINCE ARTHUR, Duke of Connaught. The usual salutes were fired by the batteries and the 62nd St. John Volunteer Battalion shared in this as in the other celebrations. A ball was held in the evening and on the following day there were more salutes and the usual rejoicing. On September 10th, H. R. H. visited Fredericton, where Lieutenant STRATTON's company paid the usual honors.

In the fall rifle competition Gunner PALLEN of Major GILLESPIE's battery won both first prizes, the Prince of Wales' cup and medal, and the event was duly celebrated at Chatham by his comrades.

There was another Fenian scare this year, which, though it did not immediately culminate, caused unusual preparations to be made. The 62nd Battalion were ordered to be in readiness but there does not seem to have been any call for the services of the artillery.

The next year, 1870, was uneventful. Probably the most disagreeable feature of it was a review on 24th May during a snow storm. The artillery had ten guns on parade, three drawn by horses and the rest by hand. A royal salute was fired at noon and the shivering soldiers took but little comfort from the fact that the weather was so exceptional as to become historic.

No. 3, the Portland battery which has always displayed a great deal of enterprise in social affairs made arrangements for holding a picnic on the 9th August, at Oak Point, on the St. John river. No doubt it was successful but the newspapers of the day do not record it. Gunner JOSEPH EWING, who afterwards obtained command of the battery got his first step this year, being appointed second lieutenant.

The next year opened with a ball on St. Valentine's day by

Captain KERR's battery. The Queen's birthday was observed by a review under circumstances much more favorable than those of the previous year. Salutes were fired by all the batteries during the morning and at noon they joined with the Royal Artillery, while the 62nd fired a *feu de joie*. The latter corps presented an address to their retiring Lieutenant-Colonel, CHARLES R. RAY.

The artillery inspection was held on 3rd October by Lieutenant-Colonel MAUNSELL and Major JAGO, at which the brigade turned out about two hundred strong. In the evening the officers gave a dinner to the inspecting officer.

In the same month Lord LISGAR again passed through the city, and the artillery fired the customary salutes. The 62nd Battalion does not appear to have taken part at this time as it had, most unfortunately, been disbanded some time before for non-compliance with a general order, and was then only in the process of re-organization. Since this time the two corps have gone on side by side, each emulating the other's successes and sharing the trials and disappointments incident to militia service. Major MELICK, the senior regimental major, retired on 7th December, 1871, with the rank of lieutenant-colonel. He was succeeded by Brevet Major PICK. The junior, Major MOUNT, also retired with rank of brevet lieutenant-colonel, and was succeeded by Major MARTIN HUNTER PETERS. Captain J. ALFRED RING then succeeded to the command of No. 2 battery, Carleton, which he held for thirteen years.

1872 is remembered as the year of the first brigade camp at the Barrack Square, St. John, where two hundred and fifty officers and men of the artillery, with a volunteer band, assembled on August 23rd. All the city batteries turned out and were joined by those of Woodstock and Chatham. A church

              Lieut. Bell, Major Gillespie, Lieut. Fraser,   Lieut.-Col. Otty.
Capt. Kane,   Lieut. Ewing,   Lieut.-Col. Foster, Asst. Surgeon Andrews,
   Lieut. Armstrong, Lieut. Carleton, Lieut.-Col. Jago, Adjt. Underhill,   Capt. Ring,
              B . Major Cunard,   Major Pick,   Major Peters.

OFFICERS CAMP, 1872.

parade to St. Paul's church was held on Sunday, the 25th inst., and the Chatham battery returned to their home on the 29th. The prize for the best shot in the brigade was awarded to Bomb. J. BROWN of No. 10, now No. 4 company, and Mrs. JAGO's prize fell to No. 1 battery. Inspection was held on the 30th and the men made a very creditable showing. In a few days they had become accustomed to camp life and acquired a degree of proficiency that weeks of drill under other conditions would not have given them. In this year JOHN A. KANE became Captain of No. 1 battery, in which position he served until 1885, maintaining a good standard of efficiency. Captain KANE's services as an officer began in No. 10, under Captain KERR, in 1869. He afterwards had as lieutenant Mr., now Major, DRURY of the Royal Canadian Artillery, and this officer is a grandson of the late Lieutenant-Colonel RICHARD HAYNE.

In March of the following year No. 10 battery lost a valuable officer by the death of Captain JOHN KING, who had reorganized the battery in the previous year, it having become non-effective. His funeral, which took place on the 10th March, was attended by members of the battery and of the Masonic order. The interment was in the burial ground on Lancaster Heights. He was succeeded in command by an enthusiastic volunteer officer, Captain ANDREW J. ARMSTRONG. whose services must be frequently referred to in this volume.

During 1873 New Brunswick was honored by a visit from the new governor-general, LORD DUFFERIN, who arrived in St. John by the western train on 19th August and was received by salutes from all the batteries and the ringing of the church bells. The 62nd Battalion furnished a guard of honor, and addresses were presented by the civic officials and various public bodies. The citizens vied with each other to do honor to the popular representative of royalty and he was well entertained during his stay in St. John. A drawing room was held on the 20th which was attended by the officers of militia corps in large numbers. The next day's celebrations included one of the regattas for which the city is famous, and on the following day His Excellency visited the capital of the province when the military honors were done by a provisional company under command of Captain BECKWITH. This gentleman, who had been adjutant of the 71st Battalion, had for some years previous assembled a number of men to fire the customary salute at the opening of the sessions of the House of Assembly. This led him to think of the formation of an artillery company, and about 1870 he, with Mr. JOHN ALLEN, son of the Chief Justice, as a prospective lieutenant, made up a roll of men willing to join such an organization. This was forwarded by the D. A. G. with his recommendation, but no reply was received by Captain BECKWITH from headquarters. About a year afterwards Captain BECKWITH was advised by Colonel P. ROBERTSON ROSS, then commanding the Canadian militia, to forward another application, which he did, but like the preceding one it received no official answer. It afterwards transpired that the authorities at headquarters were willing to establish a field battery, but thought Fredericton to be too far inland for the useful service of a garrison battery, and the matter dropped. An effort to raise a battery among the I. C. R. employees at Moncton was also discouraged, and though a service roll was forwarded the movement went no further.

An unfortunate accident marred the pleasant progress of the governor-general through the province. When at Chatham

Captain GILLESPIE's battery turned out to salute, and probably through the hurry of enthusiasm there was some oversight in the service of the vent or sponging out the gun. Whatever the cause may have been it is sad to relate that two men, Gunners J. MURRAY and R. STEEL, lost their lives by a premature discharge. An inquiry was ordered and the cause was reported to have been an unavoidable accident. The event cast a gloom over the battery and greatly lessened its efficiency for some time.

At the competition in September Mrs. JAGO's silver cup was won by Sergeant C. BELYEA of No. 3 battery, and the officers silver cup by No. 2 battery. Captain CUNARD, a valuable officer, afterwards district storekeeper, assumed command of No. 3 this year in succession to Brevet Major FARMER, who became quartermaster in place of W. A. LOCKHART.

Early in the following year, on the appointment of Lieutenant-Governor TILLEY, a levee was held in St. John, and the event was celebrated by a salute from the guns of Captain KANE's battery. Captain G. FRED RING and Lieutenant-Colonel SAUNDERS were appointed provincial aides-de-camp, and Lieutenant-Colonel JAGO with Captains F. B. HAZEN and LIKELY attended with a guard of honor. An address was presented to the new governor by the corporation of St. John, he having for many years represented that constituency both in the local and federal parliaments.

On the 26th February there was a grand gathering in Smith's Hall, when the prizes won at the autumn competition were presented by Lieutenant-Colonel MAUNSELL. The great event of the year, however, was 'Camp Dufferin,' held at the Barrack Square, which opened on the 23rd July, and consisted of No. 1 battery under Captain KANE, with Lieutenants DRURY and Wallace ; No. 2 under Captain Ring, Lieutenants Carleton and Lander ; No. 3 under Captain Cunard, Lieutenants Scott and Ewing : No. 7 under Captain Gillespie and Lieutenant Fraser, and No. 10 under Captain Armstrong and Lieutenants King and Till. Lieutenant-Colonel Maunsell was commandant of the camp; Lieutenant D. G. Smith supply officer, and 217 officers and men were under canvas. The force paraded to St. Paul's church on the 26th, and next day Lieutenant-Governor Tilley and suite paid a visit to the camp. The usual competition was held and resulted in the winning by No. 10 of the first prize ; Nos. 2 and 3 tied for the second. No. 10 also won a cup presented by Lieutenant-Colonel Thurgar, and Quartermaster Sergeant Armstrong of No. 3 won a silver medal presented by Lieutenant-Colonel Thurgar, jr. During the camp Gunner Samuel McIntyre of No. 3 was taken ill, and his death in August caused sadness to his comrades in their recollection of a pleasant camp. He was buried with military honors by his battery. The year closes with a more pleasant event in the marriage of Captain Cunard on 2nd December. The gallant captain entertained the men of No. 3 at supper on the evening preceding the ceremony and received a royal salute from his congratulatory gunners. During the year No. 5 battery, Woodstock, was made a field battery and ceased to be connected with the brigade. No. 9 battery, St. George, was transferred to the infantry of Charlotte county, and No. 8 at St. Stephen had become non-effective.

The year 1875 is practically without record except that No. 3 battery with its usual enterprise held a soiree in the Portland Temperance hall which closed with a dance, about ninety couples being on the floor.

In this year Lieutenant-Colonel JAGO was appointed assistant inspector of artillery for New Brunswick and Nova Scotia.

A very important step was taken by the officers of the brigade on the 21st January, 1876, when they assembled in Lieutenant-Colonel FOSTER's office to consider the formation of the Dominion Artillery Association. In 1873 a Provincial association had been brought into existence, entirely through the efforts of Lieutenant-Colonel JAGO, but owing to the small number of batteries and the limited membership, it had not been able to accomplish very much. It had, however, laid the foundation of good work in this direction and emphasized the necessity for such an organization. Lieutenant-Colonel MAUNSELL, who presided at the meeting, was appointed a delegate to represent the brigade at the organization meeting in Ottawa.

No. 3 battery laid another comrade, Gunner LANE DUNHAM, to rest on the 2nd February, escorting the remains from Fort Howe to Lancaster Heights. The firing party was under command of Lieutenant EWING.

The brigade lost a good friend and excellent officer by the resignation of Lieutenant-Colonel JAGO of the post of assistant adjutant-general of artillery. He sailed for England in April, previous to which he was presented with an address at the Park Hotel by the officers of the artillery. The address was read by Lieutenant-Colonel FOSTER, and Majors PICK, PETERS and FARMER, Captains UNDERHILL, CUNARD, KANE, RING, ARMSTRONG, Lieutenants DRURY, WALLACE and KING, and Surgeon DANIEL, were present. He left St. John on the 20th, the band of the 62nd Battalion playing a farewell, and the batteries firing a salute.

The artillery, together with the engineers and 62nd Battalion, were called out on the 12th of July in aid of the civil power, a disturbance being apprehended on the occasion of the Orange celebration. But happily it was found that the good citizens of St. John were so peaceably disposed that the services of the militia were not required, and after being a few hours under arms Lieutenant-Colonel FOSTER dismissed the force. Only one man was shot that day. He was in the procession and carried a revolver. By some carelessness in handling it was accidentally discharged, causing him a flesh wound in the thigh, and this was the only blood shed!

The first competition for prizes offered by the Dominion Artillery Association was held in August and the winners were as follows:

No. 1 Battery.
1st, Corporal ROBERTS,
2nd, Sergeant MCGAW,
3rd, Gunner MCILWAINE.

No. 2 Battery.
1st, Lieutenant LANDER,
2nd, Captain RING,
3rd, Gunner J. J. GORDON,

No. 3 Battery.
1st, Gunner DARRAH,
2nd, Gunner GRAHAM,
3rd, Sergeant BROWN.

No. 10 Battery.
1st, Sergeant DUNLOP,
2nd, Sergeant C. F. LANGAN,
3rd, Sergeant MAGEE.

The prizes were presented in the Carleton City Hall on the 5th September.

It is worthy of note that with the many apparent disadvantages under which the corps was laboring, the inspector of

Artillery, Lieutenant-Colonel STRANGE, should have been able to say in 1871 that with the exception of the New Brunswick Artillery, he believed few batteries in the Dominion had made gunnery their main object. This opinion was strongly supported by Lieutenant-Colonel JAGO, who had done his best to bring up the efficiency of the corps, and who felt that it was at that time the best in the Dominion. Again, in 1876, Lieutenant-Colonel STRANGE in his annual report said :

"The gun drill and practice of the brigade was very good. And I am of opinion that with the exception of the men of the two gunnery schools, who practically are regular soldiers, the New Brunswick Garrison Artillery is unsurpassed among those I have seen in the Dominion. I have less hesitation in paying this tribute to their efficiency, because I can claim no part of the credit of their instruction, which must be given to my late assistant, Lieutenant-Colonel DARREL JAGO, late Royal Artillery, and to Lieutenant-Colonel FOSTER, who has for many years commanded them and labored for their efficiency, no doubt assisted by the commanding officers of batteries, and by his adjutant, Major UNDERHILL, who has a first-class certificate from the Kingston Gunnery School. Major CUNARD'S, No. 3 battery, was not drawn for drill this year, but they performed their duties without pay, which marks the *esprit* that exists in the New Brunswick Artillery."

In this period there are but a few other changes to be specially noted, most of the appointments being dealt with only in the appendix. Surgeon BERRYMAN retired in 1875 being succeeded by J. W. DANIEL, M. D., in 1876. The latter had been appointed assistant surgeon in 1875 in succession to JOSEPH ANDREWS, M. D., who had left the province. Dr. ANDREWS was re-appointed assistant surgeon in 1883 and still holds that rank. Dr. STEPHEN SMITH, assistant surgeon of the old corps, was transferred to the Woodstock field battery at the time of its becoming a separate organization.

CHAPTER XV.

1877-1884.

Great Fire at St. John—Services of the Artillery—Mining the Walls —A Brave Rescue—Visit of H. R. H. the Princess Louise and the Marquis of Lorne—Celebration of the Loyalist Centennial— Retirement of Lieutenant-Colonel Foster.

THE year 1877 will long be a memorable one in the annals of St. John, distinguished as it was by the greatest of the many conflagrations by which the city has been visited. Breaking out at half-past two o'clock on Wednesday afternoon, June 20th, in nine hours the entire business portion of the city and a great part of the residential district was destroyed. The loss was enormous in proportion to the size and wealth of the city. But the same qualities which have made good artillerymen of the sons of the city, pluck, intelligence and determination, have long since raised a newer and better St. John in the place of the desolated city. One great loss, however, can never be made good. The city of the loyalists was filled with mementoes of her founders and possessed a vast store of collected information which would have been of great use to the archivist and the historian. These were destroyed and among them many a muster roll and reminiscence of the old days of the volunteer artillery. Throughout the hours of panic on that memorable June day the militia of the city proved themselves worthy of their calling, and during the period of insecurity which followed, the peace and safety of the city largely depended upon their efforts.

The old barracks, with the uniforms of Nos. 1 and 10 batteries and of the 62nd Battalion, were destroyed despite the brave efforts of men of both corps led by Lieutenant-Colonel MAUNSELL, D. A. G., Brigade-Major MACSHANE, Lieutenant-Colonel BLAINE, Captain HALL and others.

Lieutenant-Colonel FOSTER was then the senior officer in St. John, and two days after the fire he was requested by Mayor EARLE, Alderman JOHN KERR and WM. ELDER, Esq., J. P., to provide a military force to guard the unopened vaults of the banks and large business houses which were exposed to the depredations of a lawless element. Private properties, too, and the temporary quarters of such banks as were able to resume business required more protection than could be afforded by the small police force. A force was at once raised from the artillery, Nos. 2 and 3 batteries at first principally contributing the men, owing to the loss of uniforms which the other batteries had sustained. To No. 3 battery is due the credit of having the first men on duty after the requisition was made on the morning of the 22nd June. The detail was composed as follows:—

  Brevet Major WM. CUNARD, commanding.
  First Lieutenant JOSEPH EWING.
  Sergeants: J. S. BROWN, T. A. GRAHAM.
  Corporals: JOHN VINCENT, J. R ANDREWS.
  Bombardiers: W. BELL, W. MCJUNKIN, WM. LEE.
Gunners: JOS. LEE, A. LONG, S. TORREY, C. GARRETT, JOHN SPEIGHT, JAMES LEE, G. CRAWFORD, C. YOUNG, JUSTUS MOWRY, H. SAUNDERS, W. MORGAN, R. A. C. BROWN, JOHN ANDREWS, W. CRAWFORD, R. CARLIN.

The detachment mustered pursuant to orders at their drill room, Temperance Hall, Simonds street, Portland, at 2 p. m., and marched thence to Charlotte street, opposite the country market, where at 2.30 p. m. men were told off for duty. The first work was the mining of the front wall of the Post Office on Prince William street and the posting of sentries at several points. Other men of the artillery, as well as a portion of the 62nd Battalion, were soon on duty. The latter corps, whose uniforms were destroyed, obtained a supply from the stores of the 74th Battalion. The artillery were on duty from 22nd June to 5th July and contributed a force varying from seventy to ninety-two officers and men. A camp was formed on King Square and guards were detailed for day and night duty. Besides this the artillery were employed in the demolition of dangerous walls which were everywhere standing and threatening the safety of laborers and passers-by. In this service the men faced danger as great as that of the battle field, and the reader is reminded of the sad fate of the late Major SHORT of "B." battery, R. C. A., when reading the following extract from STEWART'S HISTORY OF THE FIRE, which tells of a narrow escape of Sergeant LAMB of the artillery :

"At the blowing down of the walls of the post office an act of valour was performed by some men belonging to the artillery which deserves prominent mention. Major CUNARD, Captain A. J. ARMSTRONG and Lieutenants INCH and EWING, together with a detachment of the Brigade of New Brunswick Artillery, under the command of Lieutenant-Colonel S. K. FOSTER, marched to Prince William street and proceeded to blow down the walls of the post office. Sentries were posted all around a circle of nearly two hundred yards, and everything being in readiness the work was begun. Two bags of powder were placed against the building with the length of spouting which would contain the port fire fuse that was to connect with the powder. Two charges went off and the effect on the walls was slight. The men thought of the expediency of placing a charge against the inside as well as one on the outside of the building. The trains were laid and fuses lit, but some loose powder igniting in a moment with the train it exploded with a deafening crash before the men could get away, and half of the wall facing Prince William street came down as if a thunderbolt had struck it. Gunner JOHN NIXON, of No. 2 battery, was covered with the debris but escaped uninjured save a few scratches on the arm and a cut or two. Gunner WALTER LAMB, of No. 10 battery, was struck down and everyone deemed him dead, the smoke and debris completely hiding him. The second 70 pound blast was still burning, and was momentarily expected to go off, when LAMB'S hand was seen to raise over his head and touch his cap. In a moment five men, unmindful of the terrible fate which threatened them, rushed in and bravely dragged from the mass of ruins their fallen comrade. He was borne away just as the second charge went off with a roar carrying away at a bound the remainder of the wall. Stones and bricks flew in every direction, and JOHN ANDERSON, who was standing on Germain street, but whose presence there was unknown, fell badly wounded. He was conveyed to the hospital and died in a few days. The names of the five artillerymen who behaved so bravely are, Lieutenant INCH, No. 10, Lieutenant WM. KING, No. 10, Corporal J. R. ANDREWS, No. 3, Corporal ANDERSON, No. 1, and Gunner R. McJUNKIN, No. 10. Captain RING, of Carleton battery, was standing within three paces of Gunner LAMB when he fell. His escape was certainly miraculous.

This explosion also severely injured Lieutenant EWING of No. 3, who was within a few yards of the building. He had to be carried away. He remembers Corporal ANDREWS and three other men running from King street to the assistance of Gunner LAMB and extricating him at the peril of their lives. Their bravery, strange to say, never received official recognition from headquarters.

The force was strengthened on the arrival of H. M. S. *Argus* from Halifax with the marine artillery and some soldiers of the 97th Regiment. The whole force was under Lieutenant-Colonel FOSTER, who was then the senior lieutenant-colonel in the Dominion. The militia were specially commended for their services by the D. A. G. in his annual report. He said:

Lieutenant-Colonel FOSTER has informed me that while the presence of a considerable armed force was absolutely necessary in preserving law and order at such a time as this, when thousands of able-bodied men were thrown out of employment and left without house or home, all, or nearly all, of the arduous duties of guards and picquets devolved upon the force of active militia of St. John, then under arms, the individual members of which were, in many instances, themselves left without house or home, and most creditable, I consider, to them, to the officer in command (Lieutenant-Colonel FOSTER), and to their officers and men generally, was the discipline maintained, as well as the manner in which duties were performed.

One of those little incidents occurred during the time the volunteers were on duty which illustrates the absurdity to which technical questions of authority may sometimes come. The chief of police, JOHN R. MARSHALL, whose long service in the artillery has before been mentioned, apparently thought that notwithstanding the presence of the soldiery he was still responsible for the peace of the city, and by some oversight no orders appear to have been issued as to the co-operation of the military with the police force or that any respect should be shown to its officers. Consequently we find one of the newspapers abusing the chief of police in round terms for having forced a sentry, and there is, on file, a report from Lieutenant-Colonel BLAINE to the effect that the chief refused to answer the challenge of the sentry at the Bank of New Brunswick, on Carleton street, but, revolver in hand, drove him back on his comrades. The attention of the civic authorities was called to the affair, but presumably a better understanding was arrived at as the matter dropped.

Owing to the loss of clothing and want of drill accommodation, the annual drill of the corps for the year was much interfered with. The erection of a new drill shed, which is still in use, was begun, but, unfortunately, the distance of the site from the centre of population and the inadequate accommodation of the building has always militated against the interests of the St. John force. For a city of the size and importance of St. John the facilities for drill and military association are, in this respect, far inferior to those of any other part of the Dominion, and it is the hope of all that before long some better provision may be made for the force, which of all departments of the public service, gives most and gets least. The armament of Fort Dufferin was completed in this year by the addition of five 64-pr. rifled guns.

The year 1878 opened with considerable uneasiness in Europe, and for a time it seemed probable that another great war would be added to the world's history. So great did the danger appear that preparations were made among the colonial forces for local defence, and on 22nd May orders were issued to the corps in the New Brunswick district to hold themselves in readiness for any service. At Deer Island, St. George, St. Andrews and St. Stephen, being exposed places, the men were directed to have the arms in their possession at once. Even before this Lieutenant-Colonel FOSTER issued a regimental order for batteries Nos. 1, 2, 3 and 10 to recruit to their full strength and to be held in readiness for immediate duty at Fort Dufferin, Partridge Island, Fort Howe, Carleton Heights, Dorchester battery and Red Head battery should a sudden emergency arise. The defences at Fort Dufferin and St. Andrews were strengthened, and the report of the D. A. G. for the year commends Brevet Lieutenant-Colonel UNDERHILL, Captain POLLEYS and Captain Ring, of the artillery; Captain PERLEY, of the engineers; Lieutenant-Colonel MACSHANE, Brigade-Major and Lieutenant-Colonel CUNARD, district storekeeper, for their services in these necessary works. An offer for service abroad was also made by Brevet Lieutenant-Colonel UNDERHILL of two batteries from the brigade. Lieutenant-Colonel MAUNSELL, D. A. G., also says :

"When offers to serve in any part of the world, at home or abroad, were being freely made on the part of a large portion of the active force of this district, it was deemed advisable to issue orders to all corps to hold themselves in readiness for any service, and while, in every instance, these orders were obeyed with alacrity, I must advert to the systematic way in which the Garrison Artillery at St. John (Lieutenant-Colonel FOSTER five batteries) were detailed for duty at the forts and batteries, with the view to every officer, non-commissioned officer and man knowing the part he would have to occupy for the defence of the important harbor of St. John "

The corps was this year inspected by Lieutenant-Colonel STRANGE, inspector of artillery, who found the New Brunswick artillery together with those of Montreal the only really efficient artillery forces in the Dominion. Credit is given to Captain POLLEYS, of St. Andrews, who had successfully reorganized a battery at that important position.

A curious survival of an old volunteer custom is found in the records of this year. On 22nd July No. 1 battery met at the Orange Hall, Simonds street, and elected their non-commissioned officers. On 27th December the Portland battery celebrated their anniversary in a very successful manner among those present being Brigade-Major MACSHANE, Lieutenant-Colonel CUNARD and Captain EWING.

In this year also a new battery, No. 9, was formed under Captain THOMAS W. LANDER, at Fairville, in the county of St. John. Captain LANDER had been a lieutenant in No. 2 battery. FREDERICK H. ELLIS was gazetted as first lieutenant, and a very efficient battery was raised.

During the early part of 1879 the corps were equipped with new helmets which added much to their appearance in the ceremonial display upon the arrival of H. R. H. the PRINCESS LOUISE and His Excellency the Governor-General. The vice-regal party arrived at St. John on 6th August and the city was again *en fête* to honor another member of the royal family. Besides all the St. John batteries, a squadron of the 8th cavalry under Major DOMVILLE, the 62nd battalion under Lieutenant-Colonel BLAINE, and N. B. Engineer Company under Captain PERLEY, took part in the ceremonies of welcome. Lieutenant-Colonel MAUNSELL, D. A. G., was in command of the whole force. The 62nd battalion furnished a guard of honor at the railway station, and the arrival of the party was announced by salutes from No. 1 battery, Captain KERR, near the residence of Hon. ISAAC BURPEE, at Mount Pleasant; No. 3, Captain EWING, at Zion Church, and No. 10, Captain ARMSTRONG, at Wright street hill. It was the proud duty of Captain ARMSTRONG to hoist the royal ensign and fire the royal salute of twenty-one guns. The men of the force who were not engaged in saluting lined the streets through which the party passed on their way to Reed's Castle, the home of Captain R. R. REED, a veteran artillery officer, which had been placed at the disposal of the visitors. Upon their visit to Carleton the following day Captain RING'S, No. 2, battery fired a salute and a similar honor was tendered at Fredericton, on the 9th, by Captain BECKWITH'S company. Upon the return of the party to St. John on the 12th Captain LANDER'S battery fired a salute from Lancaster Heights, and upon their departure from the city the 62nd again furnished a guard of honor, and Captains KANE and ARMSTRONG fired the parting salute. The services of the force on this important occasion were acknowledged by a general order to which in district orders Lieutenant-Colonel MAUNSELL added his thanks for the splendid work which had been done and his gratification at the neat appearance and cheerful obedience of the men.

On the 17th January of this year Captain POLLEY's battery at St. Andrews rendered aid to the civil power on the occasion of the execution of T. DOWD, a murderer. An anticipated riot was prevented by prompt action and 'the ready response of the battery.

The next year was an eventful one for the corps. The annual inspection was held in August, Lieutenant-Colonel PRICE LEWES being the inspecting officer. At gun practice No. 10 battery, Captain ARMSTRONG, won a silver mounted clarionet, and No. 1, Captain KANE, a silver plated clarionet, both the gifts of Mr. G. J. PINE, of England, formerly of St. John. At the inspection Lieutenant-Colonel FOSTER said he had attended drill for fifty-three years and had never missed being present. Even assuming that the veteran officer was speaking generally, his was a splendid record and worthy of imitation by all officers. Few, of course, can serve for such a long period, but all can make it possible that their service shall be uninterrupted. Lieutenant-Colonel PRICE LEWES, in his report for the year, called attention to the fact that Lieutenant-Colonel FOSTER had served for over fifty years and deserved the highest credit for the efficiency of his brigade referred to in past reports. He suggested, in view of his advanced age, that he should relinquish the active command of the brigade and be appointed to the honorary command. This but foreshadowed the severance of the happy relations which had so long existed between a worthy officer and the command by which he was regarded with respect and affection.

The Provincial Exhibition was opened in St. John on 5th October, with great brilliancy and display, by Lieutenant-Governor TILLEY, who was accompanied by Lieutenant-Governor HAVILAND, of P. E. I., and many other distinguished statesmen and officials. The salute was fired from the guns of No. 10 battery and the officers of city corps attended in uniform.

In December, to the regret of the whole force, Lieutenant-Colonel MAUNSELL, D. A. G., was transferred to another district and was succeeded by Lieutenant-Colonel TAYLOR, who proved during his administration to be a competent officer with ambition similar to that of his predecessor for the encouragement and improvement of every branch of the service. Lieutenant-Colonel MAUNSELL was tendered a farewell dinner at the Dufferin Hotel, St. John, at which Lieutenant-Colonel FOSTER occupied the chair.

On January 20th of the succeeding year a very pleasant gathering was held at the residence of Captain ARMSTRONG on the occasion of the presentation to him by the non-commissioned officers and men of his battery of a handsome framed photograph of the officers and men of his command. The presentation was made by Lieutenant KING, and testified that the Captain ARMSTRONG of that day was as popular as is the Major ARMSTRONG of to-day among all ranks of the militia. A supper was served, at which Captain ARMSTRONG occupied the chair, supported by Lieutenant-Colonel BLAINE and Lieutenant-Colonel FOSTER. The vice chair was filled by Lieutenant KING who had on either hand Major FARMER and Lieutenant-Colonel CUNARD. Among those present were Captain KANE, Lieutenant STEVEN, Surgeon DANIEL, Sergeant-Major HUGHES and Sergeant LANGAN. In response to the toast of the 'N. B. B. G. A.' Lieutenant-Colonel FOSTER reviewed the history of the corps and repeated his claim, which is now thoroughly substantiated, that it is the oldest military organization in the Maritime Provinces. To this statement we may now add the wider field of Canada.

In this year Lieutenant-Colonel PRICE LEWES resigned his position of assistant inspector of artillery, and since then no officer of this rank has been resident in New Brunswick.

The camp at Sussex was augmented for the 1st July by the addition of the N. B. B. G. A., the 63rd Rifles and 66th Princess Louise Fusiliers, from Halifax, and on this occasion the whole force was reviewed by His Excellency the Governor-General, a total strength of three thousand one hundred and seventy-nine being present.

The annual inspection was this year held at Fort Dufferin by Major-General LUARD and Lieutenant-Colonel IRWIN, inspector of artillery. It is to be regretted that one of those periods of depression which occur in every organization had overtaken the force and that it was not able to maintain its previous high character for efficiency. The attendance was good and the inspecting officer recognized that there was material for doing excellent work but with the exception of some detachments it had not been properly developed. But the brigade has always possessed a spirit of determination to surmount difficulties and correct deficiencies as soon as they are pointed out and thus animated have now more than regained the position which they previously held.

In 1881 was inaugurated the first of those artillery competitions which have done so much to improve our force and to bring us into touch with the artillery of the mother country. Lieutenant-Colonel OSWALD, of the Montreal brigade, had the honor of commanding the first Shoeburyness team and of bringing to Canada in triumph the prize offered by the Governor-General for shifting ordnance.

Next year the old custom of a salute on Loyalists' day was revived, one being fired at 7 o'clock in the evening by Captain ARMSTRONG's men. An entertainment commemorative of the day was held, and the citizens generally began to prepare for the centennial celebration to be held in the following year. Only Nos. 1, 2 and 10 of the city batteries drilled this year, and No. 7 at Chatham. The system of credits for the Dominion Artillery Association prizes was extended to the Garrison Artillery, and this measure more than any other has been of benefit to the force. It has encouraged a competitive spirit from Vancouver to Halifax and stimulated all ranks to efforts which no other method could have induced. Since this time, too, the force has had the undivided attention of Lieutenant-Colonel IRWIN, as inspector, and to him is due the credit for the high standard which has steadily been kept before it. The result of the inspection was a considerable improvement upon that of the previous year. In the competition, which was made upon a basis considerably different from the present, No. 1 made 125.6; No. 2, 75.6; No. 7, 38.2; and No. 10, 93.6. No. 1 took third place in the Dominion.

The celebration of the Centennial year, 1883, like everything else of deep interest to the community, was of great importance to the corps. Formed by the loyalist fathers of the city, for the defence of their infant colony, but a decade after their exile, the corps has always felt the influence of loyalist tradition. Then, too, its veteran commander was of loyalist descent and felt most deeply the importance of an impressive celebration of the hundredth anniversary of his forefathers' stand for British government. Accordingly active preparations were made in which not only the artillerymen as militia, but as citizens participated, and it was fitting that at midnight of the 17th of May, just as the first century faded into the second, the guns of the loyal artillery fired a salute at the Old Burying ground, where slumbered men who had founded a city and strengthened a nation. The night was calm and the echoes of the guns could be heard far away reverberating among the hills surrounding the city, as the chimes of Trinity church rang out on the midnight stillness. At seven o'clock the next morning a salute was fired consisting of fifty guns from No. 1, Captain KANE, and of a like number from No. 2, Captain RING. There was no turn out of the militia as a body, the idea being to reproduce the early life of the city, and in this the volunteers ably assisted. In the great procession which traversed all the principal thoroughfares of the city no pageant was more conspicuous than that of the 'Artillery Company of 1793.' The uniform and equipment were faithfully reproduced, and indeed this was characteristic of the whole parade. From the Indian in his canoe, who greeted the Loyalists with a rifle shot on their landing, to the representation of the 104th Regiment on their famous march, every detail was a faithful reproduction of the original. The celebration of this centennial did much to arouse interest both in military and historical matters. True is the saying of EDMUND BURKE, 'People will not look forward to posterity who never look backward to their ancestors,' and equally true is its converse.

A church parade was held at St. Paul's Church on 17th September of that year, the corps being under the command of the major, Brevet Lieutenant-Colonel M. H. PETERS. The sermon was preached by Rev. F. S. SILL. On this occasion the corps was headed by its fife and drum band.

The opening of the Dominion Exhibition on October 1st was signalized by a salute from No. 10 battery followed by H. M. S. *Garnet*, then in harbor, running up the American flag and firing a royal salute. This courtesy was an acknowledgment of the American salute to the British flag at Yorktown. The U. S. S. *Alliance*, Commander REED, immediately responded with a salute, and thus, in the harbor of the Loyalists was evidenced a reconciliation, effected by the community of ancestry and the healing hand of time.

Inspection was held on 9th October by Lieutenant-Colonel COTTON, assistant inspector of artillery, who, in his report adverted to the intended retirement of Lieutenant-Colonel FOSTER, and congratulated him on the state in which he would hand over the brigade. On 12th December, 1883, the formal announcement was made that Lieutenant-Colonel STEPHEN KENT FOSTER was permitted to retire retaining rank, and thus ended the honorable service of a gentleman whose first artillery commission bears the date of the 25th April, 1834, a continuous service of nearly half a century as an officer of his well loved corps, and much more than that as a member of the militia. Consequent upon his retirement the command of the brigade devolved upon Brevet Lieutenant-Colonel M. H. PETERS, who, being over the prescribed age could not be promoted to the regular command.

In 1884 Staff-Sergeant WALLING was sent from Quebec to instruct a team for the competition which was held at the latter place in September and in which the brigade had the honor of taking second place in the "B" or "go-as-you please" shift. Before leaving St. John Sergeant WALLING was given a supper by the non-commissioned officers of the brigade.

At the annual inspection Major-General MIDDLETON was

present and expressed himself as much pleased with the appearance and work of the men. During the year Major and Brevet Lieutenant-Colonel PICK and Brevet Lieutenant-Colonel and Adjutant UNDERHILL retired retaining their rank, and No. 7 battery at Chatham was removed from the list. The other batteries outside of St. John had all become non-effective. These and other anticipated changes temporarily operated against the efficiency of the corps.

In this year another change was made in the staff of the province, Lieutenant-Colonel MAUNSELL returning to the office of D. A. G. He was heartily welcomed back to the position which he has since held, and in which it is the hope of every volunteer he may long continue.

LIEUT.-COLONEL ARMSTRONG.

CHAPTER XVI.

1885–1893.

Lieutenant-Colonel Armstrong Takes Command—North-West Rebellion—Shoeburyness—Death of Lieutenant-Colonel Peters—The Queen's Jubilee—Death of Lieutenant-Colonel Foster—Two Carnivals—Death of Major Seely—Building of Drill Sheds—Promotion of Major Gordon—Dawn of the Centennial.

ON 9th January, 1885, an announcement of considerable importance to the corps appeared in general orders. It was that Major JOHN R. ARMSTRONG, of the 8th Cavalry had been appointed specially and provisionally to the command of the brigade. The step had been rendered absolutely necessary, but for some time the friends of the artillery were anxious as to the effect which it would have upon the force.

Fortunately the corps appreciated the advisability of the appointment and the reasons which required the ordinary rules of promotion to be set aside. Some of the officers, however, felt that they could no longer continue in their positions, and a number of resignations were received. This, of course, must be regretted, as it is always unpleasant to see men who have served for a long time severing the ties which bind them to the force, but it must be admitted by all, from the standpoint of the present day, that the new commanding officer won the confidence of the brigade, was successful in filling up the vacancies, and that under him the corps has since equalled if not excelled its previous record. Lieutenant-Colonel ARMSTRONG had in 1865 been a private in the University Rifles at

King's College, Windsor, N. S., and afterwards a gunner in B. LESTER PETERS' battery. He was then appointed a lieutenant in the reserve militia and promoted to a captaincy therein. In June, 1880, he received a commission as major in the Princess Louise Hussars.

Soon afterwards, by general order, No. 10 battery became No. 4 and No. 9 was changed to No. 5. The idea of maintaining batteries outside of St. John was abandoned and the brigade was placed on the same footing as it is to-day.

In March Brevet Lieutenant-Colonel PETERS retired retaining his rank. His was a long military career. In 1836 and 1837 he had drilled in an infantry company at Fredericton, under command of Captain FISHER, father of the late Judge FISHER. In the fall of the latter year he enlisted in the York Light Dragoons, under Lieutenant-Colonel, the late Judge WILMOT. In 1839 he was on service in the 'Aroostook war,' the dragoons being employed in conveying despatches from Woodstock to St. John, a work of no small difficulty in those ante-railroad days. His corps was then on duty about four months. In 1846 Lieutenant-Colonel PETERS came to St. John to practice his profession, that of medicine, and he there joined the Queen's New Brunswick Rangers under Lieutenant-Colonel, the Hon. JOHN H. GRAY, remaining in that corps until he was transferred to No. 2 battery of the N. B. Regiment of Artillery at Carleton, of which he had command for many years, as before stated. Lieutenant-Colonel PETERS always took the warmest interest in all things pertaining to the militia, and his record of nearly fifty years of service almost equals that of his commanding officer. The regret was general that his age prevented Lieutenant-Colonel PETERS from obtaining the command of the brigade, a reward which he had fully earned by years of arduous work and zealous service. About this time several other changes occurred. Paymaster KING retired with his rank, and was succeeded by one of the truest friends of the corps, the late Captain GEORGE F. SMITH. Later in the year Captains RING, EWING and LANDER retired. As Captain KANE had already been succeeded by GEORGE B. SEELY, this made an entire change of captains throughout the brigade, with the exception of No. 4 battery, of which Captain A. J. ARMSTRONG retained command. There were but few lieutenants who had served in the old establishment and it was difficult work for new men to prepare the corps for inspection. The loss of old and valued officers who had given many years of service to the corps and who had gained for it many successes, was deeply regretted on all hands, but at that time the step seemed to be necessary in their judgment. It is with pleasure that the brigade of to-day realizes that many of these officers who retired are among its most active supporters and warmest well-wishers.

A school of instruction for officers was opened in March and conducted by Lieutenant, afterwards Captain and Adjutant LANGAN and Sergeant-Major HUGHES. Later in the year the services of Corporal DONNINGTON, R. A., from Halifax were obtained.

The news of the fight at Duck Lake, on 28th March, alarmed the country and showed that the uprising of RIEL had attained the full proportion of a rebellion. The enthusiasm of the militia of this province knew no bounds, and when on the 11th May there sounded in New Brunswick the 'trumpet call throughout the land' that 'needs scarce repeated be' there was a ready response. Lieutenant-Colonel ARMSTRONG offered the services of the brigade. The lot, however, fell to their brethren of the 62nd battalion, who, in the short space of a week were *en route*. The scene of their embarkation at the I. C. R. station is one that will never fade from the memories of those who witnessed it. Though their services were not eventually required yet while immediate employment was expected our sister corps displayed the readiness to face danger in the discharge of duty which is characteristic of the true British soldier.

Though the artillery did not participate in the conflict yet Captain HARRISON, who lately commanded No. 3 company, saw service in the Queen's Own Rifles, and Corporal RICHARDSON, who is referred to elsewhere, served in "A" battery.

In September busbies were adopted as the brigade headdress replacing the helmets and were provided at regimental expense. In the same month No. 5 battery, at the Orange hall, Fairville, presented their retiring captain, THOMAS W. LANDER, with an address and gold headed ebony cane.

On October 4th a church parade was held at St. Paul's church, the sermon being preached by Rev. MR. WALKER. The next day the corps was inspected by Lieutenant-Colonel IRWIN whose report says: 'Their improvement since last year is most marked, and the interest shown by officers and non-commissioned officers in acquiring a knowledge of their duties promises well for increased efficiency in the future.'

The following was the establishment of battery officers at the inspection :

    No. 1—*Captain*, GEO. B. SEELY.
       Lieutenant, S. D. CRAWFORD.
       Second Lieutenant, R. R. RITCHIE.
    No. 2—*Lieutenant Commanding*, JOHN J. GORDON.
       Second Lieutenant, GEO. K. MCLEOD.
    No. 3—*Lieutenant Commanding*, HEDLEY V. COOPER.
       Second Lieutenant, WM. M. BOTSFORD.

No. 4— *Captain*, A. J. ARMSTRONG.
Lieutenant, Arthur S. BENN.
Second Lieutenant, GEO. W. JONES.
No. 5—*Lieutenant Commanding*, E. J. SCAMMELL.
Second Lieutenant, E. H. TURNBULL.

In November Lieutenant-Colonel ARMSTRONG, Captain SEELY, Lieutenants BOTSFORD, JONES and SCAMMELL attended a special course at Quebec and obtained the necessary certificates to enable their rank to be confirmed. Surgeon DANIEL also attended the course, and though the obtaining of a certificate was unnecessary for his position, showed great proficiency in the examination and received one of the highest certificates ever taken by an officer of the corps at the school. He is probably the only regimental surgeon in Canada who has also the qualification of a combatant officer. At the close of the year the lieutenant-colonel was appointed provincial A. D. C. to the Lieutenant-Governor.

The formation of a band had already been made and on New Year's day, 1886, they appeared wearing the new busbies.

At the annual meeting of the officers it was decided to present a gold medal for a skating competition to be held in the Lansdowne Rink. The medal was accordingly prepared and competed for. Paymaster SMITH offered a prize for shifting ordnance.

This year it was decided to send another artillery team to compete at Shoeburyness and the choice of commanding officer fell upon Lieutenant-Colonel ARMSTRONG. The brigade was also represented by Sergeant ALBERT K. PRATT, of No. 1 battery, while Sergeant GOOD, of the Woodstock field battery was also contributed by New Brunswick. Captain, now Major C. W. DRURY, R. C. A., a former officer of the brigade, was the adjutant of the team. After practice at Quebec the team sailed for England on 22nd July and arrived at London on the 31st. The competition took place in the following week and the Canadian team was most successful. In the competition for the Montreal Merchants' Challenge Cup, which had previously been won by the British team, the Canadians fired against a detachment selected by lot from the winning detachments of the week previous. The choice fell on the team which had the highest score in the grand aggregate. Yet the Canadian team won the prize and also the Marquis of Londonderry's Challenge Cup and the Governor-General's Cup for a special shift. They also won from ninety-two detachments nine silver cups presented by Sir RICHARD WALLACE, Bart., M. P., the first prize in a 64-pr. firing competition, besides receiving a certificate of merit in the 10 inch R. M. L. gun competition. The record of the team is a high one, and the regiment is deservedly proud of the fact that it was commanded by the same officer who is at the head of the corps.

Captain ARMSTRONG obtained the majority this year and dur the absence of the cólonel was in command of the brigade. Lieutenants GORDON, BOTSFORD, JONES and SCAMMELL were promoted to the captaincy of Nos. 2, 3, 4 and 5 batteries.

On the 1st of July the corps held a programme of sports on the Barrack square which was largely attended, and the events included a shift to give the spectators an idea of the work to be performed by the Shoeburyness team in England. An accident unfortunately prevented the shift being done in fast time.

The year was essentially one of church parades. No. 3 held the first at St. Luke's church, and later in the summer Nos. 2 and 5 attended service at Carleton Presbyterian church.

MAJOR A. J. ARMSTRONG.

Besides these there was the brigade church parade at St. Paul's church on July 12th, when Canon DeVeber preached. This parade was under command of Major Armstrong.

On the morning of September 29th the brigade, under Major Armstrong and headed by the band, marched to the residence of Lieutenant-Colonel Armstrong, on Wellington Row, and welcomed home their commanding officer with a general salute and an address of congratulation from the major who had so ably looked after the interests of the corps during the colonel's absence.

At the inspection on 8th October, Lieutenant-Colonel Maunsell, D. A. G., presented Lieutenant Harrison with the North-West medal and Lieutenant-Colonel Irwin handed a similar memento to Sergeant Richardson, who had been promoted to staff sergeant. The result of the inspection was that No. 4 battery made 109 points out of a possible 129, and took second place in the general efficiency competition though, unfortunately, at that time there was no second prize among garrison batteries. After inspection a dinner was given at the Dufferin hotel by the corps to Lieutenant-Colonel Armstrong for the celebration of the victories achieved by the Shoeburyness team. Major Armstrong presided ; on his right sat the guest of the evening, and on his left Lieutenant-Colonel Maunsell, D. A. G.

It was soon to be the turn of the gallant major to be honored at festivities of a similar character. He would himself probably say that the greatest honor that an officer can receive is one paid to him by the men who have been under his command, and one of the proudest moments of his life was on the 5th November when at a supper which he gave to No. 4 battery, his old command, he was presented with a beautifully illuminated address and a handsome walking stick bearing the inscription :—

Presented to
Major A. J. ARMSTRONG,
by the
Non-commissioned Officers and Gunners
No. 4 Battery, N. B. B. G. A.,
1886.

The corps was not destined to have the new major long in the saddle, though while life lasts he will always be with them in spirit. In February of the next year he was appointed district storekeeper for the Province of New Brunswick, and his pleasant companionship with the corps came to an end so far as the militia lists can testify.

At the annual meeting of officers on 14th March, 1887, a vote of thanks was passed to BLAIR BOTSFORD, Esq., of Dorchester, N. B., for the gift of a valuable challenge cup which has since been competed for among the batteries by the non-commissioned officers' answers to questions. In case of a tie it is decided by the officers' answers to their questions. The officers also passed the following resolution upon the death of the late Brevet Lieutenant-Colonel PETERS which occurred on 5th February, 1887 : —

Whereas, The late Lieutenant-Colonel MARTIN HUNTER PETERS, lately in command of this corps, has departed this life, having served with the militia volunteers of this province for a period of over forty years ; therefore

Resolved, That the officers of the New Brunswick Brigade Garrison Artillery do hereby place on record their feelings of respect and esteem for the late Lieutenant-Colonel PETERS. Always willing to devote his time, attention and ability to the service of his country, and in aid of his fellow men, he at last lost his life in the commendable effort of saving his neighbors' property from destruction by fire ; and further

Brevet Lieut.-Colonel MARTIN HUNTER PETERS.

Resolved, That a copy of this resolution be forwarded to the widow of the late Lieutenant-Colonel PETERS with the sincere condolence of the members of this brigade.

This year forms another landmark for the St. John militia. It being the Jubilee year of HER MAJESTY'S accession to the throne, it was the feeling of all that it should be fittingly celebrated, and this feeling was naturally very strong among the militia. Accordingly a grand demonstration was planned by the city force, which should include the 'trooping of the colors' a ceremony that had not been performed in St. John since the departure of the regular troops. The 21st June was observed as the official holiday, and at 2 p. m. on that day were brigaded under Lieutenant-Colonel BLAINE, the artillery commanded by Lieutenant-Colonel ARMSTRONG, the 62nd battalion under Major TUCKER, and the St. John Rifle Company, Captain HARTT. Major MARKHAM of the 8th Princess Louise Regiment of cavalry acted as orderly officer. Arrived at the Market Square the artillery were posted on the south, the 62nd and Rifle Company on the north while the ceremony of trooping the color was performed. The artillery then took up their position on the North Wharf and a *feu de joie* was fired by the brigade, the artillery firing seven rounds from their guns three times. The brigade then marched past twice and after several manœuvres a hollow square was formed, two volleys fired and the brigade reformed in line and advanced in review order. Further detail of the events of the day is unnecessary. Suffice it to say that on all hands there was loud praise for the citizen soldiery of all ranks, and that all did their best to honor the Sovereign whose regnal jubilee was a festival of rejoicing throughout her mighty empire.

On August 21st the corps attended divine service at St.

Stephen's church, where an excellent address was given by Rev. Dr. MACRAE. Inspection took place on the following day when Lieutenant-Colonel IRWIN, the inspecting officer, handed to Gunner EDWARDS, of No. 3 battery, a gold maltese cross, the gift of Lieutenant HARRISON, for attendance at drill. In the evening there was a regimental dinner at the Dufferin hotel which passed off with all the pleasantness usual to such affairs. In the following month at the competition at the Island of Orleans No. 4 battery won the Montreal Challenge Cup for highest 40-pr. aggregate from twenty competing detachments. This battery was again second in general efficiency, though for this there was no prize. No. 1 took fourth place.

At the annual meeting held 18th March of the succeeding year it became the sad duty of the officers to again record the passing away of another who had lately been associated with the corps. The death of Lieutenant-Colonel FOSTER was the subject of the following resolutions :

Whereas, On the 20th December last, Lieutenant-Colonel STEPHEN KENT FOSTER departed this life, full of years and in the enjoyment to the greatest extent of the respect and esteem of the public ; and

Whereas, Colonel FOSTER was appointed lieutenant in the corps April 26th, 1834 ; captain, March 31st, 1841 ; major, August 14th, 1848 ; lieutenant-colonel, December 6th 1859, retiring in 1884 ; and thus served as an officer of the corps continuously for the exceptionally long period of half a century, and was for twenty-five years of this period its commanding officer ; therefore

Resolved, That we, the officers of the N. B. B. G. A., hereby express our appreciation of the personal worth of our late commander, and our admiration of his untiring zeal, and the ability he displayed in keeping his corps in a condition of strength and efficiency for so many years—no small achievement, and one demanding more than average executive powers ;

nor would we forget those pleasant traits of disposition which gained for him the affectionate regard of the officers and men under his command, and made his death a personal loss to so many; and further

Resolved, That the above resolutions be entered on the records of the brigade, and a copy sent to the family of the late Colonel FOSTER.

No. 2 battery, under Captain GORDON, developed considerable energy this year. They obtained subscriptions from the citizens for the erection of a band stand on the Market square, Carleton, which has since been frequently used greatly to the pleasure of the residents of that side of the harbor. The stand was opened on the evening of 10th July, No. 2 battery, headed by the Carleton Serenade Band, marching from their quarters to the square, forming a circle about the stand and firing three volleys. The citizens, by subscription, presented a silver cup to the battery which has since been annually competed for on the 1st July. The church parade was held on 19th August, at St. John's church, Rev. JOHN DESOYRES officiating, and inspection took place on the 22nd by Lieutenant-Colonel IRWIN. The result was highly satisfactory, No. 1 battery winning the second prize, the Lansdowne cup, for general efficiency, with 126 points out of a possible 148. No. 4 battery was not far behind, taking third place with 119 points. At the Island of Orleans, Captain CRAWFORD, of No. 3, won the officers' first prize, following in the footsteps of his colonel who had won it in the year previous. The corps gave a ball on 28th September at which they entertained over four hundred guests. The affair took place in Berryman's hall and no labor was spared to make the surroundings as attractive as possible. The dance was popularly voted the most successful of society events for many years, and the brigade was much encouraged to repeat the entertainment in subsequent years.

No. 2 battery in this year decided to build a drill shed for themselves and started out to raise the funds by a series of concerts. One was held in the Carleton City Hall on November 29th at which a good programme was given. Among the principal features was the revival of the old 'Chesapeake and Shannon,' which has since been the marching song of that battery.

One of Lieutenant-Colonel ARMSTRONG'S Christmas boxes this year was an appointment as A. D. C. to His Excellency the Governor-General.

In February, 1889, Captain SEELY was promoted to the majority, and in the following May Captain Crawford of No. 3 battery was transferred to No. 1 ; Lieutenant McLEOD being promoted to the captaincy of No. 3. Major SEELY was presented with a handsome gold headed cane by his battery upon his promotion.

The winter carnival, held on 27th February, was participated in by the artillery as the following newspaper extract will show:

"'To the artillery belongs the honor of a fine historic representation, and to Portland battery credit must be given for a tableau expressive of loyalty. No. 1 and No. 4 batteries joined in a scene illustrative of the overland journey of the Imperial troops in 1861, when all England and America were excited over the seizure by the latter power of MASON and SLIDELL, the Confederate commissioners to England. It is fresh in the recollection of many persons how the troops were hurried out to Canada and up through our province to Quebec. The transport arrangements of the home authorities were well imitated yesterday by the artillery, and effective scenes were presented by the sledges where artillerymen wrapped in their great coats were seated in the rough and ready conveyances. Following the teams with the men were other teams laden with field pieces, wheels and limbers. The teams had the mottoes, 'Trent Affair,' Riviere du Loup ' via Nerepis ' 'via Fredericton,' 'St.

John the winter port in '61, why not '89?' More teams followed laden with the knapsacks and other equipments of the men.

No. 3's show was really fine. On arches over their sledges were the mottoes 'Long live Victoria' and 'Every ready,' besides others. Under a canopy stood a number of non-commissioned officers and men in full uniform with fixed swords. At the rear of the sledge was a brass field piece.

The display was fine and was much enhanced by the thought that, if needed, gallant No. 3 would stand by their motto of 'Ever ready.' The whole parade of the artillery was headed by a sleigh containing Lieutenant-Colonel J. R. ARMSTRONG, Major A. J. ARMSTRONG, Surgeon DANIEL, Captain G. B. SEELY, Captain G. W. JONES, Lieutenant W. W. WHITE.

If 1887 was distinctively 'Jubilee Year,' 1889 was Carnival year. July 23rd was the day of the Summer Carnival, the enjoyment of which was much enhanced by the presence in port of H. M. S. *Tourmaline*. In the evening a brigade was formed under Lieutenant-Colonel BLAINE consisting of the blue jackets of the warship with their field pieces, the marines, artillery, 62nd, and rifle company. The color was trooped on the Market square, and the marines under Lieutenant HENDERSON, R. M. L. I., performed the bayonet exercise with beautiful precision. The blue jackets, under Lieutenant BARTON, R. N., next gave an exhibition of field gun drill which drew forth the applause of thousands of spectators. The brigade marched past in column and quarter column and returned to the drill shed where Lieutenant-Colonel MAUNSELL, D. A. G., addressed the men.

At inspection Corporal SULLIVAN, of No. 3, won Lieutenant HARRISON's prize, a breast-pin, for best attendance at drill in his battery. No. 4 battery secured the Botsford cup. The church parade was held at St. Luke's church, on August 11th, Rev. L. G. STEVENS preaching the sermon.

The next year the brigade sustained a severe loss by the sudden death on March 21st of Major GEORGE B. SEELY, who, in a few years had risen to the second position in the corps and was respected for his ability and kindliness of heart. Many a young officer was encouraged by him, and many an older one strengthened by his wise and timely advice. With a hopeful career before him at the bar of his province, his death was not merely a loss to a single organization but to the community. When but a lad of fifteen, the Fenian trouble broke out, and young SEELY, then a member of a school cadet corps, enlisted in a company of York county militia and went to the front. His record as an officer in the corps has been already told. Owing to his illness being of a contagious nature the funeral was private, but the officers of the brigade followed the hearse to the railway station from whence the body was taken to Fredericton, where it was interred. The Infantry School corps there preceded the hearse and as the body of Major SEELY was laid to rest by the side of his father three volleys paid sorrowful tribute to the departed. His death cast a gloom over the annual meeting which was held on March 31st, and at which the following resolutions were adopted: —

Whereas, We are called upon to mourn the loss by death of Major GEO. B. SEELY, of this corps;

Resolved, That we, the officers of the N. B. B. G. A., place on record an expression of our deep sorrow and regret for the loss of a brother officer, who, since his connection with this corps in 1885 has taken the greatest interest in it, and has been both a strength and an ornament thereto.

As a battery officer he was not only respected and beloved by his men, but by his painstaking attention to his military duties, indefatigable zeal and honorable ambition to place his command at the head of the list, he succeeded in gaining for No. 1 battery a position for efficiency which was second to but one

LIEUT. JONES, LIEUT. SCAMMELL, SURGEON DANIEL, LIEUT.-COL. ARMSTRONG, CAPT. SEELY, LIEUT. BOTSFORD.
OFFICERS' SPECIAL CLASS, QUEBEC, 1885.

in the whole artillery of Canada. As a member of the regimental committee his cool, clear judgment was invaluable, and he was ever ready and willing to give to its deliberations the benefit of his presence and advice.

We admired him for his manly bearing, his intellectual ability, his firm integrity and his patriotism; we loved him for his constant courtesy, his fidelity and his kindness of heart.

Resolved, That we send a copy of the foregoing resolutions to his widowed mother, to whom we would also most respectfully extend our warmest sympathy in her deep affliction.

In that year the brigade obtained from the city of St. John two lots of land on Winslow street, Carleton, for the erection of a drill shed. The corps during the year built a shed on Fort Howe for No. 3 battery at a cost of about $1000, of which only $250 was contributed by the government. A manual of rifle and artillery exercises was published by the corps, the work being compiled by Captain LANGAN and Lieutenant BAXTER. Church parade was again held at St. John's church, and the sermon preached by Rev. JOHN DESOYRES, the rector. Inspection was held on August 28th, and on the 29th the officers entertained Lieutenant-Colonel IRWIN at dinner at the Dufferin hotel. No. 1 battery was successful in winning the Botsford cup, and the event was duly celebrated by a supper given by its officers to the battery on the evening of September 8th. In the fall of this year His Excellency the Governor-General and LADY STANLEY OF PRESTON visited the city. A salute was fired from Fort Howe on the arrival of the train. On the 18th December the death occurred of Lieutenant-Colonel JAGO to whom frequent reference has before been made in these pages.

In 1891 the corps provided a drill shed for Carleton battery which however was not completed in time for occupation for the purposes of that year's drill. The cost was $1200, of which the government gave the small grant of $250. At the annual church parade to St. John's church on August 30th, a number of the officers of H. M. S. *Tourmaline*, which was again in port, accompanied the staff of the brigade. Rev. G. E. LLOYD, formerly chaplain of the Queen's Own Rifles, preached the sermon. On September 2nd the bluejackets of the *Tourmaline* joined with the artillery and 62nd in another demonstration which was quite as successful as the one previously mentioned. After the parade the men of the several corps were entertained at the drill shed by His Worship Mayor PETERS.

The inspection by Lieutenant-Colonel MONTIZAMBERT resulted in No. 1 battery winning third prize, $25, in the general efficiency with 247 out of a possible 260 points. The Botsford cup was also won by this very efficient battery.

Another brilliant event in the social history of the corps was the ball held in the assembly rooms of the Mechanics' Institute, on April 30th following. The brigade again entertained some hundreds of their friends. Among those invited were the officers of Infantry School Corps, Fredericton; 8th Cavalry, Halifax Garrison Artillery; Brighton Engineers; 66th P. L. F., Halifax; 62nd, 66th, 71st and 74th Battalions, and the St. John Rifle Company. This year's inspection found both Nos. 1 and 4 in the third place with 244 points each. They divided the prize. No. 4 was the winner of the Botsford cup. All of the city corps attended service on the same day, August 21st. A brigade was formed which was afterwards separated, the artillery going to St. John's church and the 62nd and Rifle company to the Mission church. The vacant majority was filled on 16th December by the promotion of Captain GORDON, of No. 2 battery, who was succeeded in the command of the battery by Lieutenant BAXTER. On New Year's day, 1893, the new major received a testimonial of the esteem in which he was held by his old command. At the 'At Home' given by the band, Captain BAXTER read an address from the battery and presented Major GORDON with a neat gold headed cane suitably inscribed. On the same day a brief historical sketch of the corps, the precursor of this volume, was published in the Canadian Military Gazette.

The Dominion Artillery Association at their annual meeting in the following year chose Lieutenant-Colonel ARMSTRONG as their president.

At the regimental meeting on March 27th, 1893, the following was adopted :—

'*Resolved*, That the officers of the New Brunswick Brigade
'of Garrison Artillery desire to express to Lieutenant-Colonel
'ARBUTHNOT BLAINE, late commanding the 62nd St. John
'Fusiliers, and senior officer at this station, upon his retire-
'ment therefrom, their appreciation of his long and successful
'work in the militia service, and their sincere hope that he
'may live for many years to see the continued prosperity of
'the force which has so warm a place in his heart.'

It was also resolved to celebrate the centenary of the corps in a suitable manner. How that was done must be told in another chapter.

CHAPTER XVII.

THE SERGEANT-MAJOR AND NON-COMMISSIONED OFFICERS.

HIGH in importance among the elements of a successful corps are the non-commissioned officers. It is not necessary to repeat the trite language of the drill books as a definition of their duties. No mere words can describe their usefulness, and their duties can only be learned by experience and common sense. Much of the success which has attended our corps in the past and a great measure of its present strength lies in the ability and good judgment of the men who wear the stripes. Under the present excellent system, which requires each non-commissioned officer to answer a number of questions each year ensuring some theoretical knowledge on their part, and by the judicious selections for appointment which have been made in all the companies, the efficiency of the non-commissioned officers has been maintained. Too much importance cannot be attached to the manner in which a recruit receives his first instruction, and as this is generally given by a sergeant or corporal, their ranks should be held in high regard. An excellent feature of the regiment is that many of its officers have served in the ranks and are, by practice, well acquainted with the adaptation of drill to the needs of the soldier and the service.

Among the non-commissioned officers of the regiment the Sergeant-Major is of course chief in rank, but more than that he is first in the affections both of officers and men. His connection with our force dates from 1862 when he came to St. John from Halifax in the gunboat *Spiteful*. Sergeant-Major SAMUEL HUGHES was then in "K" battery, 4th brigade, R. A., under Captain STRANGWAYS, and at St. John was with his battery transferred to Captain MORRIS' "A" battery, 8th brigade. He arrived in St. John October 31st, 1862, and for thirty-three years has been a resident of the city. For some years he was occasionally detailed to give instruction to the local batteries in field gun drill, and in 1866 on the strong representation of Major JAGO was transferred to the N. B. Regiment of Artillery, being at the same time placed on the Coast Guard, R. A., as brigade sergeant-major. The latter step gave him a permanent rank in the Imperial force, while in the militia artillery he became regimental sergeant-major. Since that time his service has been constant. Many officers of our corps since that time have passed through his hands for instruction, and hundreds of recruits have been by him initiated into the mysteries of drill. With the right siege train at Sebastopol he took part in four bombardments, was wounded on 6th June and 7th September, 1855, being present at the fall of the great fortress, and proudly wears the reward of his services in the Crimean medals. Every officer and man of the corps will join in saying that the tokens of honor were never displayed on a braver or more faithful breast. Sergeant-Major HUGHES was born at Porthywayne, Shropshire, on the borders of Wales, on 25th July, 1835, and has therefore recently completed his sixtieth year. May he many times again appear on parade with the corps for which he has worked so strenuously and which is so greatly indebted to him.

A quarter of a century ago he was held in such esteem by

the corps, that, at a parade in Merritt's building, he was presented by the brigade, through Lieutenant-Colonel FOSTER, with a handsome gold watch, bearing the following inscription:

"Presented to
Sergeant-Major S. HUGHES, R. A.,
by the officers, non-commissioned officers and gunners of
Batteries 1, 2, 3, 10, N. B. B. Garrison Artillery,
Dominion of Canada, January 27th, 1870."

The following address accompanied the gift:

New Brunswick Brigade of Garrison Artillery,
Headquarters, St. John, N. B.,
Dominion of Canada, January 27, 1870.

Sergeant-Major HUGHES, R. A.:

The staff officers of the brigade, and the officers, non-commissioned officers and gunners of batteries Nos. 1, 2, 3 and 10, under the respective commands of Major GEORGE H. PICK, Major M. H. PETERS, Major R. FARMER and Captain JOHN KERR, have great pleasure in recording their unanimous approval of the faithful and efficient manner in which you have discharged the duty of your position of drill instructor to this portion of the brigade, from the date of your appointment in September, 1863, to the present time.

On several occasions during that period the batteries were inspected by Major-General Sir H. DOYLE, and other government officers of Her Majesty's Service, all of whom bestowed the highest encomiums on the practical results of your tuition.

As drill instructor to the corps, your ability and happy manner of imparting knowledge, have secured our fullest confidence, and as a man, your exemplary conduct has won our highest respect and esteem.

As a small token of our friendship we ask you to accept this gold watch and chain; and our best wishes for your future happiness and prosperity.

(Signed)   S. K. FOSTER,
Lieutenant-Colonel commanding.

SERGEANT-MAJOR HUGHES.

Sergeant HUGHES responded as follows:

Lieutenant-Colonel Foster and Staff Officers of the Brigade of Garrison Artillery of New Brunswick:

Majors PICK, PETERS and FARMER, and Captain KERR, together with the respective non-commissioned officers and gunners under their respective commands, having declared through you their approval of the manner in which I have discharged my duty as drill instructor, and also referred to the flattering remarks made on several occasions by General Sir C. HASTINGS DOYLE in reference to the high state of discipline which you have acquired, nothing, sir, can possibly be more gratifying to the British soldier than to know his humble services have met with the approbation of his commanding and other officers, also the non-commissioned officers and gunners of the portion of the service to which he belongs. And with reference to the discipline of these batteries, I have only to state that when I consider the facilities granted by my officers and the untiring zeal and determination of the non-commissioned officers and gunners to approach as near as possible the perfection of Her Majesty's artillery of the regular army, that had we failed to elicit favorable remarks from Sir C. HASTINGS DOYLE, I would have decidedly looked upon myself, and myself alone, as the person to blame; but I have also to add the testimony of a gentleman of long military experience, and who has witnessed the manœuvuring of volunteers in different parts of the several provinces in our Dominion, that the artillery to which we have the honor to belong will bear favorable comparison with those he has seen in other places.

And with reference to the gold watch and chain—a token of your kindness to me, which I neither expected nor deserved —a present which, notwithstanding its great value, shall be prized by me as a great treasure, chiefly as a memento of the happy years I have spent with the Volunteer Artillery of St. John, New Brunswick, and for which I can only return you all my sincere thanks.

The sergeant-major, besides his other decorations, has also received the medal bestowed for long service and good conduct, one of the proudest emblems which a soldier can display. A portion of the period of service for which this **medal was** granted was spent in the regiment.

Though the corps did not directly contribute to the force engaged in the suppression of the rebellion in the North-West, yet, as before mentioned, one officer, Captain HARRISON, saw service, though before he was connected with the brigade. The corps had another representative in the field in the person of Corporal THOMAS RICHARDSON of No. 4 battery, who, while attending a short course at "A" battery, Quebec, volunteered and went to the front. He served in the engagements at Fish Creek and Batoche. Upon his return he was banquetted at the Clarendon Hotel by his comrades of No. 4, and was presented by Lieutenant-Colonel ARMSTRONG with a handsome meerschaum pipe, on the silver ferrule of which the names of the battles were engraved. The pipe was the gift of No. 4 Battery, and was accepted by the recipient with modest thanks.

CHAPTER XVIII.

THE BAND.

The Music of the Corps and Its Makers—Formation of the Band—What Has Been Done and Who Have Done It—Present Membership.

THE Artillery band has become such a leading organization among the musical circles of Saint John, that in a history of the corps it requires to be dealt with by itself. Of course, like the rest of the regiment, much of its work is of a routine character which would be very dry reading, but, nevertheless, it has been the patient performance of just such routine work which has enabled the band to occupy the same relative position among other bands as the corps does among other corps, and that is, be it modestly said, a high one for efficiency. Prior to 1885 the artillery had to depend upon hiring the services of civilian bands or at times to rely on such a fife and drum organization as could be got together. The latter was at times very good while at other periods probably the less said about it the better. Upon the present lieutenant-colonel assuming command it was decided to bring the musical department into line with the other work of the corps, and, by great good fortune, the brigade possessed the right man to do it. He was soon put in the right place and to Captain S. D. CRAWFORD, for many years president of the band committee, is almost entirely due the great success with which the band has met and the steady increase in its efficiency. Nor has his task been unattended with difficulty for the selection and maintenance of an efficient musical organization is probably one of the most difficult tasks which can be undertaken.

The right man must be selected and the tuition must be carefully watched. Engagements for the services of the band have to be made with a due regard to the interests of the corps and with consideration for the fact that almost every engagement takes at least a portion of the men from their daily vocations. All of these things have been well and carefully done and the corps appreciates the fact that the success is due to the enthusiasm and untiring energy of the president of the band committee. In 1885 there existed what was known as the City Brass Band. They were unpretentious musicians but anxious for improvement, and for a chance to show what they could do under favorable conditions. Negotiations were carried on for some time which resulted in the appearance of the band in the uniform of the corps, on October 1st, 1885. Three days later the band accompanied the brigade to divine service. The leader was MICHAEL MADIGAN, a veteran of the Crimean war. The men enrolled were:—

JAMES HOLMAN,	ALBERT BURGESS,
CHARLES H. SMITH,	JOHN M. JENKINS,
WM. DUNCAN,	WM. MITCHELL,
THOS. DUNCAN,	SAMUEL PATTERSON,
J. A. LIPSETT,	ALBERT WATTERS,
JOSEPH MATTHEWS,	A. J. CHARLTON,

and soon afterwards JOHN PENFOLD, FRED. MENELEY and FRED. W. AMLAND were added to the roll.

At the inspection of 1885 the corps had music, not, perhaps, of a very ambitious character, but the men who made it were bound that it should be improved. It was then a difficult matter for the infant band to obtain engagements, and Mr. A. B. COLWELL, afterwards an enthusiastic member who contributed an excellent newspaper sketch of its history, is authority for the statement that members of other bands would

CAPTAIN S. D. CRAWFORD,
(President of the Band Committee.)

not give their assistance even for pay. In the next year Mr. COLWELL and JAMES SULLIVAN joined the band, and contributed much to its efficiency. During the winter of 1886 the band was instructed by M. J. PENFOLD, of the Royal Irish Rifles, but his removal to Halifax, after a few months' service, left them again without a tutor. The corps provided a set of new instruments in this year, and near its close CHARLES H. WILLIAMS, who had formerly been band sergeant on H. M. S. *Royal Alfred*, was engaged as bandmaster. Under his tuition they came on rapidly and were emboldened to enter the lists in a band competition in which the 62nd battalion and the City Cornet bands took part. This was in 1887, and the tyros received honorable mention from the judge,. Bandmaster COOLE, of the 2nd battalion York and Lancaster Regiment. In the previous summer the boys had secured an engagement with the St. John firemen who visited Halifax to participate in a tournament. They acquitted themselves so creditably that the obtaining of engagements became no longer difficult. Their progress continued in the right direction under MR. WILLIAMS until, in 1889, it was felt by the band committee that the exclusive services of a bandmaster were required for so good an organization, Mr. WILLIAMS being instructor for three city bands. Mr. J. M. WHITE then took up the baton which he wielded until the end of the year, when the present bandmaster, THOMAS W. HORSMAN, took charge. The result has been surprising, for today the Artillery band acknowledges no superior in the Maritime Provinces and possibly the field of competition might be more extended. Mr. HORSMAN, who was born in Leeds, England, in 1857, enrolled as a bandsman in the 2nd battalion Royal West Kent Regiment when but 14 years of age. His studies on the baritone showed such proficiency that he was sent by the officers of his regiment to Kneller Hall, where the more promising musicians of war receive their education. Here he spent two years under instruction and was made the euphonium soloist of the Hall. He rejoined his regiment, now known as the 97th, at Bermuda, in 1874, and has since followed its fortunes in Halifax, Gibraltar and South Africa, in which latter place it was stationed during the Boer expedition in 1879-80. The regiment was then sent to Dublin where the subject of this sketch obtained his discharge. He then came to Halifax and played in the band of the Halifax Garrison Artillery and that of the 63rd Rifles until he removed to St. John to take charge of the band of this corps. Mr. HORSMAN volunteered for service in the North-West campaign and went to the front as a sergeant in No. 2 company of the Halifax Garrison Artillery.

It may be said of our band that since its formation it has shared in every event in which the corps has taken part. In the hours of gaiety it has furnished music for the ballroom, and in those of mourning its strains of sorrow have expressed the sentiments of the regiment.

The whole cost of maintaining the band has been borne by the officers of the corps without calling on the public for any assistance. The present set of instruments is worth about $1500, and additions in number and value are yearly being made.

The Christmas season of 1890 found the boys so jubilant over their successes that they serenaded many of the officers of the corps. They also acknowledged the arduous work done on their behalf by Captain CRAWFORD by presenting him with an address and a souvenir of the occasion. A presentation was also made to Bandmaster HORSMAN, evidencing the good feeling which then and ever since has existed between him and his men.

On New Year's day, 1891, the band held an "At Home" in their rehearsal rooms, to which, besides the officers and non-commissioned officers of the corps, many prominent citizens and friends of the band were invited. This event has become a custom, which was unfortunately interrupted in the present year because of the death of a near relative of one of the bandsmen. These social gatherings have always been of an exceedingly pleasant nature and have done much to familiarize both the corps and the public with the *personnel* and work of the band.

On 17th May, 1892, the band, under the auspices of the officers of the corps gave a concert in the Opera House, St. John, which was spoken of in the highest terms. On this occasion the band was assisted by Mrs. JOHN BLACK, Miss PIDGEON and Mr. A. M. F. CUSTANCE, three well-known vocalists.

The band paid a visit to Charlottetown, P. E. I., in July, where they entered into a band competition and were awarded the first prize.

Their participation in the celebration of the centennial of the corps appears elsewhere and space forbids an extended notice of the many functions in which they have taken part. In 1895 they added a new feature to their annual programme by giving a special "At Home" to their lady friends on February 4th, which, it is almost needless to say, proved a most enjoyable affair. The present membership and instrumentation of the band is as follows:

BANDMASTER.
Thomas W. Horsman.
SERGEANTS.
Arthur B. Farmer.   Fred Meneley.
CLARIONETS.
F. H. Watson,   F. W. Amland,   H. S. Crawford,
D. Stewart,   W. Noakes,   W. Burton,   T. Horsman.

FLUTE.   OBOE.   PICCOLO.
R. E. Crawford.   A. Cook.   W. G. V. Stokes.

BASSOON.
J. W. Stanley.

HORNS.
W. Moore,   F. McFeters,   M. H. Wilson,   J. McLeod.

CORNETS.
T. W. Horsman,   W. H. McIntyre,   F. N. Jordan,
F. Horsman,   R. McMurray,   H. McClaskey,   L. Corey.

TROMBONES.
W. Mitchell,   W. H. Wilson,   N. Hutchinson, (Bass).

BARITONE.   EUPHONIUM.   ALTO CLARIONET.
F. McNichol.   Allan G. Crawford.   F. W. Eddlestone.

BASSES.
Arthur B. Farmer,   Fred Meneley (BB b).   J. Kane.

DRUMS AND CYMBALS.
W. R. Browne, (Bass Drum).   J. A. Lipsett, (Side Drum.)
J. Stewart, (Cymbals).

CHAPTER XIX.

THE FORTIFICATIONS.

IT has never been said of the gunners of New Brunswick that
'They lay along the battery's side,
Beneath the smoking cannon,—'
and, therefore, but little interest is attached to the few points where guns and embrasures denote the posts of the artilleryman. Yet some of the fortifications have been the scene of battles and others have been beautified by the magic of romance. At St. John, within a radius of little more than a mile, are three points of interest, one of which recalls the days when the lilies of France waved over Acadie; another, the love story of a British soldier who rose from the ranks to a seat in his country's parliament; while the third stands as a memorial of the days of 1812, an object lesson in stone of the advance of the science of war. The three points are the 'Old Fort,' as it is commonly called, or Fort LaTour; Fort Howe; and the Martello Tower on Lancaster Heights. Besides these there are Dorchester battery, Red Head battery, the defences on Partridge Island and Fort Dufferin.

The story of Fort LaTour is one of tragic interest. Shortly before the Treaty of Saint Germain in 1632, by which Acadie was ceded to the crown of France, preparation had been made by that country for taking possession of the territory. Accordingly, about 1631, CHARLES DE LATOUR commenced building a fort at the mouth of the Saint John river on the western side of the harbor, on a small neck of land opposite Navy Island. This fort was not completed until about 1635. It was about 180 feet square and was palisaded. Much of the material for the construction of the bastions seems to have been taken from what is now the channel between the site of the fort and Navy Island, and it is probable that the channel was widened by design as well as by nature. Prior to the completion of the fort LaTour had been appointed governor of the eastern district of Acadie, practically comprising Nova Scotia, while D'Aulnay Charnisay was given the command over the western district, or New Brunswick as it is now called. This demarcation of boundaries found LaTour with a large and well fortified position within Charnisay's territory, while at Port Royal Charnisay held an equally important post within the jurisdiction of LaTour.

Charnisay displayed the utmost jealousy of LaTour and assiduously endeavored to undermine his influence at the court of France. After years of scheming he succeeded and was empowered to seize both LaTour and his wife and send them prisoners to France upon charges of treason. He made several attempts to capture the fort at Saint John but was always repulsed, LaTour on one occasion having obtained assistance from Rochelle, the Huguenot stronghold, and on another from the merchants of Boston. But he was not always destined to be so fortunate. During his absence in April, 1645, when the fort was commanded by Madame LaTour and a small garrison, Charnisay again attacked it. The garrison led by the noble woman repulsed the invaders and they drew off having suffered considerable loss. But treachery accomplished that which arms could not achieve. A Swiss sentry revealed to Charnisay the weakness of the fort and he tried a land attack. Once again the gallant lady roused the defenders and inspired them by an exhibition of her personal courage. CHARNISAY finding himself again in danger of being defeated, proposed honorable terms of surrender for the capitulation of the garrison. Madame LA TOUR seeing no hope of the siege being raised, and trusting the word of a soldier, on Easter Sunday, April 16 of that year, opened the gates to the victor, who gave immediate orders that the garrison be hanged, sparing the lives of only two, Madame LaTour and a soldier who consented to become the executioner of the others. Broken hearted with grief the noble lady died soon afterwards and was buried somewhere near the ' Old Fort ' in a grave that is unknown today. This scene of heroism was captured by the British under Colonel MONCKTON in 1758, and was afterwards known as ' Fort Frederick.' Mention was made of it in the first chapter when the defences of the city were strengthened in anticipation of a French invasion in 1793.

On the opposite bank of the river, near RANKINE'S wharf, CHARNISAY also had built a fort, portions of which may yet be distinctly traced. While excavating for a sewer a few years ago the workmen found a number of cannon balls of small calibre.

Fort Howe, situated on a rocky eminence in the old Parish of Portland, now part of the City of Saint John, was garrisoned by a corps under Major GUILFORD STUDHOLM in 1777-78, in consequence of a threatened revolt of the Indian tribes, and was for many years the chief military post at Saint John. In 1784 Lieutenant-Colonel ROBERT MORSE, R. E., reported to Sir GUY CARLETON, general and commander-in-chief, upon this and all other fortifications in the Province of Nova Scotia. The report is published in the Dominion archives for 1884, and is a very interesting document. Lieutenant-Colonel MORSE was not greatly impressed with the utility of the defences at this post where, he thought, too little land had been reserved for defensive purposes. The fort had then accommodation for 12 officers and 100 soldiers. It was armed with 2 18-pr., 4 6-pr., and 2 4-pr., iron guns besides 2 5½-inch brass mortars. This fort was abandoned as a military position in 1821, the last regiment stationed there being the 74th under Lieutenant-Colonel FRENCH. The ordnance store and wharf were at York Point, the store houses being on the site now occupied by Messrs. STARR, and the wharf was afterwards called HARE's wharf. The old store houses still standing on the skirt of the hill on the Rockland road were the married officers, quarters. The brick shoe factory on Paradise Row opposite the mission church of ST. JOHN THE BAPTIST, is on the site of the officers' mess. The 'King's store house,' was on the corner of Main and Mill streets, while the 'Red Store' or commissariat was at the head of Long wharf.

The romance of Fort Howe is that of WILLIAM COBBETT, who was stationed there about 1783. COBBETT was born in 1762 at Farnham, in Surrey, England, and was a field laborer. He became a soldier, and while at Fort Howe was a sergeant-major of infantry. While walking out with some companions early on a winter's morning he first saw his future wife, who was a daughter of a sergeant of artillery. Four years afterwards, upon obtaining his discharge, COBBETT was married to the girl whom he had seen on that winter's morning scrubbing out a washing tub on the snow at daybreak. After his marriage COBBETT lived for some time in France studying the language. He removed to Philadelphia, where he compiled a French and English grammar. After remaining in the United States for about eight years he returned to England, where he established a considerable reputation as the author of 'Rural Rides,' 'Cottage Economy,' the 'Protestant Reformation,' and works on America. At last, after the passing of the first Reform Bill in 1832, he was elected member of Parliament for Oldham. He was entirely self-taught and thus describes the conditions under which he acquired a knowledge of grammar:

"I learned grammar when I was a private soldier on the pay of sixpence a day. The edge of my berth, or that of the guardbed, was my seat to study in; my knapsack was my bookcase; a bit of wood, lying on my lap, was my writing table; and the task did not demand anything like a year of my life. I had no money to purchase candle or oil; in winter time it was barely that I could get any evening light but that of the fire, and only my turn even of that. And if I, under such circumstances and without parent or friend to advise or encourage me, accomplished this undertaking, what excuse can there be for any youth, however pressed with business, or however circumstanced as to room or other conveniences.

To buy a pen or sheet of paper I was compelled to forego some portion of food, though in a state of half-starvation. I had no moment of time that I could call my own, and I had to read and to write amidst the talking, laughing, singing, whistling and brawling of at least half a score of the most thoughtless of men, and that, too, in their hours of freedom from all control. Think not lightly of the farthing that I had to give, now and then, for ink, pen or paper. That farthing was, alas! a great sum to me. I was as tall as I am now; I had great health and great exercise. The whole of the money, not expended for us at market, was twopence a week for each man. I remember—and well I may, that, upon one occasion I, after all absolutely necessary expenses, had on a Friday, made a shift to have a half-penny in reserve, which I had destined for the purchase of a red herring in the morning; but when I pulled off my clothes at night, so hungry, then, as to be hardly able to endure life, I found that I had lost my half-penny! I buried my head under my miserable sheet and rug, and cried like a child!

And again, I say, if I, under circumstances like these could encounter and overcome this task, is there, can there be in the whole world, a youth who can find an excuse for the non-performance? What youth, who shall read this, will not be ashamed to say, that he is not able to find time and opportunity for this most essential of all the branches of book-learning?"

A newspaper item in the year 1800 refers to the arrival of COBBETT at Halifax on the 6th June on his way from New York to England, and suggests, with bated breath, that he was 'said to have dined with the DUKE OF KENT.' The item also tells that he had landed before in Halifax as a 'simple corporal.'

The Martello Tower on Lancaster Heights is of the same character of defensive work as the towers at Quebec. On a height between two and three hundred feet above the sea level it is an imposing object and looks as though it should have a more thrilling history than that which it possesses. Its building was begun in 1800 and was not finished until 1813. Nearly all the stone used in its construction was carried by soldiers on hand barrows from the sea beach, half a mile away, through a forest and up a steep hill to its site. Hundreds of men must have toiled at the making of the old tower, which was probably impregnable in those days but which could not long withstand the Palliser shot and the armour piercing projectiles of modern days. It was originally mounted with four 48-pr. and two 24-pr. guns but for many years the armament was reduced to two 33-pr. carronades. During the Fenian scare in 1866 the roof was taken off and guns were mounted, but they have long since been removed. Opposite the tower on the adjacent hill there used to be a wooden block house the main portion of which was raised some distance from the ground. It had accommodation for forty men, and was called Fort Drummond. It fell into decay and was torn down some years ago. It has often been proposed that the old tower should be razed and a modern fortification substituted for it upon the commanding height. The suggestions have even gone so far as to include a Royal School of Artillery stationed there, but desirable as that may be to the people of St. John the removal of the historic sentinel of the past would be deprecated by all who feel an interest in the days and things of old. Should the old fabric ever be removed, however, its memory will be perpetuated in the following admirable lines, which, by special permission of their author, PATRICK MC-CARTHY, Esq., alderman of the city of St. John, are here reproduced :—

THE MARTELLO TOWER.

Upon a craggy crest
Proudly it stands,
Its profile outlined 'gainst the azure arch
Of Heaven's dome ; right regally it bears
The footmarks of Decay's destructive march ;
Still solid as the cliff wherefrom it rears
Its rough hewn, stony breast
In circling bands
Of masonry, that brave the gales of Time
Which round its tap'ring sides so fiercely bellow ;
And veils of fog and shrouds of icy rime
Have left few tarnishings on stone or lime,
About the old Martello.

Massive the noble tower
Seems to the sight,
Suggesting foemen fierce, and siege and death
And kindred horrors of grim, gory, fray ;

It sentinels the broad expanse beneath
Of city, river, harbor, beach and bay,
    And in unconscious power
      Looms on the height,
A grand memorial of the years bygone,
Which has with age, like olden wine, grown mellow;
It now keeps ward ungarrisoned upon
The sunny slopes that garnish West Saint John,
    Around the old Martello.

    It recks not of the chill,
      Weird, winter storm,
That plays against its eaves as seasons roll
Into the past; nor spring's delicious breeze
Which sighs on bursting buds, and wakes man's soul
To joy; nor summer sun, which glints the trees,
    And gilds the purling rill
      With lustrous charm;
Nor autumn's breath, which turns the purest green
Of nature's costume to the "sere and yellow;"
Ah! well has it withstood climatic spleen;
The weather's shocks as yet almost unseen
    Upon the old Martello.

    Stately upon the site
      It meets the gaze;
Its rubble wall a softened, brownish grey;
A sturdy structure of that by-past age
Which now, thank God, has pass'd for aye away;
Much better work have we than war to wage,
    Or deadly foes to smite
      In these new days,

MARTELLO TOWER.

When strangers meet as once met only friends,
And each gives kindly greeting to his fellow;
And Peace, with her twin sister, Learning tends
For ancient hate of race to make amends,
   Beneath the old Martello.

The Imperial barracks used to be on the ground at Lower Cove now occupied by the drill shed and as a parade ground. They were erected about 1819-20, and were destroyed in the fire of 1877 with the exception of two stone buildings on Sidney street which still remain.

About 1812-13 a wooden block house was erected on King street, east, at the intersection of Wentworth street. Traverses were also cut in the solid rock for a two gun battery, but when the level of King street was reduced some years ago all trace disappeared of the eminence on which the block house and battery stood.

Besides these there were four batteries on the line of the shore of the harbor and Courtenay Bay, called the 'Graveyard battery,' 'Southern battery,' 'Blockhouse battery,' and the 'Eastern battery,' or 'Fort Johnston' on Pitt street, fronting on Courtenay Bay. It is difficult at the present time to get any authentic account of the building of these batteries. General opinion places the time of erection about the commencement of the war of 1812, with the exception of the battery at the foot of Sidney street, called the 'Southern battery.' In the newspaper account of the arrival of PRINCE EDWARD, DUKE OF KENT, in 1794, quoted in the second chapter, it is stated that a royal salute was fired from 'Dorchester battery.' This name has always been applied to the Barrack batteries and it is probable that the 'Southern battery' is the oldest of the fortifications on the

Barrack grounds. The reminiscences of JAMES BUSTIN given in the third chapter are interesting in this connection.

The fort at Red Head was constructed in 1863 and 1864. It is a spacious work, and if mounted with modern ordnance would be an effective defence to the harbor. The large battery at Negrotown Point, now known as Fort Dufferin was also constructed before Confederation. It received its present armament in 1877, and is the battery used for shell practice when competition is held at local headquarters. Within a few years the guns and carriages at Partridge Island have been removed to the ordnance yard, and there is at present no armament at this station.

One other fortification has been mentioned in the chapter which treats of the Fenian scare. It is called 'Fort Tipperary,' and is situated at St. Andrews, commanding the harbor of that town. The armament is not extensive, and since the cessation of artillery work at that place but little attention has been given to it.

CHAPTER XX.

1893-1896.

The Fourth of May—Centennial Salute and Concerts—The Ball—Death of Paymaster Smith—Colors of an old Corps laid at Rest—Visit of the Earl of Aberdeen—Death of Judge Peters—Inspections—Change of Designation—Conclusion.

AS the centennial year would begin very early in the drill season it was not thought to be advisable to have any military demonstration upon the 4th May, but the firing of a salute of one hundred guns, for which authority was sought and obtained. At this, the first day of the second century of the corps, the officers were:

Lieutenant-Colonel, JOHN RUSSELL ARMSTRONG.
Major, JOHN JAMES GORDON.

No. 1--*Captain,* STANLEY DOUGLAS CRAWFORD,
Lieutenant, WALTER WOODWORTH WHITE.

No. 2--*Captain,* JOHN BABINGTON MACAULAY BAXTER,
Lieutenant, HERBERT CHIPMAN TILLEY,
Second Lieutenant, ARTHUR DRAKE WETMORE.

No. 3--*Captain, N. W.* CHARLES FREDERICK HARRISON,
Lieutenant, ROBERT HUNTLEY GORDON,
Second Lieutenant, WALTER EDWARD FOSTER.

No. 4—*Captain,* GEORGE WEST JONES,
Lieutenant, THOMAS EDWARD GRINDON ARMSTRONG.
Second Lieutenant, FREDERICK CAVERHILL JONES.

No. 5—*Captain,* JAMES ALBERT EDWARD STEEVES,
Lieutenant, FREDERICK LANDON TEMPLE,
Second Lieutenant, ROBERT PATTISON FOSTER.

Adjutant, Captain GEORGE KERR MCLEOD.
Paymaster, GEORGE FREDERICK SMITH.
Quartermaster, Major RICHARD FARMER.
Surgeon, JOHN WATERHOUSE DANIEL, M. D.
Assistant Surgeon, JOSEPH ANDREWS, M. D.

The names of the men who composed the corps during the year, as taken from the pay lists, are given in an appendix.

Before the hundredth anniversary was reached the name of the corps was changed, the establishment lists making it the 'New Brunswick Battalion of Garrison Artillery.' However technically correct the new designation may have been considered, it did not find favor with the corps, nor was the change from 'batteries' to 'companies' thought to be either euphonious or necessary.

It was arranged that the salute should be fired from Dorchester battery, Fort Dufferin, Martello Tower and Fort Howe. At sunrise the Union Jack was floating above the forts and soon after some of the men were on hand eager to participate in the celebration. Some mischievous persons had spiked the vent of the gun at Martello Tower and an attempt was made to put the guns at Fort Howe out of service, which was partly successful, only one gun being capable of use. Punctually at nine o'clock the salute began, No. 2 firing the first gun from Fort Dufferin. In twenty minutes the salute was over and the smoke as of battle hung in wreaths over the historic heights of the city. The following are the officers, non-commissioned officers and men who took part in the saluting:

Lieutenant-Colonel Armstrong, *Major* Gordon.

Captains, George W. Jones, S. D. Crawford, C. F. Harrison, and J. B. M. Baxter.

Lieutenants,—R. H. Gordon, H. C. Tilley, W. E. Foster and Fred L. Temple.

Medical Officers,—Surgeon Daniel, Assistant Surgeon Andrews, Captain and Dr. J. A. E. Steeves, and Lieutenant and Dr. W. W. White.

Sergeant-Major, —Samuel Hughes.

Staff Sergeants,—James Brown, Thomas W. Horsman.

Sergeants,—Walter Lamb, Joshua P. Clayton, Joseph F. Smith, Joseph Nealy, John C. Edwards, William G. H. Kilpatrick, W. H. Sulis.

Corporals,—Fred V. Hatt, W. deBowes, Frank A. Courtenay, John W. Sarah, Robert McJunkin, Edwin Ougler, Robert G. Fulton, Fred Globe.

Bombardiers, —Fred H. Slipp, Frank L. Perry.

Gunners,—Frank W. Laskey, J. D. Charlton, T. S. Irvine, Robert J. Armstrong, H. Chandler, R. Sprowson, L. Kershaw, Frank Forrest, J. F. Berton, R. D. Robertson, L. Philips, F. Banks, John Stewart, W. P. McColgan, F. E. Thomas, A. W. McInnis, R. M. Graham, R. A. McHarg, George Dunlavy, Richard D. Damery, E. Allan, William Clark, Joseph Laskey, James Huey, George M. Boyd, Arthur W. Machum, Nelson Parlee, Wm. McCauley, William Maxwell, Geo. W. Lee, William Prime, Walter McH. Olive, Walter P. Dunham, William T. Lanyon, and Richard W. Craft.

In the evening despite unfavorable weather the old Mechanics' Institute was filled to the doors for the centennial concert given by the band of the corps, assisted by Mrs. C. W. HARRISON, (Sackville), Mr. GERSHON S. MAYES, and the Germain Street Quartette. Mrs. HARRISON in her selections "The Daughter of the Regiment" and "Lo, Here the gentle Lark," won round after round of applause, to which she responded with "Jock o' Hazeldean." Mr. MAYES' splendid rendition of the "Death of Nelson" evoked the military ardor of the audience, which rose to enthusiasm over his encore "The Boys of the old Brigade." Bandsmen STOKES, FARMER, WATSON, and McKAY, contributed instrumental numbers which were much appreciated. Many of the selections were arranged by Bandmaster HORSMAN, and, above all, the marked success of the concert was due to the untiring energy of Captain CRAWFORD, president of the band committee.

Loyalists' Day was celebrated by 18 guns from No. 1, Captain CRAWFORD'S company, while on the Queen's Birthday, No. 2, Captain BAXTER fired the usual salute. The guns of No. 1 were again heard on 14th June, being the occasion of the wedding of Lieutenant W. W. WHITE. A similar service had been rendered by No. 3 a few years before at the marriage of Captain McLEOD.

The next in the series of celebrations was a smoking concert for the men, held in Berryman's Hall, on 21st June. About two hundred members of the battalion with their friends were present and an enjoyable time was spent. Captain GEO. W. JONES presided and a short programme was carried out. The band contributed several instrumental pieces; Gunner TONGE of No. 4 gave a comic song; Captain BAXTER read a humorous selection; an exhibition of sleight of hand work was given by Mr. J. S. MACLAREN; a song was sung by C. T. GILLESPIE, and Major GORDON danced a Highland fling in full native costume. Besides this Lieutenant-Colonel ARMSTRONG read an historical sketch of the corps; Sergeant KILPATRICK of No. 3 gave a song; the LEAMAN BROS. two bright little chaps sang their amusing songs and Captain HARTT, late of the Rifle company, contributed a couple of vocal selections. Light refreshments were served during the evening. Officers of the 8th cavalry and 62nd

Fusiliers were present in uniform, and the smoking concert was voted a very enjoyable affair.

On the 27th July the corps together with the Rifle company had a march out in the evening, and on the following Sunday both bodies paraded for divine service and marched to St. JOHN's church, where the sermon was preached by the Rev. JOHN DE SOYRES. Major MARKHAM of the 8th cavalry was on the staff and the Rifle company was under command of Captain E. A. Smith. Inspection followed on 3rd August, that of No. 2 company for gun drill being held at the Carleton armory on the succeeding evening. The result of the inspection was gratifying. Out of a total strength of 232, there were 215 of all ranks present and the absentees accounted for. No. 1, Captain CRAWFORD, took the second prize for general efficiency with 243 points, while No. 4, Captain JONES, was not far behind with 235. Nos. 3 and 4 companies tied for the Botsford cup, which went under the rules to No. 4. The centennial photograph of the officers of the corps was taken on the 4th August.

About this time H. M. S. *Blake* arrived in port and a ball was tendered by the corps to the officers of the ship. Owing to her short stay in port the invitation had to be declined.

On the 4th December Lieutenant-Governor BOYD, of New Bruunswick, died. At the state funeral Lieutenant-Colonel ARMSTRONG was in charge of the procession, assisted by Chief of Police CLARK of St. John, and officers of militia formed an escort to the body. On the 18th of the same month Captain ROBERT REED, whose name appears in the earlier portion of this history, passed away, thus breaking one of the few remaining links between the old organization and the present.

The last event in the celebration of the centennial, a

grand ball given on the 29th December at the Assembly Rooms of the Mechanics' Institute, was an unqualified success. The rooms were elaborately decorated for the occasion. As the guests entered they were confronted by a large field gun, behind which was a collection of fire arms showing the advances made by modern science. In the ball room the massive pillars were trimmed with spruce and ornamented with bayonets. At the eastern end of the room, on a background enclosed by the colors of the regiment, were the letters "N. B. B. G. A." in blue, and under them "1793-1893" in red. Opposite this was a portrait of the QUEEN, on either side of which were small flags. There were around the walls, at regular intervals, stars of bayonets, surmounted by flags and alternated with pictures, among which were photographs of present and past officers of the corps. In an alcove stood two 6-pr. guns with their side arms complete. The supper room was handsomely fitted up, the table being decorated with natural flowers. Upon it were displayed the Botsford cup and the general efficiency prize won by No. 1 company. A large number of guests were entertained, and it is safe to say that the artillery centennial ball will not soon be forgotten.

As light is succeeded by darkness, so in human affairs joy gives place to sadness, and the pleasure of the centennial year was soon to be shadowed by the thought that one more of the best loved officers of the corps would never again take part in its festivities or join in its councils. Sad, indeed, was the news of the death of Captain and Paymaster GEORGE F. SMITH, who passed away on the 6th March following. A well-known shipowner, respected for his high sense of honor and absolute integrity as well as beloved for his kindliness and charm of manner, his death was regretted by the citizens at large, toward whom he had discharged many public duties. To the corps it was a deeper blow. Captain SMITH had been active in his assistance to the commanding officer in the time when help was needed upon his assuming the command, and during the succeeding nine years his best services were always at the disposal of the corps in which he took the warmest interest. He had been identified with the old PETERS' battery, and, indeed, with almost every athletic movement in the city. A vestry man of St. John's church, an ex-president of the Union Club and a prominent supporter of the Neptune Rowing Club and the Athletic Association, he was above all best known as a gentleman in every sense of the word. The corps signified their feeling of the loss which they had sustained in the following resolutions:

Resolved, that the officers of the New Brunswick Battalion Garrison Artillery hereby express their sense of the great loss that they have sustained through the death of their brother officer, Captain and Paymaster, G. F SMITH. For many years he served in the ranks as a gunner, then as a non-commissioned officer, and for the past nine years on the staff. During all this period he showed his unswerving interest in the welfare of the corps, and his example and advice were at all times prized in the highest degree by all its members. His abilities, his urbanity, his decision of character, his courageousness of opinion, his mature judgment, as well as his physique, in every way made him the model of a good officer and soldier ;.and further

Resolved, that the officers attend the funeral in a body as a mark of respect; and further

Resolved, that a copy of these resolutions be sent to Mrs. SMITH, with the respectful condolence of the corps.

At the funeral the Artillery band assisted, and several of the officers formed an escort, the remainder together with officers of other corps joining in the procession.

On the 29th July of this year the artillery were called on

by ex-Mayor PETERS to perform an unusual service for militia corps, that of presenting to a church the colors of a regiment that they might be laid at rest. Mr. PETERS was in possession of the colors of the 1st Battalion St. John Light Infantry, and desired to have them placed in ST. PAUL'S church. The event cannot be better described than by the following extract from the 'Daily Sun' newspaper of the next day:—

"At sharp half-past two yesterday when the battalion assembled in the drill shed there was the best of weather—a little hot and dusty, perhaps, but tempered now and again with a cool breeze. The battalion fell in with Lieutenant-Colonel ARMSTRONG in command, and Major JONES appeared for the first time in his new rank. In the absence, through illness, of Captain CRAWFORD, Captain WHITE took charge of No. 1 company with Lieutenant B. R. ARMSTRONG as subaltern. No. 2 company (Carleton) was under command of Captain BAXTER, with Lieutenants TILLEY and SCOVIL.; No. 3, under Captain GORDON, with Lieutenant FOSTER; and No. 4, under Captain ARMSTRONG, with Lieutenants JONES and SKINNER. On the staff were Quartermaster GORDON, Surgeon ANDREWS and a number of the retired officers of the City Light Infantry whose colors were to be presented, and also retired officers of the artillery. Among them were: A. A. STOCKTON, M. P. P., Captain CHARLES CAMPBELL, Lieutenant W. ROXBOROUGH, Captain J. ALFRED RING, Lieutenant McKINNEY and Captain A. W. LOVETT. Major MARKHAM, of the 8th Cavalry, and Major A. J. ARMSTRONG, of the district staff, and Majors STURDEE, HARTT and MAGEE, with Surgeon WALKER, Rev. Fr. DAVENPORT, chaplain, and Lieutenant MACMICHAEL, of the 62nd, also attended on the staff.

On the Barrack square the battalion was drawn up in line in two ranks, and at 3 o'clock the color party, from No. 3 company, appeared with the colors guarded by fixed bayonets. They were received with a general salute and the colors taken over by Lieutenants TILLEY and FOSTER, the senior subalterns on parade. The band played Auld Lang Syne and the National Anthem.

The battalion then marched in fours from the left of companies.

No. 2 company, with fixed bayonets and arms sloped. being the escort. At King street near Charlotte, Lieutenant-Colonel IRWIN, inspector of artillery, was received with a salute as he joined the staff. At the church, line was formed facing the edifice and the colors again saluted, after which column of half companies was formed to the left, and the column retiring formed quarter column on No. 1, which was in rear. They then marched past in column of half companies by the right, and afterwards in quarter column by the left, with changed ranks. Line was again formed facing the church, and after a general salute the companies entered and took their places in the church, the officers occupying seats in the east side of the south transept.

No. 3 company, with bayonets fixed, then entered the church and was stationed in the centre aisle with shouldered arms. The color party passed through the main entrance, and was received with presented arms, after which the company formed up, facing the chancel. THOMAS W. PETERS then stepped forward and, addressing the rector, said that the ceremony took place at the request of old officers of the battalion, and that he presented the flags for that purpose, they having come into his possession through his father, who, as colonel, had the custody of them. The battalion was the first of the city militia corps under the old system, and had been in existence for many years, but the loss of the old files of newspapers from 1838 to 1843 rendered it impossible to fix the date of the presentation with precision. Among its officers had been Sir LEONARD TILLEY, the ex-Governor of the Province, and W. O. SMITH, once Mayor of the city. The colors had never seen active service, but he had no doubt that those who bore them then would have stood by them manfully had they been called on to do so, and he was equally sure that those who laid them to rest in the sacred edifice were imbued with the loyal spirit and determination of their forefathers.

Mr. PETERS then took the colors from Lieutenants TILLEY and FOSTER and handed them to Rev. Mr. DICKER, the rector, who in turn passed them to Canon DEVEBER, by whom they were placed in the chancel.

Rev. Mr. DICKER then read a formal acceptance of the colors for the purpose of repose, after which a short evening service was conducted and Rev. Archdeacon BRIGSTOCKE delivered an address.

The escort again saluted the colors, while the National Anthem was played, after which and the recessional the troops left the church and formed again on the street. They marched back to the drill shed, where after an expression of thanks from Lieutenant-Colonel ARMSTRONG, to the retired and visiting officers who had so kindly assisted in the ceremony and a few words of encouragement to the officers and men under his command for the way in which their work had been performed, the battalion dispersed.

This year's inspection held on the 30th July and succeeding days was a rigid test of the corps and resulted in No. 4 company Captain T. E. G. ARMSTRONG winning the second general efficiency prize with 231 points. This company also took the Botsford cup. The illness of Capt. CRAWFORD of No. 1, and a severe family affliction which he had sustained, called forth the sympathy of every officer and man in the battalion.

Major JONES donated a handsome silver cup for competition among the companies, and desired that it should be awarded upon the general efficiency points exclusive of those for officers questions. It was won for the first time by No. 1 company.

His Excellency the EARL OF ABERDEEN, Governor-General of Canada, and the COUNTESS OF ABERDEEN, visited St. John for the first time on 13th August. Owing to the late hour of their arrival there was no demonstration until the next morning, when at the opening of the reception in the Common Council chamber No. 3 company, under Captain GORDON, fired a salute of nineteen guns from King street east, the 62nd Fusiliers furnishing a guard of honor. Upon their departure for Fredericton the next day a salute was fired from Fort Howe by a detachment from No. 4 company. On Thursday evening, 14th August, a levee was held in the Mechanics'

Institute at which the officers of the artillery, among others, were present.

Gunner FREDERICK M. BURGESS, of No. 3 company, who was accidentally drowned on 13th August was buried with military honors by his company. The loss of the yacht 'Primrose' in a sudden squall during a race in St. John harbor on 21st August also deprived No. 4 company of a member, Corporal T. H. BARTLETT. His last military service was the firing of the salute on the departure of the Governor-General. The company presented his widow with a resolution of sympathy suitably engrossed and a substantial testimonial.

Judge B. LESTER PETERS, the captain of the old 'Kid Glove' battery, was also on 25th November numbered among those departed. At his funeral which took place on 28th November, the Lieutenant-Colonel and officers of the corps attended. Outside of the pall-bearers walked thirty members of the old battery. They were George E. Thomas, James F. Robertson, Joseph Allison, W. A. Lockhart, W. E. Vroom, John H. Parks, F. W. Wisdom, John C. Miles, S. K. Wilson, J. Fred Lawton, C. Fred Langan, Chas. Campbell, Arthur W. Lovett, Joseph B. Stubbs, R. H. Arnold, John McLauchlan, D. D. Robertson, Frank O. Allison, Frank Gallagher, P. R. Inches, M. D., J. Morris Robinson, G. Ludlow Robinson, George K. Berton, J. S. Kaye, C. U. Hanford, Charles McLauchlan, E. G. Scovil, George B. Hegan, Albert S. Hay and Frank Lansdowne.

At the regimental meeting on 23rd March of the following year, Major JONES formally presented to the corps the cup which is known by his name, and received a hearty vote of thanks for his handsome gift.

Loyalists' Day was again celebrated by a salute from Fort Dufferin by No. 2 company, and later in the year, upon the return of Major MARKHAM of the 8th Princess Louise Hussars, the commandant of the Bisley team of 1895, to his home in Saint John, he was serenaded by the Artillery band.

On August 10th No. 2 company attended divine service at St. GEORGE'S church, Carleton, where an excellent sermon was preached by the rector, Rev. W. H. SAMPSON.

The Artillery, 62nd Fusiliers and Rifle company were brigaded, under Lieutenant-Colonel ARMSTRONG, for service at TRINITY church on the 29th of the same month, and an appropriate address was delivered by Rev. Father DAVENPORT, chaplain of the 62nd battalion.

Inspection was held on 22nd October and following days by Lieutenant-Colonel MONTIZAMBERT, and resulted in the winning by No. 1 company, Captain CRAWFORD, of the second general efficiency prize with 246 points, only two points behind the highest score made. This company also won the Jones and Botsford cups. No. 2 company stood second in the battalion and fifth in the Dominion with 237 points.

After the inspection the inspecting officer was entertained at supper at the Union Club and a very enjoyable evening was spent.

On the 16th December, LANGFORD McFREDERICK, a gunner in No. 2 company was accidentally killed while at work. His funeral which took place on the 19th December, was attended by the company in uniform and the usual honors were paid. The death on 17th January, 1896, of Paymaster Sergeant FRED L. HEA, removed an active and useful non-commissioned officer from the staff. The officers of the corps attended the interment.

In the preceding November a change occurred in the adjutancy, Captain WHITE being transferred from No. 5 company to that position. Since the roll of the centennial year there

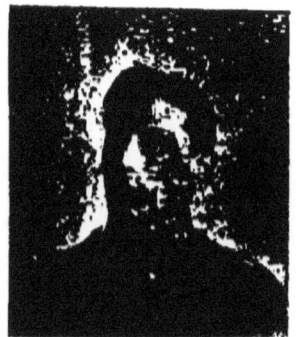

Lieut. F. A. Foster,   Lieut. E. R. Jones,   Lieut. A. C. H. Gray,
Lieut. S. A. M. Skinner,   Lieut. B. R. Armstrong

JUNIOR OFFICERS, 1893-96.

have been but two changes in the staff non-commissioned officers. Sergeant THOMAS H. JOHNSTON of No. 2 became Orderly Room Clerk in October, 1895, and upon the death of Staff-sergeant HEA was transferred to the appointment of Paymaster-sergeant. Sergeant JOHN C. EDWARDS of No. 3 was then appointed Orderly Room Clerk. The only staff sergeant who has not as yet received special mention is Quartermaster Sergeant JAMES BROWN, whose attachment to the force has caused him to serve in it for upwards of thirty-seven years.

On January 30th, 1896, No. 4 company, by invitation of Captain T. E. G. ARMSTRONG, had a sleigh drive and supper, an event of which the guests will long have a pleasant recollection.

In the early part of this year Lieutenant TEMPLE succeeded to the command of No. 5 company; Second Lieutenant B. R. ARMSTRONG was promoted to the first lieutenancy in No. 1, and ERNEST RAY JONES was appointed second lieutenant in No. 5.

At the close of the previous year the designation of the corps was again changed, the new title being "New Brunswick Regiment, Canadian Artillery." Practically a reversion to the title by which the corps was first known, the change was a welcome one to the regiment. Equal pleasure was not afforded, however, by the numbering of the corps as "3rd," while the beginning of its regimental history is at least eighteen years earlier than that of the Montreal regiment, which is second, and over thirty years earlier than that of Halifax, which is styled the first. It is hoped that in time due recognition will be given to the continuity of the history of our corps and that the right of the regiment to the first place on the list will be acknowledged. It is submitted that the pages of this history contain ample and incontrovertible evidence in support of the claim.

The story of our corps is now brought to a close. It can not be said to be replete with incidents of sensational nature, yet neither is it a record of which the citizens who are its members need be ashamed. The feeling grows that war as a means of settling international questions must in time give way to a more enlightened and more highly developed system. Arbitration replaces carnage and the student succeeds the soldier. Yet war has not been without its use nor battle without humanity. The soldier and the best soldier has thought for his age as deeply as the statesman, and by his success has taught that science, not numbers, is truly power. Nor, when war has become a matter of history will its influence for good have passed away. The spirit of fairness and honor which has characterized the soldier in all ages will survive to ennoble more peaceful arts and will have its weight in the settlement of the future problems of the world. To an unthinking portion of the public, no doubt, the maintenance of a militia seems well nigh useless, but to those who appreciate the *morale* of such a force its utility is apparent. The lad who dons a uniform feeling that it is the outward and visible emblem of identification with his country, becomes a better citizen because of his aspiration. In the ranks he acquires that spirit of comradeship, and devotion to an ideal, which, in its application through all the departments of the life of the nation conduces to a grander fulfilment of the destinies of the race. 'Shoulder to shoulder' he realizes, is the secret of success. True discipline, he finds, is after all not an arrogant exercise of authority but a wise direction of his individuality so that it may best combine with that of others towards the attainment of a desired object. With proficiency in his work grows the ability to apply in the larger sphere of the exercise of his rights and duties as a citizen, the lessons which he learns as a soldier. The importance of good direction, the sacredness of honor and the glory of devotion to principle become factors in his daily life and he also feels that in the organization of which he has become a member, there are no limits to his ambition, but those of ability and fidelity. Such is the teaching of a military force, and such, as well as the important duty of being thoroughly trained and available for the defence of his country, are reasons why the youth of our land should enrol themselves in its ranks with the encouragement, approbation and active assistance of every true citizen and patriot. Nor should the social side be overlooked. In the ranks, there is that feeling of unity—of comradeship—which lives in grateful memory through the after life of the volunteer as well as of the soldier. With a sadness that is not all sorrow it causes the old man to say:—

> "Where are the boys of the Old Brigade,
> Where are the lads we knew?"

who in his youth resonantly sang:

> "Steadily, shoulder to shoulder,
> Steadily, side by side,
> Ready and strong
> We are marching along,
> Like the boys of the Old Brigade!"

APPENDICES.

CENTENNIAL BATTERY ROLLS—1893.

NO. 1 BATTERY.

Captain, Stanley D. Crawford.
Lieutenant, Walter W. White, M. D.
Second Lieutenant, Gordon S. McLeod.
Staff Sergeant, Paymaster's Clerk. Fred L. Hea.
Sergeants, Walter Lamb, Joshua P. Clayton.
Corporals, George A. Foster, James W. Clayton, David E. Brown.

Gunners :—

James A. Lindsay,	Louis Philips,	Richard D. Damery,
Frank Anderson,	Henry Chandler,	Thomas Pilling,
John Pilling,	James H. Barton.	Arthur W. McInnis,
Gilford Humphrey,	Lambert Kershaw,	Wm. P. McColgan,
Henry Ricketts,	William Sprowson,	James L. Lamb,
Fredcrick Withers,	George Barnes,	Robert W. Graham,
John Stewart,	William Muirhead,	David S. Betz,
George Cook,	John Ricketts,	William C. Brown,
Robert Sprowson,	Thomas Marshall,	Frank G. Berton,
Ernest E. Thomas,	Fred'rk Stephenson,	Frank W. Laskey,
James Pilling,	Neil A. Seely,	Frank Forrest,
John F. Berton,	Albert E. Coates,	Robert A. McHarg.

NO. 2 BATTERY.

Captain, John B. M. Baxter,
Lieutenant, Herbert C. Tilley,
Second Lieutenant, Arthur D. Wetmore.
Sergeants, Thos. H. Johnston, Joseph F. Smith, Joseph Nealy.
Corporals, Edwin Ougler, Frederick Globe, Robert G. Fulton.
Bombardiers, Frank L. Perry, Frederick H. Slipp.

Gunners :—

George O. Trafton,	Jas. M. McLennan,	Gilbert J. Mayes,
George W. Lee,	George M. Palmer,	Walter P. Dunham,

APPENDICES.

George R. Forbes, Richard W. Craft, James Sullivan,
James B. Nichols, William T. Lanyon, Federick Bartlett,
George E. Olive, George H. Seely, Wm. J. Cunningham,
Willard Crawford, Ezekiel McLeod, Herbert P. Gardiner,
Ernest Perry, Bernard G. Ring, L. Edwin Rolston,
Walter McH. Olive, George Sullivan, John Lawton,
John J. Sinclair, Harry B. Duke, George Dunlavy,
William Prime, John A. Pollock, Joel H. Waters,
James F. Belyea, William Maxwell, William Foster,
Trumpeter, Frank A. Hea.

No. 3 Battery.

Captain, Charles F. Harrison,
Lieutenant, Robert H. Gordon,
Second Lieutenant, Walter E. Foster,
Sergeants, John C. Edwards, Wm. G. H. Kilpatrick, A. Lingley,
Corporals, John W. Sarah, Robert McJunkin, John Robinson.

Gunners:—

James Sears, George W. Boyd, Noble Clark,
Herbert Parlee, James Huey, Robt. McKenzie,
Fred'rk W. Marshall, George S. Bishop, Joseph Laskey,
William McCauley, Fred A. Boyd, Nelson Parlee,
Thomas E. Powers, Alfred Wood, Arthur Parlee,
William Henery, Frank E. Whelpley, Edward S. Day,
Frederick Burgess, Arthur T. Irvine, James Semple,
Robert Moore, Ernest Allan, August Stoerger,
Edward Newport, Smith Foster, David B. Laskey,
Herbert Williams, George Richardson, William Clark,
John Whitmore, Howard M. Barnes George F. Clark,
Arthur W. Machum, James Mercer, David Speight.

No. 4 Battery.

Captain, George W. Jones,
Lieutenant, T. Edward G. Armstrong,
Second Lieutenant, Frederick C. Jones.
Regt. Sergeant-Major, Samuel Hughes,
Sergeants, William H. Sulis, Jas. A. Brown, James B. Thompson,
Corporals, Henry Bartlett, Frederick V. Hatt, John T. McGowan,

CENTENNIAL ROLLS.

Gunners :—

James E. Earle,	John H. Tonge,	George Runciman,
Wm. F. Harrison,	Harry P. Robertson,	Frederick Rubins,
Frederick A. Foster,	Fred C. Cummings,	Robt. M. Bartsch,
Herbert W. Splane,	Harry E. Hall,	Robt. D. Robertson,
Edward D. Outram,	W. Arthur Boyd,	Stanley Dixon,
Percy G. Hall,	Bev. R. Armstrong,	Fred'rk W. McLean,
Robt. J. Armstrong,	Charles W. Barlow,	Harold Wright,
Ernest Law,	Wm. A. Robertson,	T. Sterrie Irvine,
James A. Nicholson,	Frank A. Charlton,	Edward T. Bell,
Frederick Tracy,	Louis H. Rainnie,	Charles Lawton,
Joshua O. Charlton,	Arthur C. Ellis,	Fred'rk T. Chesley.
Fred'rk C. Folkins,	Alonzo G. Sulis,	

No. 5 BATTERY.

Captain, James A. E. Steeves, M. D.
Lieutenant, Frederick L. Temple.
Second Lieutenant, E. Walter B. Scovil.
Sergeants, Arthur B. Farmer, Frederick Meneley, Thomas Richardson.
Corporals, Wallace F. Beatty, Samuel J. McGowan.

Gunners —

Aaron D. Colwell,	Albert Harris,	James O. McKay,
James Kitchen,	Edwin Stirling,	Edgar Rowe,
William H. Wilson,	Wm. C. Thornhill,	James Stewart,
Edward K. McKay,	David Stewart,	William Warren,
Fred'rk W. Amland,	Wm. H. McIntyre,	Frederick Eddleston,
William G. Stokes,	James W. Manson,	J. Hamblet Wood,
William F. Moore,	William Mitchell,	Frank Bankes,
Burton Griffin,	Matthew S. Adams,	Charles J. Turner,
John H. Daley,	Allan S. Crawford,	Robert McKay,
Frederick H.Watson,	Harold S. Crawford,	William deBowes,
James Knowles,	John A. Lipsett,	Thos. F. Thompson.
Charles Brigden,		

Quartermaster Sergeant, James Brown.
Band Master, Thomas W. Horsman.
Orderly Room Clerk, Thomas A. Crockett.

APPENDICES.

REGIMENTAL FIELD AND

Date.	Lieut. Colonel.	Majors.	Adjutant.
1838 28 Feb.	Richard Hayne, (*Capt. R. A.*) *Provincial A. D. C., 7 May,* *'41; 7 Oct. '54; 26 Oct. '61.* *Ass't Adj't General 4 April,* *'48; Adj't Gen'l 20 May,'51; Q.* *M. G. 1 Jan. '62, to 5 Jan. '64.* *Col. Commandant 22 March,* *'65.*		
8 May.		George F. Street, (*Capt. 1st York Batt'n 22 Nov.* *'38.*)	
9 May.			Edward Pick, (*2d Lt. 10 May, '58.*)
25 June.			
1840. 17 March.			John C. Allen, *Prov'l A.D.C. 5 July, '44.*
1841. 30 March.		Thomas L. Nicholson.	
26 April.			
1845. 30 Oct.			
1848. 10 Aug.		Stephen Kent Foster, *Bt. Lt-Col. 6 Dec. '59;*	
1849. 20 Sept.			
1850. 20 Sept.			J. Mount,
6 Dec.		Charles J. Melick *Bt. Lt. Col. 10 Jan, '66; Bri-* *gade, 26 May,'69. Retired with* *rank of Lt. Col. 7 Dec, '71.*	
1860. 7 Feb.			

STAFF OFFICERS, 1838-1896.

Paymaster.	Quartermaster.	Surgeon.	Assistant Surgeon.
James W. Boyd. (*Capt.*)			
		J. Toldervy, M. D., (*from 3rd Batt'n York.*)	
	E. B. Peters, 1st Lieut. 30 Mar. '41.		
			LeBaron Botsford, M. D, *Retired with rank of Surgeon-Major,* 18 Ap'l, '66.
Frederick A. Wiggins, (*Capt.*) *Retired with rank of Major* 19 June, '67.			
			Stephen Smith, M, D., Brigade, 26 *May,* '69; *transferred to Woodstock Field Batt.,* 24 Ap'l, '74.

APPENDICES.

REGIMENTAL FIELD AND

Date.	Lieut. Colonel.	Majors.	Adjutant.
1864, 28 March.			
1865, 29 March.	Stephen Kent Foster, Brigade, *26 May, '69, Retired with rank Lt Dec. '84.*		
5 April.		James F. Berton,	
1866, 18 April.			
1867, 19 June.		J. Mount, Brigade, *26 May,'69, Retired with rank Bt. Lt. Col. 7 Dec. '71.*	
17 July.			Jacob Day Underhill, Brigade, *26 May, 69; Bt. Major, 2 Jan, '72; Bt. Lt. Col, 2 Jan. '77. Retired with rank 28 March, '84.*
1871, 7 Dec.	Brigade—Dominion of	Canada, 26 May, 1869. George Hamilton Pick, *Bt. Lt. Col. 7 Nov, '71. Retired with rank 14 Mar., '84.*	
1872, 12 July.		Martin Hunter Peters, *r, b, 1st, Bt. Lt. Col, 30 Jan. '72, Retired retaining rank 20 March, '85.*	
1874, 4 Sept.			
1875, 3 Sept.			
1876, 11 Aug.			
1881, 25 Feb'y.			
1883, 14 Sept.			
1885, 9 Jan'y.	John Russell Armstrong, *from 8th Cavalry—specially and provisionally—confirmation of rank 22 Nov, '85, r. s. a. 1st.*		

STAFF OFFICERS--Continued.

Paymaster.	Quartermaster.	Surgeon.	Assistant Surgeon.
	W. Albert Lockhart, Brigade, 26 May, '69; Resigned 12 July, '72.		
		John Berryman, M. D., Brigade, 26 July, '69; Resigned 17 Sept. '75.	Joseph Lordly Bunting, M. D
Stephen Kent Foster, jr. (*Capt.*) Brigade, 26 May, '69.			
	Richard Farmer, Bt. Major, 27 Feb, '67; Retired with Hon. rank of Major 28 July, '94.		Joseph Andrews, M. D.
			J. W. Daniel, M. D., vice Andrews, left limits.
		J. W. Daniel, M. D., r s. a. 1st.	
Wm. Arthur King, *Hon. Capt.* 25 Feb. '81. Retired with rank 27 Feb. '85.			Joseph Andrews, M.D.

APPENDICES.

REGIMENTAL FIELD AND

Date.	Lieut. Colonel.	Majors.	Adjutant.
1885. 27 Feb.			
10 April.			Charles Frederick Langan, *g. s. 1st. Lieut. 24 June,'81;* to command No. *2 Co'y.,* 4 June, '86.
1886. 18 June.			C. F. Langan, *Re-appointed, Capt. 4 June, '86. Retired retaining rank, 24 Dec., '91.*
22 Oct.		Andrew J. Armstrong. *r. s a. 1st. To District Staff, 1 Feb. '87.*	
1889. 12 Feb.		George Bliss Seely, *r. s. a. 1st. Died 21 March, '90.*	
1892. 2 Jan.			George Kerr McLeod, *Capt. r. s. a. 1st. Removed having left limits, 9 Nov., '95.*
16 Dec.		John James Gordon, *r. s. a. 1st. To Quartermaster, 28 July, '94.*	
1894. 28 July.		George West Jones, *r. s. a. 1st.*	
1895. 9 Nov.			Walter Woodworth White, *r. s. a. 1st. Capt. 1 June, '94.*

STAFF OFFICERS--Continued.

Paymaster.	Quartermaster.	Surgeon.	Assistant Surgeon.
George Frederick Smith, *Died 6 March, '94.*			
	John James Gordon, *Major 16 Dec., '92.*		

NOTE.--The word 'Brigade' is used to designate those officers of the N. B. Regiment who were continued in their positions by the G. O. constituting the N. B. Brigade of Garrison Artillery. This order was dated 26th May, 1869.

THE COLVILLE COMPANY (At St. John).

Date.	Captain.	Lieutenant.	Second Lieutenant.
1793. 4 May.	John Colville.	Thomas Gilbert.	John Ward.
1808. (or before)	Andrew Crookshank, Died 14 Feb., 1815. James Potter, (See p. 34)	William Donald.	David Waterbury
1816. 10 August.		David Waterbury.	Caleb Ward.
1821. May 1, (about)	David Waterbury, Retired with rank of Major, 3 Sept., 1822.	Caleb Ward.	John C. Waterbury.
Sept. 3.		Thomas Barlow.	
1822. Sept. 3.	John C. Waterbury, Retired with rank 4 July, '26.	Thomas T. Hanford.	George Waterbury.
1827. 9 January.	Thomas Barlow, Retired with rank of Major, 28 Feb., '38.		
1833. 13 April.		George Waterbury. v. Hanford, deceased. Retired with rank 3 Nov.'38.	
14 April.			Robert Robertson (Sergt).
15 April.			Charles J. Melick.
1839. 8 March.		Charles J. Melick.	
9 March.	Robert Robertson, vice Barlow, Retired with rank, 10 Apr. '43.		
23 April.			Lewis Durant, vice Melick, promoted.
1843. 10 April.	Charles J. Melick, Major 6 Dec., '59, vice G. F. Street, deceased.		

THE COLVILLE COMPANY--Continued.

Date.	Captain.	Lieutenant.	Second Lieutenant.
1843, 12 April.		Lewis Durant.	
1843. 11 August.			James G. Melick.
1860. 24 January.	Lewis Durant, *Retired with rank 18 Mar., '61.*	James G. Melick. Thomas Coke Humbert.	
June 27.		Alexander Rankine, *vice Humbert resigned.*	
1861. 13 April.	James G. Melick, *Retired with rank 13 April, '61.*		
13 April.	Alexander Rankine, *Retired with rank 24 Feb., '63.*		
23 April.		Wm. Fred'rk Deacon.	Roger Hunter.
1862. 14 Nov.	Samuel R. Thomson.		
1864. 8 July.		Christopher Murray.	
20 July.		Roger Hunter.	
1865. 4 January.		Owen Jones, *from Charlotte Co.*	
1866. 10 January.	Christopher Murray.	(*Sergt.*) Stephen Kent Foster *Captain and Paymaster, 19 June, '67.*	

By M. G. O. 20 March, 1868, the services of this battery were dispensed with.

(Signature of First Captain)

APPENDICES.

CAPTAIN NICHOLSON'S BATTERY,
FROM 1st BATTALION CITY MILITIA.

Date.	Captain.	Lieutenant.	Second Lieutenant.
1833.			
8 Oct.	Thomas L. Nicholson, *Capt. 31 Aug., '30; 2nd Major 30 March, '41.*	John Pollok, *Retired with rank on account of ill health 10 April '43.*	
9 October.			Charters Simonds, *Left limits. 11 April, '43.*
10 October.			Wm. Ross.
1838.			
M. G. O. 25 June.			
1841.			
30 March.	William Hughson, *Resigned 12 Aug., '48.*		
1843.			
10 April.		William Wright, *To Ranney's 11 Aug., '45.*	
11 April.			C. C. Stewart
1846.			
20 January.			Robert Reed, *Dated from 10 Oct., '45.*
1843.			
12 August.	C. C. Stewart, *Retired with rank 1 July, '59.*		
13 August.			Robert Sweet.

Did not re-enrol under Act of 1862.

B. LESTER PETER'S BATTERY.

Date.	Captain.	Lieutenant.	Second Lieutenant.
1861.			
25 March.	B. Lester Peters, *From St. John City Militia. Bt. Lieut.-Col. 1 Oct., '66.*	Robert R. Sneden, *Lieut. 14 Nov., '59; Capt. 10 Oct., '66* George J. Thomas, *Lieut. 14 Nov., '59.*	F. G. W. Lansdowne, *2nd Lieut. 3 Jan., '60; 1st Lieut. 8 July, '64.*

There was no change in the officers of this battery.

OFFICERS' SERVICE LISTS. 237

CAPTAIN RANNEY'S BATTERY.
ARTILLERY ATTACHED TO RIFLE BATTALION (2nd Battalion St. John City.)

Date.	Captain.	Lieutenant.	Second Lieutenant.
1834. 20 April.	William Parker Ranney.	William Hughson, *Lieut. 5 Nov., '33, 2nd Battalion St.John City Militia.*	N. W. Wallop. Frederick A. Wiggins, *Paymaster 20 Sept., '49.*
26 April.			S. K. Foster, *Lieut. 12 Nov., '33, 2nd Batt. St.John City Militia. Commission dated 25 April '34.*
1841. 31 March.	Stephen Kent Foster, *Major 10 Aug., '48, vice Nicholson deceased; Lt.-Col. 6 Dec., '59.*		
1843. 10 April.		William Wright.	
1848. 11 August.	Wm. Wright. *(from Hughson's), Retired with rank 1 July, '59.*		
12 August.			John R. Marshall.
1859. 6 December.	John R. Marshall, *vice Wright.*	George F Thompson. Robert J. Leonard.	Francis Smith.

Did not re-enrol under Act of 1862.

CAPTAIN McLAUCHLAN'S BATTERY (Carleton).

Date.	Captain.	Lieutenant.	Second Lieutenant.
1860. 17 April.	John McLauchlan, *Retired with rank 9 Feb., '64.*	Richard Newell Knight. *Resigned 3 Oct., '62.*	Thos. Mitchell McLachlan.
20 August.			George Hunter Clark. *Resigned Jan. 13. '62.*
1862. 18 Sept.		Thomas M. McLachlan.	
19 Sept.		William J. McCordock, (*Sergt.*)	
1864. 11 February.	Thomas M. McLachlan.		

Services of the battery dispensed with 8 March, 1865.

No. 1 (CAPTAIN PICK'S) BATTERY.

Date.	Captain.	Lieutenant.	Second Lieutenant.
1859. Nov. 14.	James Mount, late R. A.	George Hamilton Pick. Robert R. Sneden, *Transferred 25 March, '61.* George Thomas, *Transferred 25 March, '61.*	NOTE.—The lieutenants appointments are dated Nov. 14, '59, while Mount to adjutancy is dated Sept. 20, '59.
1860. January 3.	George Hamilton Pick, *Bt. Major 7 Nov., '66; (1st class certificate 3 Nov., '71) Bt. Lt.-Col., 7 Nov, 71; To majority 7 Dec., '71.*		Francis Gilbert Ward Lansdowne, *(Sergt.) transferred 25 March, '61.*
1861. April 13.		William J. Shannon, *(Sergt.) Retired with rank 20 July, '64,* John M. Taylor, *(Sergt.) Retired with rank 20 July, '64.*	
1864. 13 July.			Jacob Day Underhill.
14 Dec.		Jacob Day Underhill, *Capt. 2nd Jan., '67. Adj't 17 July, '67.*	
1866. 21 February.			James McNichol, jr.
7 Nov.			John R. Smith, *Retired 7 Nov., '66.*
1867. 30 January.		James McNichol.	
1871. 6 April.		John Alexander Kane, *From No. 10 (prov.) g. v.b. 2nd, 9 Feb., '72.*	
13 Sept.			(Sergt.) John E. Bell, *(prov.) g. c. 22 May, '72.*
1872. 23 February.	John Alexander Kane, *g. v. b. 2nd. Retired with rank 20 Mar., '85.*		
31 May.		John E. Bell, *g. c. (Left limits.)*	Andrew J. Armstrong, *(prov.) g. c. 2nd, 19 June '72.*
1874. 2 January.		Charles William Drury, *(prov.) g. s, 1st s. c, 13 Oct. '74; g. s, 1st l,c. 2 July,'75. Transferred to 'A' Battery as Lieut., 23 Feb., '77.*	Matthew Wallace *(prov.) vice Armstrong to No. 10; Resigned 3 Oct., '79.*

No. 1 (CAPTAIN PICK'S) BATTERY—Continued.

Date.	Captain.	Lieutenant.	Second Lieutenant.
1877. 21 Dec.		Joseph Howe, *g. s, 1st s, c., 30 Nov., '77; 2nd class, l. c 8 Nov., '78.*	
1879. 3 October.		George Kerr Berton, *v. b* (*prov.*) *from retired list of Captains, vice Howe, left limits.*	
1881. 24 June.		Charles Frederick Langan, *g s 1st s. c 22 Jan., '76. Transferred to adjutancy.*	Stanley Douglas Crawford, (*prov.*) *g. s. 2nd, 6 April, '82.*
1885. 20 March.	George Bliss Seely, *m. s. 2nd, 22 March, '72; r. s. a. 1st, 22 Nov., '85; Promoted to majority 12 Feb., '89.*		
10 April.		Stanley Douglas Crawford, *g. s. 2nd; transferred to Captaincy No. 3, 3 June, '87.*	Robert Rankin Ritchie, (*prov.*) *r.s.a. 1st. 20 April, '86.*
1887. 17 June.		Robert Rankin Ritchie, *r. s. a. 1st. Resigned 29 Nov., '89.*	
16 Sept.			John Edward Earle Dickson, (*prov.*) *Resigned 20 June, '90.*
1889. 31 Ma .	Stanley Douglas Crawford, *Capt. 3 June, '87, from No. 3.*		
29 Nov.		Walter Woodworth White, *r. s. a. 1st, from No. 2; transferred to No 5 and promoted 1 June, '94.*	
1890. 20 June.			Herbert Chipman Tilley, (*prov.*) *from No. 5; r. s. a. 2nd, 18 May, '92; transferred to No. 2 and promoted 20 Jan., '93.*
1893. 23 June.			Gordon Sutherland McLeod (*prov.*) *Transferred to No. 3, 12 Oct., '95.*
1894. 28 July.			Gunner Beverley Robinson Armstrong (*prov.*) *r. s. a. 1st, 9 Sept., '95.*
1895. 12 Oct.			Arthur Cavendish Hamilton Gray, (*prov.*)
21 Dec.		Beverley Robinson Armstrong, *r. s. a. 1st.*	

No. 2 (CAPTAIN ADAMS') BATTERY.

Date	Captain.	Lieutenant.	Second Lieutenant.
1859, Dec. 6,	Josiah Adams. *Retired with rank 24 Feb., '63; Died 31 May, '68.*	Joseph Coram, Edwin J. Wetmore.	George J. Stackhouse.
1860, June 27.		James Quinton, *vice Coram resigned. To St. John Co. Militia 27 Oct., '63.*	
1861, Sept. 2.			Martin Hunter Peters, *vice Stackhouse resigned*
1862, July 11.	Martin Hunter Peters, *Bt. Major 30 Jan., '67 ; 1st class certif. 3 Nov., '71 ; Reg. Major 7 Dec., '71 ; Bt. Lt.-Col. 30 Jan., '72.*		
1867, Jan. 31.		James Alfred Ring, (*prov.*) *g. v. b. 2nd, 9 Feb., '72.*	
1871, May 19.			James Carleton (*prov.*). *Retired Sept. 17, '75.*
1872, February 23.	James Alfred Ring, *g. r. b. 2nd. Retired with rank 14 Aug., '85.*		
1875, Sept. 17.			Thomas Wm. Lander (*prov.*) *vice Carleton resigned. Transferred to No. 9 31 May, '78.*
1878, 5 July.			Wm. Jas. Kingston, (*prov.*) *vice Lander.*
1881, 5 August.		(*Sergt.*) James Hersey Easty, (*prov.*)	(*Sergt.*) Bernard Trestrum Ring, *vice Kingston left limits.*
1885, 15 May.		John James Gordon (*prov.*) *vice Easty ; r. s. a. 1st, 27 March, '86.*	
4 Sept.			George Kerr McLeod (*prov.*) *vice Ring left limits. r. s. a. 1st, 15 May, '86. Transferred to No. 3 11 March, '87.*
1886, 4 June.	C. Fred Langan, *from adjutancy. Transferred to adjutancy 18 June, '86.*		
18 June.	John James Gordon, *r. s. a 1st. To majority 16 Dec., '92.*		

No. 2 (CAPTAIN ADAMS') BATTERY.—*Continued.*

Date.	Captain.	Lieutenant.	Second Lieutenant.
1886. 30 July.		Albert Arthur Clark (*prov.*)	
1887. 5 August.			Walter Woodworth White, (*prov.*) *r. s. a. 1st, 10 Sept.* '89 ; *transferred to No. 1 and promoted 29 Nov,* '89.
1889. 31 May.		(*Bomb.*) John Babington Macaulay Baxter (*prov.*) *vice Clark resigned ; r.s.a. 1st, 10 Sept.,* '89.	
1891. 28 August.			Arthur Drake Wetmore, *from No. 4 28 Aug.* '91. *Struck off list 10 Nov ,* '94.
1892. 16 Dec.	John Babington Macaulay Baxter *r. s. a 1st, vice Gordon promoted.*		
1893. 20 January.		Herbert Chipman Tilley, *r. s. a. 2nd, from No. 1.*	
1894. 10 Nov.			Frederick Arthur Foster, (*prov.*) *r.s.a. 2nd, 27 Aug.,* '95.

No. 3 (CAPTAIN HURD PETERS') BATTERY.

Date.	Captain.	Lieutenant.	Second Lieutenant.
1860. January 4.	Hurd Peters, *To St. John Co. Militia, 1 Sept.,* '63.	Alexander Rankin, *Resigned 7 April,* '63. James Kirk, *Resigned 30 June,* '63.	
1863. 27 April.			John Simonds.
27 July.			Edward Jones.
29 October.	John Simonds, *Retired with rank 29 June,* '64	Edward Jones, *Retired with rank 3 Aug.,* '64.	Richard Farmer.
1864. 8 July.	Richard Farmer, *Bt. Major 27 Feb.,* '67 ; *1st class certificate 3 Nov.,* '71 ; *Retired with brevet rank 31 May,* '72 ; *appointed quartermaster 14 June,* '72.		

No. 3 (CAPTAIN HURD PETERS') BATTERY.—*Continued*.

Date.	Captain.	Lieutenant.	Second Lieutenant.
1864. 7 Sept.		Wm. Cunard, *g. c.* 2nd, Feb., '72; *Capt.* 27 Feb.,'67.	George Garby.
14 Dec.		George Garby.	
1867. 27 March.		(*Sgt.-Major*) Thomas Scott, *g. c.* 2nd, 22 Aug., '73; retired with rank 2 June, '76.	T. Crocket.
1870. 3 June.			(*Gunner*) Joseph Ewing, (*prov*) vice Crocket left limits; 2nd class certif. 28 March, '71.
1872. 31 May.	William Cunard, *r. b., g. c.* 1st. Captain 27 Feb., '67; *Bt.Major* 27 Feb., '72; *Bt. Lieut.-Col.* 27 Feb., '77; To district storekeeper 1 July, '77.		
1876. 2 June.		Joseph Ewing.	
1877. 28 Sept.	Joseph Ewing. Retired with rank 14 Aug.,'85.		
6 April.			Lewis D. Milledge, *m. s.*
30 Nov.		Lewis D. Milledge, *g. s.* Resigned 27 Dec., '78.	
1878. 14 June.			George Frederick Cole, (*prov.*) *g. s.* 1st s, c. 31 Oct., '79.
1884. 15 August.		William Barber. (*prov.*) Resigned 10 April, '85, (Died 14 Dec., '91.)	Horace W. Cole, (*prov.*) vice George F. Cole left limits; Resigned 10 April '85.
1885. 10 April.		Hedley Vickers Cooper, Retired 4 Feb., '87.	William Murray Botsford, vice Cole, *r. s. a.* 1st, 22 Nov.. '85.
1886. 22 April.	Wm. Murray Botsford, *r.s.a.* 1st. Resigned 3 June, '87.		
16 July.			N.W. Chas. Frederick Harrison. (*prov.*) *r. s. a.* 1st, 10 Sept., '89.
1887. 11 March.		George Kerr McLeod, *r. s. a.* 1st, from No. 2.	

OFFICERS' SERVICE LISTS. 243

No. 3 (CAPTAIN HURD PETERS') BATTERY.—*Continued.*

Date.	Captain.	Lieutenant.	Second Lieutenant.
1887. 3 June.	Stanley Douglas Crawford, *g. s, 2nd, from No. 1; Transferred to No. 1 31 May, '89.*		
1889. 31 May.	George Kerr McLeod, *r.s.a. 1st. To adjutancy 22 Jan., '92.*		
29 Nov.		*N.W.* Charles Frederick Harrison, *r. s. a. 1st.*	
1890. 20 June.			Robert Huntley Gordon, (*prov.*)*r.s.a. 1st, 22 July, '92.*
1892. 22 Jan.	*N. W,* Chas. Frederick Harrison, *r s. a. 1st; Retired with rank 18 May, '94.*		
22 July.		Robert Huntley Gordon, *r. s. a. 1st.*	Walter Edward Foster, (*prov.*) *r. s. a. 1st, 4 Oct., '92.*
1894. 22 June.	Robt. Huntley Gordon, *r.s.a. 1st*	Walter Edward Foster, *r. s. a. 1st.*	
1895. 12 October.			Gordon Sutherland McLeod, (*prov.*)*from No 1 Co,*

No. 4 (Formerly No. 10) BATTERY.

Date.	Captain.	Lieutenant.	Second Lieutenant.
1869. 5 March.	John Kerr, (*prov.*) *g. c. 2nd, 6* May, '69.	John A. Kane, (*prov.*) *To No. 1 Batt. 6 April,'71.*	John Evans Daley, (*prov.*) *Subst. 20 April, '69.*
1871. 6 April.		Geo. Lawrence Foster, *m. s.*	
19 May.			(*Batt.Sgt.Major*) John King (*prov.*) *vice Daley left limits. Subst. 15 April,'72*
1872. 14 June.	John King *v. b.*		

No. 4 (Formerly No. 10) BATTERY.—*Continued.*

Date.	Captain.	Lieutenant.	Second Lieutenant.
1872. 6 Sept.		Wm. H. McColgan, (*prov*) *vice Foster left limits.* Resigned 1 Aug., '73.	James McKinney, (*prov*,) Resigned 1 Aug., '73.
1873. 1 August.	Andrew J. Armstrong, *g. c. 2nd. from No. 1 vice King deceased. g. s. 2nd, to majority 22 Oct., '86.*		
10 October.		(*Sgt.-Major*) William Arthur King, (*prov.*) *g. c. 2nd, 31 March, '74;* Paymaster 25 Feb., '81.	(*Bomb.*) George Till, (*prov.*) Resigned 11 Aug., '76.
1876. 11 August.			Robert Inch, (*prov.*)
1880. 6 February.			Wm. Alex. Douglas Steven, (*prov.*) *vice Inch left limits. g. c. 2nd, 24 March, '80.*
M. G. O. 6 Feb. '85, to be No. 4 Batt.			
1885. 6 Feb.		W. A. D. Steven, *g. c. 2nd.*	
20 April.		Arthur Shirley Benn, (*prov.*) *vice Steven; resigned 17 Aug., '88.*	George West Jones, (*prov.*) *r. s. a. 1st, 22 Nov., '85.*
1886. 22 October.	George West Jones, *r. s. a. 1st. To majority 28 July, '94.*		
1887. 7 April.			(*Corp.*) Thos. Edward Grindon Armstrong, (*prov.*) *r. s. a. 2nd, 13 June, '91.*
1888. 17 August.		Arthur Drake Wetmore, (*prov.*) *To No. 2 as 2nd Lieut. 28 Aug., '90.*	
1891. 28 August.		Thos. E. G. Armstrong, *r. s. a. 2nd.*	Frederick Caverhill Jones, (*prov.*) *r.s.a. 1st, 21 Feb., '93.*
1894. 28 July.	Thomas Edward Grindon Armstrong, *r. s. a. 2nd.*	Frederick Caverhill Jones, *r. s. a. 1st.*	Sherwood Arthur Manning Skinner, (*prov.*)

No. 5 (Formerly No. 9) BATTERY.

Date.	Captain.	Lieutenant.	Second Lieutenant.
1878. 31 May.	Thomas Wm. Lander, (*prov.*) from 2nd Lieut. No. 2; m.s. 2nd, 24 Mar, '80; Retired with infantry rank 14 Aug., '85.	Frederick H. Ellis, (*prov.*)	
1881. 19 August.		William Roxborough, vice Ellis left limits.	

Designation altered to No. 5 Battery, 6 Feb., 1885.

Date.	Captain.	Lieutenant.	Second Lieutenant.
1885. 20 April.		Edward Jewett Scammell, vice Roxborough; r. s. a. 2nd; 22 Nov., '85.	Ernest Hatheway Turnbull. (*prov.*)
1886. 22 April.	Edward Jewett Scammell, r.s.a. 2nd; Retired with rank 31 May, '89.		
7 May.		Jas. Albert Edward Steeves, (*prov.*) r. s. a. 1st, 10 Sept. '89.	
1888. 23 Nov.			Herbert Chipman Tilley, (*prov.*) to No. 1 20 June, '90.
1889. 29 Nov.	James A. E. Steeves, r, s. a. 1st. Retired with rank 1 June, '94.		
1890. 20 June.		Frederick Landon Temple, (*prov.*) r, s. a. 1st. 4 Oct., '92.	Robert Pattison Foster, (*prov.*) vice Tilley; Retired 7 July, '93.
1893. 7 July.			Edward Walter Bates Scovil, (*prov.*) vice Foster.
1894. 1 June.	Walter Woodworth White. r. s. a 1st, from No. 1 Co. Transferred to adjutancy 9 Nov., '95.		
1896. 21 Dec.	Frederick Landon Temple, r, s. a. 1st.		Ernest Ray Jones. (*prov.*)

APPENDICES.

CHARLOTTE COUNTY ARTILLERY.

Date.	Captain.	Lieutenant.	Second Lieutenant.

At Saint Andrews. 1st Battalion.

1822.
27 May.   William Whitlock.

1828.
10 May,   James Muir.   Henry Frye,
                                                                      Date of appointment unknown, was transferred to
1829.   *Sea Fencibles by mistake.*
4 February.   William Whitlock,   Thomas Berry.
               *To quartermaster 1st Battalion
               Charlotte Co. Militia, 4 April
               '42.*

1837.
6 Dec.   Henry Frye.

1842.
4 April.   Thomas B. Wilson,
               Prov. A. D. C., 22 Feb., '47.

2nd Battalion.

1828.
10 March.   William Gray.

11 March.   John Messinett.

1829.
2 July.   John Mowatt, *Lieut. from 1st* Benjamin Milliken.
               *Batt.; Retired 10 Aug., '48
               with rank of major from 21
               Aug., '48.*

1848.
10 August.   J. Messinett.

This company came into N. B. R. A. by M. G. O. 5 Dec., 1840.

*4th Battalion—At St. Stephen.

1827.
26 March.   T. or J. Armstrong.   J. Maxwell, *suspended by M.*
                                                                G. O, 8 April, '34, and reinstated by M. G. O. 17
31 March.   James Frink.   *March, '35.*

1834.
8 April.   William T. Rose,   T. Campbell, *dated 9 April.*   W. Andrews.
               *Retired with rank of major 13
               June, '66.*
9 April.   Peter Brown.

*This company came into N. B. R. A. at its formation. See No. 8 battery where Captain Clewly's appointment is in succession to Captain Rose.

WESTMORELAND COUNTY ARTILLERY.

Date.	Captain.	Lieutenant.	Second Lieutenant.

2nd Battalion.

1825.	—— Harris.	George L. Kinnear.	
		William Burnham.	
25 July.	George L. Kinnear.		George Hay.
1831.			
30 May.	William Burnham.	George Hay.	
1832.			
27 Sept.			Henry Ogden.
1833.			
3 July.			Charles Dixon.
1836.			
19 June.	George Hay,		
	Retired with rank 15 July,'39.		
21 June.		Henry Ogden	
1841.			
1 July.			Thomas Ogden.
1842.			
12 July.			Nelson Bulmer.
13 July.			Charles Palmer.

3rd Battalion.

1833.			
22 October.	Thomas B. Moore.	Elisha Stephens	
23 October.			Joseph Rodgers.
1840.			
6 July.			Solomon Stiles,
			vice Rogers deceased.
1849.			
14 July.			Robert Rogers.

Many of these names appear in almanacs without the '*art*,' which was then used to denote artillery officers. It is probable that the artillery gradually changed into infantry companies.

APPENDICES.

FREDERICTON, YORK COUNTY, ARTILLERY.

Date	Captain.	Lieutenant.	Second Lieutenant.
1st Battalion.			NOTE.—An attempt has been made to group these names in three organizations, but it is submitted without any pretension to accuracy. Recollections of these batteries are indistinct and conflicting and the organizations seem to have been somewhat irregular. The names of Isaac Naish, 1st lieutenant, and Alex. Mitchell, 2nd lieutenant, appear in M. G. O. 30 May, 1860. On 25 March, 1861, Mitchell was promoted to 1st lieutenant vice Naish deceased. They are said to have belonged to Fredericton, but nothing definite is known concerning them.
	George P. Bliss, *Bt. Major 17 Sept. '33.*	Richard Dibblee, *Lieut. 9 Jan., '26.*	
1834. 25 August.		John Saunders Shore.	
2 Sept.		Donald McLeod, *Retired with rank 13 Sept. '41.*	
1836. 18 June,	John S. Shore, *To H. M. 24th Foot.*	George M. Odell.	
1838. 8 May.			John C. Allen.
1839. 8 March.			William H. Shore.
1841. 28 July.	John C. Allen, *Prov. A. D. C. 5 July, '44.*		James Moore, *9 May, '49.*
1838. 8 May.	G. F. Berton, *from 1st York Battalion.*	James F. Berton, *from 1st York Battalion.*	
9 May.			Edward B. Peters.
1841. 23 July.	James F. Berton, *To majority 5 April, '65.*		
1855. 18 April.			Thomas Paisley, *R. A.,* (Sgt.Major.)
1864. 14 Oct.			Wm. Woodbridge Street.
1865. 7 June.			John Allen, jr.
1866. 29 August.	William W. Street.	John Allen, jr.	

Disbanded by M. G. O. 27 March, 1867.

1862. 9 Dec.	Enoch Wood Chestnut, *from 1st Battalion York Co. Retired with rank 19 April,'64.*		George Clopper Peters.
1863. 14 April.			John Matthew Stratton.
17 April.		George Clopper Peters.	

OFFICERS' SERVICE LISTS. 249

GAGETOWN, QUEENS COUNTY, ARTILLERY.

Date.	Captain.	Lieutenant.	Second Lieutenant.
1860. 27 March.	J. Warren Travis. *Transferred to 1st Battalion Queens Co. Militia, 21 Oct. '62.*	Frederick Lundrine Knox,	William J. Frost, *Struck off 3 March, '63.*
1862. 24 Nov.	Fred L. Knox, *Transferred to 1st Battalion Queens Co. Militia, 22 Dec. '63.*	Edward Simpson.	
1863. 21 April.			C. F. Hoben,

No. 4 BATTERY, ST. ANDREWS, CHARLOTTE COUNTY.

Date.	Captain.	Lieutenant.	Second Lieutenant.
1866. 14 Feb.	Henry Osburn, *from Lieut. 1st Battalion Charlotte Co. Militia. Resigned 28 Jan., '70.*	Thomas T. Odell, *from Ensign 1st Battalion Charlotte Co. Militia.*	Walter B. Morris.
11 April.			Nicholas T. Greathead, *From Ensign 1st Batt. Charlotte Co. Militia.*
12 April.		Walter B. Morris, *Resigned 28 Jan., '68.*	
1868. 29 January.		Nicholas T. Greathead, *Resigned 30 Sept., '70.*	
1870. 30 Sept.	Eber S. Polleys, (*prov.*)	William Whitlock, (*prov.*)	
1871. 2 June.			Francis G. Stoop, (*prov.*)

No. 5 BATTERY, WOODSTOCK, CARLETON COUNTY.

Date.	Captain.	Lieutenant.	Second Lieutenant.
1833. 17 Sept.	Abraham K. Smedes Wetmore, *(2nd Captaincy.)*		
1839. 8 March.	*To be captain from the unattached list; Retired with rank of major 23 June, '62.*		
9 October.			Walter D. Bedell.
1840. 5 May.		Thomas E. Perley.	
1845. 30 October.		Walter D. Bedell, *Retired with rank 24 Jan., '60*	
1848. 14 August.			Charles H. Connell.
1860. 7 February.		James Edgar.	
7 February.			Edward D. Watts.
7 February.		William Skillen, *Transferred to 1st Batt. Carleton Co. Militia, 27 Oct., '63.*	
1866. 30 May.	James Edgar.	James Grover Balloch, *Retired 7 Nov., '66,*	John Coffin Winslow.
1867. 2 January.		John Coffin Winslow.	*(Sergt.)* Wm. P. Donnell.
16 October.		William P. Donnell.	*(Sergt.)* Samuel T. Baker.
1871. 28 June.			*(Sergt.)* W. O. Raymond.

Transferred to field battery by M. G. O. 24 April, 1874.

OFFICERS' SERVICE LISTS. 251

No. 6 BATTERY, ST. GEORGE, CHARLOTTE CO.

Date.	Captain.	Lieutenant.	Second Lieutenant.
1869. 26 May.	*Authorized.*		
1870. 28 October.	M. G. O. explains that the following appointments were omitted from previous order:		
1871. 13 Sept.	James Bolton.	Mark Hall.	(*Sgt.-Major*) Joseph McCormack, (*prov.*)

No. 7 BATTERY, CHATHAM, NORTHUMBERLAND CO.

Date.	Captain.	Lieutenant.	Second Lieutenant.
1860. 6 March.	James C. E. Carmichael.	Elijah Parsons.	Thomas F. Gillespie.
1867. 28 Feb.	Thomas F. Gillespie, *v. b. 1st, 2 April, '72 ; Bt. Major 2 April, '72 ; Bt. Lieut. Col. 2 April, '77 ; Retired retaining brevet rank 12 Dec, '84.*	Francis J. Letson, *Resigned 12 June, '74.*	John F. Gemmill, *Retired 25 Nov., '70.*
1868. 3 June.			Daniel Crummin, *Removed 12 Dec,, '84.*
1870. 25 Nov.			(*Sergt.*) James Wm. Fraser, *g. v. b. 26 Aug., '72.*
1874. 12 June.		James Wm. Fraser, *g. v. b. Retired with rank 12 Dec, '84.*	

Battery non-effective and removed from list M. G. O. 12 December, 1884.

APPENDICES.

No. 8 BATTERY, ST. STEPHEN, CHARLOTTE COUNTY.

Date.	Captain.	Lieutenant.	Second Lieutenant.
1866. 2 May.		William Isaac Clewly.	Herbert Wm. Goddard.
13 June.	William Isaac Clewly, *appointed vice Rose, see Charlotte Co. Artillery, p. 246. Retired 15 July, '68.*	Edward H. Clark.	
1867. 6 February.			(*Sergt.-Major*) William H. Stevens.
17 July.		W. H. Stevens, *Resigned 26 May, '69.*	
18 July.			(*Sergt-Major*) John H. Rose.
1868. 15 July.	Edward H. Clarke, *Retired with rank 24 Mar. '71.*		
1869. 26 May.		William Vaughan.	
1871. 24 March.	John H. Rose, (*pror. and specially.*)		(*Sergt.-Major*) Thomas D. Stevenson, (*prov.*)

No. 9 BATTERY, ST. GEORGE, CHARLOTTE COUNTY.

Date.	Captain.	Lieutenant.	Second Lieutenant.
1869. 6 February.	Charles McGee, *q.f.o.*	Robert A. Stewart.	Joseph Meating.

By M. G. O. 19 June, 1874, this battery was detached from the N. B. B. G. A. and changed to a company of infantry.

INDEX.

Aberdeen, Earl and Countess of, visit St. John, 216.
Accidents, fatal, at Chatham, 149; destruction of walls at St. John, 156.
Adams, Josiah, captain, company of, 85.
Allen, John, assists in making up roll for Fredericton battery, 148.
Allen, Sir John C., lieutenant, 49, 52; adjutant, 63; provincial A. D. C., 73; resigns adjutancy, 84.
Anderson, Corporal, bravery at St. John fire, 157.
Anderson, James, private in Nicholson's, 43.
Anderson, James, corporal R. A., presentation to, 100.
Anderson, Thos. H., captain 78th, appointed Lieutenant-Colonel in charge western New Brunswick, 131.
Andrews, Joseph, M. D., assistant surgeon, 153; re-appointed, 153.
Andrews, W. lieutenant, 48, 84, 246.
Andrews, Corporal, J. R., bravery at St. John fire, 157.
Anthony, Henry, private, 5, 11; one of three survivors present at the semi-centennial, 69.
Armstrong, Andrew J., captain, 147, 173; presentation to, 163; major, 174; presentation to, 175; district storekeeper, 176.
Armstrong, Beverley R., lieutenant, 214, 219.
Armstrong, J., captain, 41.
Armstrong, John R., member of Peters' battery, 112; appointed to command of artillery, 169; his training, 170; offers services of brigade in North-west, 172; provincial A. D. C., 173; in command of Shoeburyness team, 173; welcome to on return, 175; A. D. C. to governor-general, 180; president Dominion Artillery Association, 185.
Armstrong, T. E. G., lieutenant, 207.
Armstrong, T., captain, 41.
Armstrong, quartermaster sergeant, wins prizes, 150.
Aroostook war, 54.
Arthur, Prince, visits St. John, 145.
Artillery Association, Dominion, formed, 151; Provincial formed, 151; Dominion extended to garrison artillery, 165.
Artillery, New Brunswick, first company formed, 4; muster roll, 4; rolls of 1808-9-10, 22; jubilee of, 66; centennial of, 207; centennial rolls, 225.
Artillery, New Brunswick Battalion, 208;
"   "   "   Brigade of, 143;
"   "   "   Regiment, 47;
of Canadian Artillery, 219.

Artillery, Royal, 7.
Asylum, Provincial Lunatic, laying of corner stone, 74.
'At Home,' band, 195.
Atlantic Cable, laying of, 81.

Baker, S. T., lieutenant, 250.
Balloch, Jas. G., lieutenant, 250.
Balls, 1833, 69; 1888, 179; 1892, 184; centennial, 212.
Band, the, 191; first appearance of, 173; 'At Home,' 195; concerts, 195, 209; visits Charlottetown, 195; membership and instrumentation of, 196; committee, president of, 195.
Band stand, built by No. 2 Company, 179.
Barber, William, lieutenant, 242.
Barlow, Thomas, a private, 22; becomes captain, 39; in sham fight, 44; retires, 48.
Bartlett, Corporal T. H., death of, 217.
Battalion, change of name to, 208.
Baxter, J. B. M., lieutenant, 183; assists in preparing manual, 183; Captain, 184.
Beckwith, Captain A. D., attempts to raise battery at Fredericton, 148.
Bedell, Walter D., lieutenant, 83.
Belding, Daniel, private in first company 4, 14; one of the survivors at semi-centennial, 69.
Bell, John E, lieutenant, 238.
Belyea, Sergeant C., wins cup, 149.
Benn, A. S., lieutenant, 173.
Berry, Lieutenant Thos., 41, 48.
Berryman, John, M. D., surgeon, appointed surgeon, 136, 140; retires, 153.
Berton, Geo. F., captain, 48; death of, 64.
Berton, Jas. F., lieutenant, 48; captain, 64, 83; major, 136; battery disbanded, 136; retired, 136.
Berton, W. S., bombardier Peters' battery, 114.
Blaine, Lieutenant-Colonel Arbuthnot, 62nd Battalion, resolutions on retirement of, 185.
Blake, H. M. S., visits St. John, 211.
Bliss, Geo. P., captain, 43.
Blockhouse battery, 205.
Bolton, James, captain, company of, 138.
Bonaparte, at Toulon, 2; St. Helena, 3; abdicates, 29.
Botsford, Blair, gift of cup, 176.
Botsford, LeB., assistant surgeon, 83; retires, 136.
Botsford, William M., second lieutenant, 172; captain, 174.
Boulton, Henry, wins medal, 119.

INDEX.

Bourdette, Oliver, sergeant in Colville company, 4, 9, 19.
Boyd, John, lieutenant-governor, death of, 211.
Boyd, J. W., paymaster, 47; resigned, 76.
Brigade, change of name to, 142.
Brock, Sir Isaac, rebuilding of monument, 66.
Brown, James, quartermaster-sergeant, 219; best shot, 147.
Brown, Peter, lieutenant, 84.
Browne, William, sergeant, 100.
Bulmer, Nelson, lieutenant, 247.
Bunting, J. L., gunner, wins prizes, 123, 128; assistant surgeon, 136, 149.
Burgess, Gunner Fred. M., death of, 217.
Burnham, Wm., lieutenant, 247.
Busbies, adopted as head dress, 172.
Bustin, James, reminiscences of, 29.

Cameron, John, bombardier in Peters' battery, 115.
Campbell, J., lieutenant, 48, 84.
Campbell, T., lieutenant, 246.
Camps, Barrack square, 146; 'Dufferin,' 149; Sussex, 164.
Carleton county, artillery in, 42.
Carleton, James, lieutenant, 150.
Carleton, St. John, formation of companies, 85, 86.
Carmichael, J. C. E., captain, company at Chatham, 86, 90.
Carnivals, winter, 180; summer, 181.
Carter, Major, W. F., in command during Prince of Wales' visit, 95.
Centennial battery rolls, 225.
Challenge cup, Montreal, 178.
Chamberlain, A., bombardier in Peters' battery, 115; secretary, 115.
Charlotte county, artillery in, 41.
Charnisay, d'Aulnay, attack on Fort LaTour, 198.
Chesley, John A., M. P., bombardier, 100.
Chestnut, E. W., captain, 122; retires, 126.
Chipman, Hon. Ward, 37; death, 38; house of, 17.
Chubb, John, sergeant Colville's company, 4, 9.
Church parades, 166, 174, 175, 177, 179, 181, 183, 184, 211, 214, 218.
Centennial year of corps, celebration of, 207; officers of corps in, 207; salutes fired, 208; concert, 209; smoking concert, 210; ball, 212.
Civil power, aid to, anticipated riot, 151; St. John fire, 155; upon execution, 162.
Clark, A. A., lieutenant, 241.
Clark, George Hunter, lieutenant, 97.
Clark, E. H., captain, 136.
Clewley, Lieutenant Wm., 42; captain, 134; retires, 136.
Cobbett, William, history of, 200; as an author, 201.
Cole, John Amber, brevet colonel in command of force in N. B., 131.

Cole, George F., lieutenant, 242.
Cole, Horace W., lieutenant, 242.
Colebrooke, Sir William, 64.
Colors, presented to regiment, 103; colors of St. John light infantry laid at rest, 214.
Colville, John, first captain, 4; life of, 7; death, 8; signature of, 235.
Concerts, by No. 2 Company, 180; band, 195; centennial, 209; smoking, 210.
Confederation of provinces, 137.
Connell, Chas. H., lieutenant, 83.
Cooper, H. V., lieutenant, 172.
Coram, Joseph, lieutenant, 85; resigns, 97.
Coster, G. C., wins prize, 124.
Cotton, Lieutenant-Colonel W. H., inspects, 167.
Crawford, S. D., lieutenant, 172; captain, 179; services as president of band committee, 191; presentation to, 194.
Crocket, T., lieutenant, 242.
Crookshank, Andrew, private, 5; related to Captain Colville, 8; residence, 9; history, 11; second captain, 23; member of city council, 27; death, 33.
Crummin, D., lieutenant, 251.
Cunard, William, lieutenant, 126; captain, 148; battery drills without pay, 153; on duty at fire, 155; district storekeeper, 159; commended in report, 159.

Daley, John E., lieutenant, 143.
Daniel, John W, appointed assistant surgeon, 153; surgeon, 154; obtains certificate, 173.
Davidson, F. A, W., corporal, 115.
Davis, Richard D., secretary Peters' battery, 114.
Deacon, Lieutenant W. F., 101; obtains colors 103; re-enrols battery, 122.
Defence, national, fund for, 20; contribution of artillery company to, 20.
DeVoe, Daniel, private, 5; sketch of, 13; death, 51.
Dibblee, Richard, lieutenant, 42, 48.
Dicker, Rev. A. G. H., accepts colors for St. Paul's church, 216.
Dickson, J. E. E., lieutenant, 239.
Disputed boundary, 55.
Dixon, Charles, lieutenant, 247.
Dominion Artillery Association, 151, 152.
Donnell, W. P., lieutenant, 250.
Donnington, Corporal, instructor, 171.
Dorchester battery, 5, 17, 205.
Douglas, Sir Howard, governor, 37, 38, 39.
Drill sheds, built at barracks, 159; at Portland, 183; at Carleton, 184.
Drury, C. W., lieutenant, 147, 149; adjutant Shoeburyness team, 173; major, 50.
Drummond, Major, commandant at Fort Howe, freedom of city granted to, 28.
Dufferin, Lord, visit to St. John, 147.
Dunham, Lane, gunner, death of, 151.
Durant, Lewis, sergeant, 40; exhibits model of steam engine, 65; lieutenant, 85; captain, 86; retires with rank, 101.

INDEX.

'Eastern' battery, 205.
Eastport, town of, friendly resolutions, 26.
Easty, J. H., lieutenant, 240.
Edgar, James, captain, 86.
Edwards, John C., won prize for attendance at drill, 178; appointed orderly room clerk, 219.
Ellis, Fred. H., lieutenant, 160.
European & North American Railway, salute on turning of sod, 77.
Ewing, Joseph, lieutenant, 144, 150; on duty at St. John fire and injured, 153; retires, 171.
Exhibition, Dominion, 1883, 167.
Exhibition, Provincial, 163.

Farmer, Richard, lieutenant, 124; captain, 126; muster roll of battery, 127; brevet major, 139; quartermaster, 149; retired, 231.
Fenian excitement, 130, 145.
Fire at St. John, 1877, 154; force called out, 155; blowing down of walls, 156; accident to Gunner Lamb, 156; to Lieutenant Ewing, 157; report of D. A. G. on, 158.
'Flat Feet,' 80.
Forts, The, 197; Dorchester battery, 5, 17, 205; Fort Frederick, 27, 199.
Foster, Fred. A., lieutenant, 241.
Foster, George L., sergeant, 114; lieutenant, 243.
Foster, Robert P., lieutenant, 207.
Foster, Stephen Kent, lieutenant, 44, 48, 51; assisted in celebration of Queen's coronation, 53; captain, 64; maintained efficiency of portion of regiment, 72; major, 75; brevet lieutenant-Colonel, 85; assists in reception of Prince of Wales, 96; presides at social meeting of officers, 98, speech in response to presentation of colors, 105; lieutenant-colonel, 129; commission as evidence of continuity of corps, 140; gazetted in brigade, 143; as senior officer in St. John requested to call out force for duty after fire, 155; issues orders for corps to be in readiness for emergency, 159; thanked for systematic preparation, 160; retires with rank, 167; death of, 178.
Foster, Stephen Kent, jr., bombardier, 114; corporal, 115; sergeant, 125; lieutenant, 130; called out, 131; reminiscences of Fenian scare, 133; paymaster, 136, 140, 143.
Foster, Walter E., lieutenant, 207.
Fraser, J. W., lieutenant, 150.
Frink, James, lieutenant, 246.
Frodsham, Sergeant, gunnery of, 137.
Frost, Wm. J., lieutenant, 86.
Frye, Henry, lieutenant, 246.

Gallagher, Francis, bombardier, Peters' battery, 114.
Garby, George, lieutenant, 126; called out, 131.
Gemmill, John F., lieutenant, 136.
George III, jubilee of, 23; death of, 35.

George IV, proclaimed, 35; birthday salute, 88.
Gilbert, Thos., lieutenant in Colville company, 4, 9.
Gillespie, C. T., assisted at concert, 210.
Gillespie, Thos. F., lieutenant, 86; raises battery at Chatham, 136; battery removed from list, 168.
Glasgow, H. Adam, sergeant, 85.
Goddard, H. W., lieutenant, 252.
Good, Sergeant, on Shoeburyness team, 173.
Gordon, Governor, address on Trent affair, 118; censures addresses from volunteers, 122.
Gordon, John J., lieutenant, 172; captain, 174; major, 184; presentation to, 185; quartermaster, 214, 233.
Gordon, Robert H., lieutenant, 207.
Governors and administrators of N. B.: Carleton, Thos., 3, 6, 25; Ludlow, Gabriel G., 25; Winslow, Edward, 25; Hunter, Major-General Martin, 25; Johnston, Lieutenant-Colonel George, 25; Balfour, Major-General William, 25; Smythe, Major-General G. T., 25, 33; Hailes, Lieutenant-Colonel Harris Wm., 33; Saumarez, Sir Thos., 33; Chipman, Hon. Ward, 37; Douglas, Sir Howard, 37, 38; Bliss, Hon. John M., 38; Harvey, Sir John, 55; Colebrooke, Sir William, 64; Manners-Sutton, J. H. T., 80; Gordon, Arthur H., 102, 117; Wilmot, L. A., 137; Tilley, Sir S. L., 149.
'Graveyard' battery, 205.
Gray, Arthur C. H. lieutenant, 239.
Gray, Rev. Dr., consecrates colors, 103.
Gray, Lieutenant Colonel John H., presents colors, 103.
Gray, Lieutenant William, 41.
Greathead, Nicholas T., lieutenant, 132.

Hall, Mark, lieutenant, 251.
Hanford, Thos. T., lieutenant, 36.
Harding, Geo. F., sergeant, 100.
Hare, Lieutenant Chas., brings prize into port of St. John, 29.
Harris, Captain, 42, 247.
Harrison, Chas. F., lieutenant, presented with N. W. medal, 175; captain, 207; services, 172.
Harrison, Mrs. C. W., assists at concert, 209.
Hartt, Captain, J. T. T., assists at concert,210.
Harvey, Sir John, governor during disputed boundary question, 55.
'Havelock' battery, 100.
Hayne, Lieutenant-Colonel Richard, referred to, 2; appointed to command of artillery, 46; sketch of life, 49; provincial A. D. C., 64; assistant adjutant-general, 75; adjutant-general, 76; assists in reception of Prince of Wales, 96; report for 1860, 99; provincial A. D. C., 102; quartermaster-general, 119; colonel-commandant, 129.
Hay, George, lieutenant, 247.
Hea, Fred. L., paymaster sergeant, death of 218.

Hoben, C. F., lieutenant, 249.
Holbrook, James, lieutenant, 42.
Hopkins, John, private in Nicholson's battery, 43.
Howe, Joseph, lieutenant, 239.
Hughes, Samuel, sergeant-major, instructs, 171; life of, 187; presentation to, 188.
Hughson, William, lieutenant, 43, 48; sketch of, 51.
Humbert, Thos. Coke, lieutenant, 86; resigns, 97.
Hunter, Roger, lieutenant, 101, 126.

Inch, Robert, lieutenant, bravery at St. John fire, 157.
Inches, Keir, death of, 126.
Inches, Peter R., M. D., sergeant, 114; sergeant-major, 115, 125; lieutenant and captain, 130.
Inspections, 64, 89, 98, 102, 122, 124, 127, 129, 145, 146, 153, 160, 162, 164, 165, 167, 172, 175, 178, 179, 181, 183, 184, 211, 216, 218.
Irwin, Lieutenant-Colonel D. T., inspects, 164, 165, 172, 175, 178, 179, 183, 215.

Jack, I. Allen, gunner Peters' battery, 111; secretary, 108; vice chair at last meeting, 110.
Jago, D. R., lieutenant R. A., 124; appointed captain and assistant adjutant-general of artillery, 131; arranges a system of signals during Fenian scare, 132; views on discipline, 134; assistance at Confederation, 141; inspects, 146; brevet lieutenant-colonel, 149; appointed assistant inspector of artillery, 151; forms Provincial Artillery Association, 151; resignation, 151; death, 183.
Johnston, Fort, 205.
Johnston, Thos. H., orderly room clerk, 219; paymaster's sergeant, 219.
Jones, Edward, gunner, wins Prince of Wales' medal, 114; Prince of Wales' cup, 123; gold watch, 123; lieutenant, 124.
Jones, Ernest Ray, lieutenant, 219.
Jones, F. C. lieutenant, 207.
Jones, Geo. W., lieutenant, 173; captain, 174; major, 214; presents cup for competition, 216, 217.
Jones, Thomas, captain, 43.
Jubilee of corps, celebration of, 66.
Jubilee, Queen's, celebration of, 177.

Kane, John A., lieutenant, 143; captain, 147; retires, 171.
Kent, Duchess of, death of, 102.
Kent, Duke of, visits St. John, 16; commander-in-chief, 18; address from city of St. John, 18.
Kerr, John, lieutenant, gunnery of, 137; raises a battery, 138; captain, 143; battery becomes non-effective, 147.
King, John, captain, death of, 147.
King, Wm. A., lieutenant, 150; bravery at St. John fire, 156; paymaster, 231; retires, 171.
King's New Brunswick regiment raised, 3.
Kingston, William J., lieutenant, 240.

Kinnear, Geo. L., captain, 247.
Kirk, James, lieutenant, 85; retires, 124.
Knight, R. N, lieutenant, 86; retires, 121.
Knox, F. J., lieutenant, 86; captain, 121; out of service, 124.

Lamb, Walter, gunner, injured at fire, rescue of, 157.
Lauder, Thos. W., lieutenant, 150; captain, raises battery, 160; retires, 171; presentation to, 172.
Langan, C. F., lieutenant, 171; instructor, 171; captain, 240; adjutant, 232; retired with rank, 232.
Lansdowne cup, won, 179, 216, 218.
Lansdowne, Frank G. W., sergeant, 84; lieutenant, 85; in Peters' battery, 107; lieutenant, 126.
Law, Militia, 4, 78, 119.
Lectures, 135.
Letson, F. J., lieutenant, 136.
Leonard, Robert J., lieutenant, 85.
Linde, F. R., sergeant, 100.
Lisgar, visit of Lord, 144, 146.
Lock's, Major, battery R. A. at St. John, 65.
Lockhart, W. A., treasurer Peters' battery, 114; sergeant, 114; sergeant-major, 115; quartermaster, 125, 140, 143; retires, 149; mayor of St. John, 126.
Lorne, Marquis of, visit of, 161.
Loyalists, landing of, 1; fall fleet, 2; jubilee, 44; 60th anniversary, 66; 66th anniversary, 75. 70th anniversary, 77; centennial, 165; participation of artillery in celebration,166.
Luard, Major-General, inspects, 164.

MacLaren, J. S., assists at concert, 210.
Madigan, Michael, leader of band, 192.
Markham, Major, commandant Bisley team, serenade to, 218.
Marshall, John R., recollections of, 40, 87; lieutenant, 83; captain, 85; authority during fire, 158.
Martello Tower, history of, 202; poem, 203.
Maunsell, Lieutenant-Colonel Geo. J., adjutant general of N. B., 129; transferred, 163; return of, 168.
Maxwell, J., lieutenant, 48, 84.
Mayes, G. S., assists at concert, 209.
Meating, Joseph, lieutenant, 142.
Mechanics' Institute, opening of, 65.
Mein, Lieutenant-Colonel 74th regiment, 37.
Melick, Charles J., lieutenant, 43, 48; 87; sketch of, 51; captain, 65, 83; major, 85, 140, 143; retires, 146.
Melick, James G., sergeant, 40; exhibits model of steam engine, 65; lieutenant, 86; captain, 101; retired with rank, 101.
Messinett, Lieutenant John, 41.
Middleton, Major-General, inspection by,168,
Militia Bill, debate on, 77.
Militia Law, 4, 78, 119; enrolment under, 121.
Militia Records, 40, 139.
Militia System, decadence of old, 63.
Milledge, Lewis D., lieutenant, 242.

Milliken, Benjamin, lieutenant, 246.
Minchin, Captain Geo. F., 38 ; major, 42.
Mitchell, Alexander, lieutenant, 97.
Montizambert, Lieutenant-Colonel, inspects, 184, 218.
Montreal challenge cup, 178.
Moore, James, lieutenant, 248.
Moore, Thos. B., captain, 247.
Morehouse, John, bombardier Peters' battery, 115.
Morgan, W., wins prize, 123.
Morris, Walter B., lieutenant, 130.
Morse, Lieutenant-Colonel, report on forts, 199.
Mount, James, work of, 84 ; major, 136, 140, 143 ; retires, 146.
Mowatt, Captain John, 41, 63.
Muir, Captain James, 41.
Murray, Christopher, lieutenant, 126 ; captain, 130 ; battery disbanded, 138.
Murray, J., gunner, killed by accident, 149.
Murray, Major, commanding King's N. B. regiment, 6.
Muster days, 73.

McAfee, Wm., wins medal, 129.
McCarthy, Alderman Patrick, poem by, 203.
McColgan, William H., lieutenant, 244.
McCordock, Sergeant Wm. J., 100 ; lieutenant, 121.
McCormack, Joseph, lieutenant, 251.
McFrederick, Langford, gunner, death of, 218.
McGee, Captain Charles, raises battery at St. George, 142.
McIntyre, Samuel, gunner, death of, 150.
McJunkin, R., gunner, bravery of, 157.
McKinney, James, lieutenant, 244.
McLachlan, Thos. M., lieutenant, 86 ; captain, 126 ; company disbanded, 129.
McLauchlan, John, captain, raises company, 86 ; company's presentation to instructor, 100 ; retires, 126.
McLeod, Donald, lieutenant, 43, 47.
McLeod, George K., lieutenant, 172 ; captain, 180 ; adjutant, 208.
McNair, Major 52nd regiment, 38.
McNichol, Jas., lieutenant, 136.

Naish, Isaac, lieutenant, 97.
Name of corps, 47, 208, 219.
Napier, Sergeant, wins medal, 138.
Nicholson, Thos. L., raises battery, 43, 49 ; sketch of, 52 ; major, 64 ; death of, 75.
Nile, battle of the, news at St. John, 21.
'Nippers, The,' picture of, 115.

Odell, Geo. M., lieutenant, 43, 47.
Odell, Thos. T., lieutenant, 130.
Officers, battery, 1838, 47 ; 1885, 172.
Ogden, Henry, lieutenant, 247.
Ogden, Thomas, lieutenant, 247.
Orange celebration, force called out, 151.

Osburn, Henry, captain, raises battery, 130 ; called out, 132.
Oswald, Lieutenant-Colonel, commands Shoeburyness team, 164.

Paisley, Thos., lieutenant, 83.
Pallen, Gunner, wins Prince of Wales' cup and medal, 145.
Palmer, Charles, lieutenant, 247.
Paris, treaty of, 54.
Parsons, Elijah, lieutenant, 86.
Penfold, M. J., bandmaster, 193.
Perley, Moses H., death of, 115.
Perley, Thos. E., lieutenant, 250.
Perley, W. Colebrooke, bombardier in Peters' battery, 115 ; corporal, 115, 125.
Peters, B. Lester, battery of, 101, 106 ; muster rolls, 109; meetings, 114, 125; disbandment, 116 ; death of, 217.
Peters, E. B., quartermaster, 47, 64, 83 ; lieutenant, 48.
Peters, Geo. C., lieutenant, 124.
Peters, Hurd, captain, company of, 85 ; lecture by, 100 ; retires, 124.
Peters, Martin Hunter, lieutenant, 103 ; captain, 121 ; called out, 131 ; major, 146 ; in temporary command of corps, 167 ; retires, 170 ; death of, 176.
Peters, R. Brooks, secretary, 115.
Peters, Thomas W., entertains corps at drill shed, 184 ; presents colors to St. Paul's church, 21.
Pick, Edward, adjutant, 47.
Pick, Geo. H., lieutenant, 84 ; captain, 85 ; called out, 131 ; major, 146 ; retires, 168.
Pine, Geo. J., gift to corps, 162.
Polleys, Lieutenant, commended in report, 159, 160 ; battery aids civil power, 162.
Pollok, John, lieutenant, 43, 49.
Portland battery, muster roll of, 127.
Potter, James, captain, 33, 34, 36.
Poulden, Captain, R. A., at Fredericton, 73.
Pratt, Sergeant, A. K., on Shoeburyness team, 173.
Prevost, Sir George, orders march of 104th regiment, 27.
Price-Lewes, Lieutenant-Colonel, inspector of artillery, 162 ; resigns, 164.
Prince Alfred, visit of, 101 ; salute to, 101 ; reprimand for salute, 102.
Prince Arthur, visit of, 145.
Prince Edward, see Duke of Kent.
Prince of Wales, birth of, 65 ; visit of, 91 ; companies called out, 94 ; at Fredericton, 93, 94 ; company called by his title, 93 ; general orders upon visit, 95; cup, winners of, 123, 145.
Princess Louise, visit of, 161.
Provincial corps raised, 3.

Queen's coronation, 53.
Queen's jubilee, 177.
Quinton, James, lieutenant, 97 ; transferred, 124.

INDEX.

Raid, Fenian, 1866, 131; general order upon, 135.
Railway, contract signed, salute upon, 77.
Rankin, Alexander, lieutenant, 85; retires, 124.
Rankine, Alexander, lieutenant, 97; captain, 101.
Ranney, Wm. Parker, raises battery, 43, 48; sketch of, 51; resigns, 64.
Raymond, W. O., lieutenant, 250.
Rebellion, North West, 171; services of corps offered, 171; services of Captain Harrison and Corporal Richardson, 172; medals presented, 175.
Rebellion, Papineau's, 46, 49.
Red Head, fort at, 206.
Reed, Chas. R., bombardier in Peters' battery, 115.
Reed, Robert, captain Independent Volunteers, 5.
Reed, Robert, private in Nicholson company, 43; lieutenant, 73, 83, hospitality to Princess Louise, 164; death of, 211.
Regiment, formation of, 46; officers, 46, 47; change to brigade, 1869, 140; officers of, 143; change to battalion, 208; to regiment again, 219; officers, 1883, 207.
Regiment, the 104th, raised, 27.
Reign of Terror, 2.
Richardson, Corporal Thomas, services in North West, 172, 190; presentation to, 190; medal presented, 175.
Right of Search, 24.
Ring, G. Fred, A. D. C., 149.
Ring, J. Alfred, captain, 146; commended in report, 150; retires, 171.
Ring, B. T., lieutenant, 240.
Ritchie, R. R., lieutenant, 172.
Robertson, James, F., sergeant, 84, 114; lieutenant, 130.
Robertson, Robert, lieutenant, 43, 48; sketch of, 51; captain, 65.
Rodgers, Joseph, lieutenant, 247.
Rogers, Robert, lieutenant, 247.
Rogers, Lieutenant William, 85.
Rose, John H., lieutenant, 252.
Rose, Captain Wm. T., 41, 42, 48, 84; retires as major, 134.
Ross, William, lieutenant; 43, 49.
Roxborough, Wm., lieutenant, 245.

Saunders, Lieutenant-Colonel, A. D. C., 149.
Scammell, E. J., lieutenant, 173; captain, 174.
Scott, Thos., lieutenant, 150.
Scovil, E. W, B., lieutenant, 214.
Search, right of, 24.
Seely, J. Fred., bombardier in Peters' battery, 115; corporal, 115.
Seely, Geo. B., captain, 171, 172; major 180; death of, 182.
Senhouse, H. F., asks for sleds to send sailors overland, 28.
Sergeant-Major, the, 186.
Sham fights, 44, 60.

Shannon, Geo. J., lieutenant, retired, 126.
Sherbrooke, Sir John, forwards materiel to St. John, 27.
Shoeburyness, first team sent to, 164; second team, Lieutenant-Colonel Armstrong appointed to command of, 173; success in competitions, 174.
Shore, John Saunders, lieutenant, 43; captain, 43, 47; sketch of, 50.
Shore, Colonel George, death of, 76.
Shore, Wm. H., lieutenant, 248.
Simonds, Charles, lieutenant, 43, 49.
Simonds, John, lieutenant, 122; captain, 124; retires, 126.
Simonds, Richard, raises company, 85, 99.
Simpson, Edward, lieutenant, 249.
Sketches of original members Colville company, 9 to 15.
Skillen, Wm., lieutenant, 85.
Skinner, S. A. M., lieutenant, 214.
Smith, D. G., lieutenant, supply officer, 150.
Smith, Francis, lieutenant, 85.
Smith, George F., bombardier in Peters' battery, 110. 115; appointed paymaster, 171; death, 212.
Smith, John R., lieutenant, 130.
Smith, Stephen, assistant surgeon, 140, 229; transferred to Woodstock field battery, 153.
Sneden, Robert R., lieutenant, 84; in Peters' battery, 107.
'Southern' battery, 205.
Sports, Barrack square, 1886, 174.
Stackhouse, Geo. J., lieutenant, 85.
St. Andrews, artillery at, 41.
Stanley of Preston, Lord, governor-general, visit of, 183.
Steel, R., gunner, killed by accident, 149.
Steeves, J. A. E., captain, 207.
Stephens, Elisha, lieutenant, 247.
Steven, W. A. D., lieutenant, 244.
Stevens, W. H. lieutenant, 252.
Stevenson, Thos. D., lieutenant, 252.
Stewart, C. C., captain, 83.
Stewart, Robert A., lieutenant, 142.
Stiles, Solomon, lieutenant, 247.
Stoop, Francis G., lieutenant, 249.
Strange, Lieutenant-Colonel, report of, 153, 160.
Stratton, John M., lieutenant, 124; death of 124.
Street, Geo. F., major, 47; sketch of, 50; death of, 85.
Street, W. W., lieutenant, 126.
St. Stephen, artillery at, 41.
Studholm, Major, Guilford, at Fort Howe, 199.
Sullivan, corporal, wins prize for attendance, 181.
Sussex, camp at, 1881, 164.
Sweet, Robert, lieutenant, 83.

Taylor, John M., lieutenant, retires, 126.
Temple, F. L., lieutenant, 207; captain, 219.
Thomas, George F., lieutenant, 84; in Peters' battery, 107.

INDEX 259

Thompson, Geo. F., recollections of, 44, 59, 88; lieutenant, 85.
Thompson, Rt. Hon. C. P., governor, 63.
Thomson. S. R., captain, 122; organizes battery, 130.
Till, George, lieutenant, 150.
Tilley, H. C., lieutenant, 207.
Tilley, Lieut.-Governor, Sir S. L., salute on appointment of, 149; opens exhibition, 163.
Tipperary, Fort, 207.
Toldervy, Dr. J., Surgeon, 47, 83.
Tourmaline, H. M. S., visits of, 181, 184.
Travis, J. Warren, captain, company of, 86; transferred, 121.
Trench, Lieutenant-Colonel commanding 74th, 200.
Trent affair, 117; services of artillery, 118.
Trooping the colors, 177, 181.
Tuites', Captain, battery R. A., at St. John, 65.
Turnbull, E. H., Lieutenant, 173.

Underhill, Jacob, D., lieutenant, 126; adjutant, 136, 140; commended in report, 159; offers batteries for service abroad, 160; retires, 168.

Vaughan, Wm., lieutenant, 252.
Volunteer system, new, inception of, 81; companies accepted, 82.

Wallace, Matthew, lieutenant, 150.
Walling, Staff-Sergeant, instructs in shifting, 167.
Wallop, Newton Ward, lieutenant, 44, 48, 51.
War, probability of European, 159; report of D. A. G., 160.
War with France, 1793, 3.
War with U. S. A., 1812, 25; ended, 1814, 31.
Ward, John, second lieutenant, 4; brief sketch of, 9; alderman, 19; as major, in correspondence, 33; issues order, 34; address to, 67; reply, 68; life of, 70; death, 71.
Ward, Caleb, lieutenant, 33, 34.
Ward, Clarence, assistance of, 29.
Waterbury, David, second lieutenant, 22; mentioned in correspondence, 33; first lieutenant, 34; captain, 34; sketch of, 36.
Waterbury, John C., private as John jr., 22; captain, 36; retirement and death, 39.
Waterbury, George, second lieutenant, 36; lieutenant, 48; retired with rank, 49; sketch of, 51.
Watts, Edward D., lieutenant, 86.
Westmoreland county, artillery in, 42.
Wetmore, Abraham K. S., lieutenant, 42; captain, 43, 48, 83, 99; retires, 123.
Wetmore, A. D., lieutenant, 207.
Wetmore, Edwin J., lieutenant, 85; called out, 131.
Wetmore, Lieutenant-Colonel, maintains Bolton's company, 138.
White, J. M., bandmaster, 193.
White, Walter W., lieutenant, 207; captain, 214; adjutant, 218.
Whitlock, lieutenant Wm., 41, 48, 249.
Wiggins, Fred A., lieutenant, 44, 48; sketch of, 51; paymaster, 76, 83; retires, 136.
Williams, Charles H., bandmaster, 193.
Williams, Gen. Sir F. W., suggests scheme of defence, 81; visit to St. John, 130.
Willis, Major Cuthbert, commandant at St. Andrews, 132.
Wilson, Captain Thos. B., A. D. C., 74.
Winslow, John C., lieutenant, 250.
Woodstock battery, becomes field, 150.
Wright Wm., captain, 83.

York county, artillery in, 42.
Young, Sir John (Lord Lisgar), visit of, 144, 146.

ERRATUM.—Page 200, line 8 from top, for '*French*' read '*Trench*.'

www.ingramcontent.com/pod-product-compliance
Lightning Source LLC
Chambersburg PA
CBHW021623250426
43672CB00037B/1380